Seams Unlikely

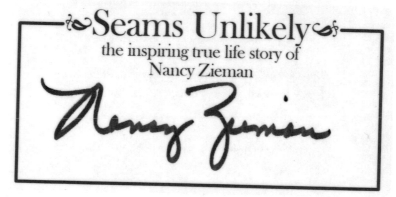

Seams Unlikely
the inspiring true life story of
Nancy Zieman

by

Nancy Zieman

with MARJORIE L. RUSSELL

Glass Road Media & Management, LLC

6017 Pine Ridge Rd, Suite 373

Naples, FL 34119

in conjunction with

Nancy Zieman Productions, LLC

215 Corporate Drive, Suite D

Beaver Dam, WI 53916-3124

Library of Congress Cataloging-in-Publication Data

Zieman, Nancy.

Seams Unlikely: The Inspiring True Life Story of Nancy Zieman/

by Nancy Zieman with Marjorie L. Russell.

p. cm.

ISBN 978-0-9884789-6-1

BIO003000 - Biography & Autobiography - Business

2013947678

For information about special discounts for bulk purchases,

please contact Nancy Zieman Productions, LLC at

920-356-9506 or springer@ziemanproductions.com

Designed by Collide Creative, www.collidecreative.com

Cover photo by Glasgow Photography, www.glasgowphoto.com

Manufactured in the United States of America

Photo credits: Unless otherwise noted, all photos are from the author's collection.

Testimonials

Here is your window to the world of PBS star, Nancy Zieman: Her struggles, her strategies, her heartaches, and her triumphs. Beyond Nancy's television fame, you will discover a real person who refused to be limited by facial paralysis, chronic pain, or financial and business challenges. Woven through each page is Nancy's constancy—and inspiring message: "If I can do it, so can you." Read it and believe.

Gail Brown
Author, columnist and frequent *Sewing With Nancy* guest

I'm humbled by the experiences Nancy has offered to my life and the millions of beloved friends she has inspired. WOW! Nancy's book is a great read and brings back many great memories for all of us that have been involved in business and life with Nancy. I admire Nancy's patience, her calm manner, her sense of humor and her family values. Nancy's book is inspiring to read. Thanks for being my friend, Nancy.

Jan Carr
President, Clover Needlecraft, Inc. USA

Not one to let life's challenges derail her ambitions, Nancy Zieman has risen to the top of the sewing and quilting world through not only business acumen, but also kindness and humility. Her forthrightness and down-to-earth telling of her story in *Seams Unlikely* reveals her true modesty and genuine gratitude for blessings, especially family, that have come her way.

Bill Gardner
Editor-in-Chief, Quilters Newsletter

I was immersed in *Seams Unlikely* from the beginning. Nancy Zieman writes of her life and of her work in this autobiography, which lets the reader understand her determination, her creativity and why she is so popular, respected and loved.

Joan Lence
Television Broadcast Consultant

Along life's journey there seems to be only a handful of people you meet that have the desire and ability to encourage and lift up those around them. The evidence of this gift is not just heard in their words, but fulfilled in their relationships with family, friends, colleagues and those in need. Nancy's creativity, professionalism and success in business deserve to be studied, but it is in the richness of her relationships that you will be most rewarded. Through the pages of *Seams Unlikely*, you'll walk with Nancy through an inspiring incredible life journey of faith, family and perseverance that will make you not only a fan, but also a friend.

Ed Moore
Founder Koala Studios

Appearances are not always as they seem. As you read Nancy Zieman's story, you'll understand that there's more to the life of this calm, professional woman who makes not only sewing, but also thirty years on television look easy. It's an amazing revelation of carrying on through humble beginnings and serious life challenges to impressive achievements and business success with credit always to the support of others. Oh, and she is humble and able to laugh at herself, too. Keep calm and carry on, Nancy—we can all be inspired by your example and life story.

Mary Mulari
Sewing teacher, author, and *Sewing With Nancy* guest

A fascinating look at the family, tradition, and entrepreneurial spirit that built a sewing career that has reached the hearts of Public Television viewers around the country. Nancy proves that she can stitch a story as well as a lined wool skirt.

Libby Peterek
Director of Web Services KLRU and Chair of PBS Digital Advisory Council

My first mistake in reading this book was starting it late at night—I couldn't put it down and had an early flight the next day. My second mistake was in reading it on the plane where I uttered sympathetic groans, shed crocodile tears and let a few peals of laughter rip from my lungs in the company of a plane full of strangers. My third mistake was in assuming I knew everything about Nancy Zieman. Her success has been built on true grit, honesty and control of her destiny. She is the American success story.

Eileen Roche
Editor, Designs in Machine Embroidery magazine

Nancy Zieman is to the sewing industry as Bill Gates is to the technology industry and Oprah to talk shows. Nancy is one of the most sought after speakers the Sewing & Stitchery Expo has ever had. Nancy is not only a legend and icon for the sewing industry; she is an educator and businesswoman extraordinaire. This book will capture your heart and your attention to the end. My heartfelt thanks go to Nancy for her willingness to support the sewing industry with such passion and grace.

Joanne Ross
Founder and Director, Sewing & Stitchery Expo

If you've ever watched *Sewing With Nancy* you will love this book! Nancy shares her childhood on the farm, her physical challenges, her growing career, and does it all with honesty, clarity and humility. I found the book spellbinding and couldn't put it down.

Natalie Sewell
Landscape Quilting Artist and Author

This book is pure Nancy! She's inspired so many of us, and in *Seams Unlikely* Nancy invites you into her life just as she invites you into her show, with wit and wisdom and humility and joy.

James Steinbach
Director, Wisconsin Public Television

To Ted and Tom

Acknowledgements

I never intended to write an autobiography. A book such as this really doesn't fit my personality. Yet, here it is!

There was a chain of events and nudges that led to the publication of *Seams Unlikely*. Let me explain.

In 2009, Marjorie Russell, the previous editor and then a freelance writer for *American Quilter* magazine, interviewed me. That was a couple years after *Sewing With Nancy's* twenty-fifth anniversary on television and Marj's assignment was to give *American Quilter* readers a glimpse into the personal and professional sides of my life. During the hour we spent together I felt a unique camaraderie with her. It was our first meeting, but I knew with certainty that our paths would cross again.

When we reached the milestone of twenty-five years on TV, co-workers and friends often said, "You should really write an autobiography!" In particular Donna Fenske and Pat Hahn, key *Sewing With Nancy* team members as well as friends, frequently nudged me in that direction during our many drives to and from the TV studio.

One day Ken Tacony, President of the Tacony Corporation and a friend and colleague, made the same suggestion, stating that a book about my journey might give others encouragement. His statement prompted me to pause and consider. I thought about Marj. If she thought it was a topic of interest and was also willing to work on it with me, I'd proceed.

After Marj's enthusiastic "Yes!" to both questions, we began working together and during the process the book seemed to take on a life of its own.

A special thank you to my mom who has been my biggest supporter and of course, to all the Zieman guys—Rich, Ted, and Tom.

Prologue

The walk from the Green Room where my makeup is applied to the studio floor takes less than a minute. All is in order. Months of preparations for a two-part broadcast celebrating *Sewing With Nancy's* thirty-year history on television will take life as cameras roll.

In terms of years, only Letterman has had a longer run.

Unlike the more than eight hundred other episodes of *Sewing With Nancy*, this one takes place in front of a studio audience. Chairs have been arranged in the cavernous studio and every one of them is filled.

The significant people of my life are in the audience—my husband and sons, my daughter-in-law, my mother and step-dad, my aunt, my sister, and one of my brothers. People I don't know as personally are here, too—fans and those accompanying them, colleagues, business associates. Special guests—people who have become my on-air and off-air friends—are rehearsed and ready for cameras to roll.

The production crew is poised. The jokes they shared through their headsets while preparing to record have been set aside and everything is business. In the control room sound levels are adjusted, tapes are cued and cameras re-checked. My director searches me out in the Green Room and gives me an uncharacteristic hug. No words exchanged, just a glance that says, "You can do it, Nancy." I fight back tears, she the same. Then she turns and heads back to the control room.

My walk down the hall is a short one, but a lot can go through your mind in a short walk. Life is full of the unexpected and I am the most unlikely of television personalities. But as this milestone is celebrated, the journey that led to this point is remembered and beginnings are acknowledged.

The audience is ready. I am ready. The countdown from the control room begins and tape rolls.

"...six...five...four..." (the audio goes silent and the floor director beats a silent three...two...one...and points at me).

"Welcome to a special broadcast of *Sewing With Nancy.*"

Chapter 1

∝

Father's Day
June 21, 1953

My mother, Barbara Larson Luedtke was ten months married, eight months pregnant, six months past her twenty-first birthday and looking forward to a whole day away from the farm with my father—Ralph Luedtke.

The morning had started cool, but was warming nicely. With house windows open, the coos of mourning doves mingled pleasantly with the lowing of cows and the wheezing of milking machines over at the barn. Skies were a clear, watery blue over fields, woods and farm buildings and it was hard to imagine better weather. The other Luedtke men—my grandfather, Leonard, and Uncle Roy—would handle evening milking without Dad. The reprieve was welcome. Life would change soon enough, and a baby, plus the demands of twice-daily milking and chores would mean a long time until my parents could claim another day as theirs alone.

Not that my mother would have complained. Their life was a practical one and they approached its demands and changes with equal acceptance. As a bride Mother moved from her parent's farm to her husband's, already well-trained in the skills required of a farm wife. She and Dad set up housekeeping in the small, one-story house built for them with lumber milled from logs cut out of the woods. Their life together had been prepared for Mother and she was prepared for it.

The navy blue maternity dress with blue and white plaid trim she wore that morning had been an indulgence at fourteen dollars. She could have sewn something and saved the money, but the dress was pretty. Mom would never make claim to being pretty—it just wasn't right to call attention to yourself that way—but wearing that dress made her feel "special." She hardly even needed maternity clothes. An attractive tall, slim, brunette woman, to others it seemed that her pregnancy had months to go, but her due date was July 26, just a month and five days away.

When Dad came in from milking, he showered and changed clothes, they ate breakfast and Mom tidied the kitchen. When they left their driveway, Dad turned right, passing the large white farmhouse where his parents and sister lived, and the barn beyond.

They headed for church first, but not to St. Peter's Lutheran down the road. St. Peter's was the church Dad attended growing up and as a bride, Mom had joined there, too. That day, though, they went back to Mother's home church, Grace Lutheran in Winchester, several miles east. A new Sunday school wing was being dedicated and my grandmother, Georgina Larson, had been on the building committee. In that region of northeast Wisconsin almost everyone was, in some way, tethered to farming. Dedication of the church's new wing was not only closure for a project that would help pass the faith of their fathers to their children, it was also a chance to celebrate the ties of community.

Mom and Dad shared a pew with her family during the service. Afterwards they greeted friends and family before heading to Mom's parent's farm. Temperatures were approaching eighty degrees by then and while the men shed jackets and rolled up shirt sleeves to expose tanned wrists, the women dished up a chicken dinner. When the dessert—strawberry shortcake—had been reduced to crumbs, Mother quickly copied my grandmother's recipe for the shortcake's baking powder biscuit cake batter and helped with dishes before she and Dad left.

They stopped to visit with more family and friends at a twenty-fifth wedding anniversary celebration before heading for a movie in Appleton, thirty minutes east. A double feature was playing at the Rio Theater, a fading relic of the opulent era of film with heavy velvet curtains, dusty upholstery and threadbare carpeting. *Fort Ti*, a 3-D movie starring George Montgomery, Joan Vohs and Phyllis Fowler, was followed by *A Queen is*

Crowned, a documentary on the coronation of England's young Queen Elizabeth II.

Dad paid for the tickets and they were handed standard 3-D movie goggles—white cardboard frames with one red and one blue lens. They found seats with a nice view of the screen and settled in.

Directed by gimmick-loving William Castle, *Fort Ti* was a story loosely based on the British and French conflict over Fort Ticonderoga during colonial America's French and Indian War. With a story line that was historically questionable, it was one of Hollywood's finest examples of screen-popping 3-D cinematography.

"There were things flying at us," Mother remembers. The couple flinched as arrows and spears shot toward them, and ducked at the threat of hurled tomahawks and swooping bats. Mother claims she was never scared, just startled by the unexpected. Then she felt a pop, and warm liquid began soaking through her dress into the cushion beneath her.

"Ralph," she whispered, "My water is breaking." He looked at her, startled. In the flickering light from the movie screen one wide eye beneath his goggles was red, the other blue.

"I'll go get the car," he whispered back. Neither panicked nor spoke aloud. He offered his arm and helped her to her feet. They slipped quickly out of their row and into the lobby. Having a big wet spot on the back of her dress was somewhat humiliating, and to this day my mother wonders what kind of mess she left behind in her vacated theater seat, but she wasn't physically uncomfortable. There was some mild cramping, but she felt no worse than during any monthly period. While Dad left to get the car, Mom hid the back of her dress and the trickle that continued to run down her legs by seeking privacy in a dark corner near a big Coca Cola machine.

In the reserve of her time and upbringing, there were some things people just didn't discuss openly. So, when a woman Mother knew saw her standing in the shadows and paused to chat, Mom did not mention that she was in labor and on her way to the hospital. As the woman returned to the movie, Dad pulled up outside and Mom ran to the car.

Their destination, Theda Clark Hospital in nearby Neenah, was about fifteen minutes away. They checked in quickly. A few minutes later, when a nurse conducted an internal exam, Mom, who still hadn't experienced heavy labor, was already nine centimeters dilated. Everything went into rapid motion. Dad was scooted into the fathers' waiting room as Mom was wheeled into delivery. A mask was placed over her face and she drifted away on a whiff of ether.

"What day is it?" She was groggy and nauseous from the ether, waking up in a hospital room with Dad standing by her bedside.

He grinned. "Father's Day."

"What do we have?" she asked and he said, "A little girl, five pounds, eight ounces, twenty-one inches long."

"Are you mad?" she asked, suddenly concerned that he might have wanted their firstborn to be a boy.

"No, of course not," he assured her and she relaxed.

Later on his way home Dad stopped to tell my mother's parents the news.

"We don't even have diapers," Grandma Larson lamented. "We haven't had a baby shower!" She was awake most of that night, planning a shopping trip to buy baby supplies.

Dad's last stop was his parent's home, next door to his own, where Grandma Luedtke thought my dad was playing some sort of prank and had to be convinced that her daughter-in-law wasn't nearby, overhearing and enjoying the joke.

My weight dropped to four pounds, twelve ounces and I was placed in an incubator. Mother and I remained in the hospital a week. When my weight once again topped five pounds, they took me home.

The day after my birth they named me Nancy Lea Luedtke—Nancy because they liked it, and Lea because it was part of my maternal great-grandmother's name, Alice Lea.

When I was born, the farm to which my parents brought me had already been in the Luedtke family for ninety-seven years. Dated 1856, eight years after Wisconsin became the thirtieth state to join the union, the deed issued to Karl Luedtke was signed by President James Buchanan. While the 1856 document refers to the acreage in northeast Wisconsin's

Winnebago County as marshland, by 1953 the farm was three hundred acres of open land plus one hundred acres of woods.

The early Luedtkes (pronounced Lid Key), were farmers, but also hunters and trappers. A German immigrant, Karl Luedtke (on early documents Karl is sometimes spelled with a C, and Luedtke is sometimes spelled without a T) was part of an 1840s influx of primarily German and Norwegian settlers who were attracted to the area by the prospect of good farmland. While most settlers cleared trees and drained marshes for pastures and fields, others started businesses and provided services to support their efforts. Churches—Lutheran mostly—sprang up every few miles, leaving the land's occupants few excuses for not exercising their faith.

As the years passed, the descendants of early settlers inherited family farms along with a strong work ethic. They tended toward stoicism, minded their own business, were reluctant to draw undue attention to themselves, quietly raised their families, and respected one another.

Almost everything in their lives centered on agriculture; and after agriculture, family; and along with family, faith; and alongside faith, community.

The one hundred acres of woods are still there—the largest group of trees remaining in Winnebago County. In 1952, before my parents married, trees from those woods were cut and milled into lumber for a small ranch-style house that my father had built for his bride at a cost of ten thousand dollars. The white-sided house was small, but it had three bedrooms, one bathroom, a utility room and a nice kitchen for that era, plus a combination living and dining room.

Hazel and Leonard Luedtke, my paternal grandparents, and Aunt Mary, lived next door in a big two-story farmhouse. Within sight to the west, but still on Luedtke property, was another ranch-style home where Uncle Roy and Aunt LaMae lived. Together my father, my grandfather and my uncle worked the Luedtke Dairy Farm, an operation that milked about thirty cows, morning and night, a bigger than average herd at that time.

My mother, Barbara Larson, grew up on a farm in a nearby unincorporated area called Larsen. (Remember, names reflect that area's Scandinavian influence. Larsons, Larsens, Olsons, Johnsons, Andersons,

Petersons, and other "sons" and "sens" populate the region.) Larsen is near Winchester, a small town in Winnebago County about six miles from the Luedtke farm. In Larsen, most of the people were of Norwegian heritage. My mother says when her Norwegian father, Loyall Larson, courted her mother, Georgina Schaefer, who was of German heritage, people in that community were concerned about the implications.

My mother's father, Loyall Larson, started out as a farmer until tuberculosis interrupted his life and he spent time in a TB sanitarium. While he was away, my grandmother, Georgina, who had my mother to care for, managed the farm with the help of a hired man. When my grandfather returned, his lungs were damaged and he gave up farming, becoming an insurance salesman to support his family. But they continued to live on the Larson farm, and it remains in our family today.

My parents met in high school. Although my reserved mother would be unlikely to mention it, she was the valedictorian of her high school class of thirty-two students. She had a talent for drawing, but did not go on to college. Instead she worked at a local bank after graduation. In the late 1940s and early 50s, her aspirations were parallel with those of many young women her age: She wanted to marry her high school sweetheart and make a family and life together.

My parents married on September 6, 1952. My mother was twenty years old and my father was twenty-three.

By the time my parents brought me home from the hospital and settled me into a small bedroom near theirs, Grandma Larson had made good on her plans to purchase baby clothes and supplies. Since I was only five pounds, she had trouble finding clothes that would fit. In that era of cottons and natural fibers, hoping that the garments would shrink, she washed the tiniest clothes she could find in hot water, dried, and then ironed them.

I was the first grandchild on both the Larson and Luedtke sides of my family. My mother was an only child. My father's brother, Roy, was married, but he and Aunt LaMae had not yet had children. So, for a while, I was the center of attention.

September 11, 1954

The dark hair I had at birth gradually disappeared, replaced by blonde that curled a little at the ends. My eyes remained blue and I had inherited my father's fair skin. Twenty-one inches in length and just five pounds at birth, I continued the trend toward being tall and slim as I grew. At nearly fourteen months I was a cheerful, happy, thriving toddler who captured hearts with my smiles.

Barbara Luedtke Eckstein
(Mother)
"She was a baby about as beautiful as anything."

The official start of autumn was nearly two weeks away, but temperatures had begun dipping toward winter. Some mornings it was difficult to know how to dress. It could be down to almost freezing at night, then in the seventies by midday.

On Friday, as she worked around the house Mother watched me more carefully than usual. She had noticed that while sitting in my high chair I pulled at my right ear. That was the only indication that something could be amiss. Otherwise I seemed fine and was not cranky or extra warm to the touch.

Mom's cousin's wedding was the next day, and she wanted me to be well for the occasion. In the evening she tucked me into my crib and checked later to make sure I slept peacefully.

Next morning, when Dad left the house for milking, it was about forty degrees. It was still a crisp fall morning later when Mom padded a few steps down the hall to get me from the small bedroom next to theirs. She remembers that I was awake, lying quietly in my crib, and not crying. But as Mother reached for me, she realized something was terribly wrong. She considered my smile the first sunlight in her day, but that day I looked up at her without smiling. The right side of my face seemed pushed downward as if a heavy hand had pressed there and the flesh beneath had failed to recognize it had lifted.

Decades later, when my mother tells of that moment, she presses hard against the right side of her face, pulling downward as if the affliction were her own. She touches a tissue to an eye and remembers. Dad was in the barn, my father's mother in the house next door. But holding me close, my mother dialed the phone to her own mother eight miles away and said, "Please come, something is wrong with Nancy."

Let me pause here for a moment and say a few words about Bell's palsy because that's what caused the paralysis on the right side of my face. It has shaped my life in many ways—directed the traffic, to offer a metaphor.

To anyone who sees me in person or on television, it is obvious that something is wrong. My face is not symmetrical.

There's also a way to check what people are asking for when they "Google" my name on the internet. Beyond all others "Nancy Zieman stroke," "Nancy Zieman face," or "Nancy Zieman mouth," are the top phrases that trigger their search. People are curious.

When I was fourteen months old, I developed Bell's palsy which affects the seventh cranial nerve. When my mother noticed me pulling at my ear, it was likely an indication of a middle ear infection. Even a mild infection can cause swelling that presses against the seventh cranial nerve at a point where the nerve travels through the skull bones. That pressure restricts the nerve's function causing muscle weakness or paralysis. That's what happened to me.

Between thirty thousand and forty thousand people in the United States are affected by Bell's palsy every year. Only about six percent do not recover fully. I am among the six percent.

My parents sought medical treatment for me, but were told my symptoms would diminish with time. The only recommended treatment was daily massages of the face to stimulate the nerve. For those who develop Bell's palsy symptoms today, corticosteroids offer some help in reducing inflammation. That treatment was not available in 1954.

Unlike many people with Bell's palsy, I do not suffer from facial numbness so I consider myself fortunate. As a child, my right eye wouldn't close, so my mother taped it shut at night. I am still unable to blink my right eye. I use eye drops to help prevent dry eye. Outside, especially when it's windy, I wear wrap-around sunglasses to protect that eye. For the same reason— protecting my right eye—I often wear them when it is raining as well.

My smile is crooked, and I speak carefully in order to speak clearly. But beyond the physical effects, one of the major effects of Bell's palsy is its assault on an individual's confidence. For more than any other reason, that is why I have chosen to write my story.

Those who know me well know that I am at heart a reserved person. My life is quite normal; I just happen to have a very public job.

Each of us faces challenges in life. Some are bigger than others. But what happens to us, does not define who we are, unless we let it.

Several years ago, when I first talked openly about my experience with Bell's palsy on an episode of *Sewing With Nancy*, I was amazed at the response. That episode has been shown numerous times in reruns and it never fails to bring more and more mail and comments from viewers. It even opened the door for my mother and me to talk about how Bell's palsy affected both of us. When I was growing up, we didn't talk about it. My parents didn't allow me to indulge in self-pity, nor did they let me slide by because of any limitations. But, my parents always wondered if there was something more they could have done, somehow that they might have prevented what happened. Then over the years as I dealt with the physical and emotional effects of Bell's palsy, my suffering became their suffering as well.

Mail and blog comments prove that something about what happened to me has helped others cope with their own challenges. I find that both humbling and exciting. If this book can help others gain the confidence to achieve in the face of challenge, that will bring me great joy.

Chapter 2

My earliest memory is of going shopping with Grandma Hazel Luedtke. My guess is I was about four years old at the time since my grandmother died when I was five. I remember sitting in the front seat (yes, children did that back then), watching her as she drove. We were headed for New London, Wisconsin, about eleven miles north of the farm.

Of course I had been off the farm before that, but what made this trip memorable, was probably that it was just Grandma and me—Grandma, me, and a bowl of bread dough in the back seat.

Life was busy for farm families and ours was no exception. There were the demands of twice-daily milking, seven days a week. There were roughly three hundred acres of tillable land, plus one hundred acres of timber or woods. Dairy cows and calves required vigilant care, milking equipment needed to be kept clean and functional, and feeding had to go on, uninterrupted, day after day. There were crops to plan in the winter, plant in the spring, cultivate in the summer, and harvest in the fall. Major equipment repair and maintenance was saved, if possible, for the winter, and fields were prepared for a new growing season as soon as weather permitted in the spring.

Those responsibilities were mostly handled by the men. The women had their own chores.

Women's duties included keeping their homes running—washing, cleaning, cooking, and tending to the needs of their children and husbands. Like most farm families, cash flow was limited, so we tried to be as self-sustaining as possible. We had a big garden that grew bigger over the years with the addition of family members. Our meat source was mostly animals raised on the farm, plus wild game of venison, duck and pheasant. Clothing, especially clothing for women and girls, was often made rather than purchased since store-bought was more expensive. Trips to the grocery store were for those items that could not be grown or made on the farm. Bread was one of those things we rarely purchased.

Bread dough needs to be punched down once during the rising process to redistribute the air pockets in the dough, making for easier shaping into loaves and more uniform baked loaves. I had likely seen my mother punch down bread dough many times in our kitchen, but that day I remember my grandmother walking hand-in-hand with me from the store, opening the back car door, washing her hands on a moistened cloth stored in a plastic bag, and punching a fist into the center of the dough. Once the dough had been punched down she calmly replaced the cloth that covered the bowl, cleaned her hands again, and we resumed shopping.

It could be that I was with my grandmother that day because my mother needed a break or had something else to do. My younger brother, John, was born when I was four, so possibly my trip with Grandma Hazel might have occurred around the time of his birth.

Whatever the reason, the point is that I grew up in the discipline of farm life where maintaining routine was critical to a smooth operation. Over the years the lessons I learned then have served me well.

Although we were somewhat isolated on the farm, I did have playmates. Uncle Roy and his wife, LaMae (we called her Auntie Mae) started having children soon after my birth. Their three oldest children—Rosemarie, Roy Jr., and Ricky—were, respectively, two, three, and four years younger than me. They often made their way "down the road" to play.

Family spacing is unusual in the Luedtke family. There are four children in my family. I'm the oldest, born in 1953. My brother, John, arrived four years later on March 2, 1957; my brother, Dean, is ten years younger than I am, born March 19, 1963; and my sister, Gina, is eighteen years younger, born on August 16, 1971.

After the first three children in Uncle Roy's family, he and Auntie Mae waited a while for their second three. My cousin, Rhonda, is nine years younger than I am, Robbie Jo is nineteen years younger, and Russell is twenty years younger.

What we played as children was an extension of our family interests. The boys had their toy tractors and trucks. My cousin, Rosemarie, and I played house and a lot of games. Mother accumulated a lot of things—especially clothing—over the years; among them were formals that she had worn for high school events or weddings in which she had been a bridesmaid. Rosemarie and I had a great time playing dress up in them.

There were five Luedtke cousins less than five years apart in age. As very young children we played under the watchful eyes of adults. As we grew older, though, we graduated to playing softball on our front lawn. Unevenly spaced trees were bases and we spent many enjoyable hours together.

Aside from cousins, the most significant young person in my life was Aunt Mary, my father's sister. She was eight years old when I was born, and lived next door with my Luedtke grandparents. She sometimes baby sat for me, and probably for John as well, but to me she was less an aunt, and more like a sister.

Within a few months of the onset of Bell's palsy that re-directed the course of my life, Grandma Larson died of kidney cancer. I have no recollection of her, but I can only guess how difficult that year must have been for my mother.

Luedtke Grandma and Grandpa were right next door, less than two hundred feet away. But soon after that shopping trip with the bread dough, Grandma Luedtke was diagnosed with breast cancer and died. I was only five years old. Grandpa Luedtke never recovered from losing her and he never remarried. Aunt Mary was thirteen when her mother died. Grandpa kept on for Mary's sake and the sake of the farm, but he suffered from depression the remainder of his life.

Mary Luedtke Rebman

(Aunt)

"We did a lot of things together, but I think Nancy perceived me as a sister a lot sooner than I did. My brother and Barbara lived next door and when Nancy was born I don't think I was happy about it at first. Her birth knocked me off my little pedestal as the youngest child in the family. I remember being jealous of her."

My maternal grandfather, Loyall Larson, remarried when I was six or seven to a very nice woman named Evelyn. Other than a brief memory of Grandma Hazel, Evelyn became the only grandmother I ever knew.

I spent a lot of time with my Larson grandparents. Staying overnight at their house was a big deal and we were very close. A very likeable man, Grandpa Larson was successful as an insurance salesman. Although tuberculosis had cut short his farming career, he understood farmers and had great rapport with them and their families.

Because we lived next door, I was close to Grandpa Luedtke. In contrast with congenial Grandpa Larson, Grandpa Luedtke was a more matter-of-fact man who loved fishing. He had a small fishing cottage on Lake Poygan about ten miles from the farm, and sometimes he took me with him. I can't remember how old I was when I first went fishing with him, but I still love to fish. The Luedtke kids were so spread out in age, but I can remember one time when he had five of us with him in the boat—me, my brother, John, and the three oldest children in Uncle Roy's family.

As a child I was infatuated by the music of Herb Alpert and the Tijuana Brass. I loved their music! As a special treat, my mother sent Herb Alpert a fan letter on my behalf and I was thrilled when I received a letter with his signature, addressed and written to me. Even today, whenever I hear the music of Herb Alpert and the Tijuana Brass, I smile at that pleasant memory.

On several surrounding farms were other relatives and friends. In our small community we knew everyone.

When we were very young, our lives were mostly centered on family and church—that was it!

On a dairy farm milking cows determines your life. Our farm supported three families and we eventually milked about one hundred cows, a lot for that time and they needed twice a day milking.

Unlike some farmers who rose between 4:00 and 5:00 a.m. to milk, Dad was in the barn for milking by 6:30 a.m., then back for evening milking around 6:30 p.m. In the hours between, my dad, my uncle and my grandfather saw to the other chores that needed tending around the farm.

Since almost everyone around us farmed, or was involved in

agriculture, most events were scheduled around farm routines. Church on Sundays was sometimes a challenge, though. The minister of St. Peter's Lutheran Church where we attended, was the pastor of two churches located about seven miles apart. So depending on his schedule we would have Sunday morning services at 9:15 or 10:30.

"Is it early Sunday or late Sunday?" Mother would ask, and the answer dictated the Sunday morning rush. If we needed to be there by 9:15, my father barely had time to eat after milking. In order to make it to church on time, he took what seemed to us the quickest shower in the world. Missing church was never an option; neither was being late.

Wisconsin is a beautiful state. The east central Fox River Valley where the Luedtke farm is located is dotted with lakes, strung together on streams and rivers like beautiful beads. Along the one hundred-eighty mile length of the north-flowing Fox River are numerous towns and cities, including Neenah, Menasha, Appleton, Oshkosh (where the river flows into, then through, huge Lake Winnebago) and the city of Green Bay where the Fox River empties into Lake Michigan. Winters are long, cold, and snowy. Summers are beautiful and mild.

Native American tribes in the area included the Winnebago (renamed Ho-Chunk in recent years), the Menominee, Ojibwa and Potawatomi. The first non-native people to arrive were probably French-Canadian trappers who found a rich supply of thick pelts. Even today there are many wild animals—hunting and fishing are popular activities. But by 1848, when Wisconsin became the thirtieth state to join the union, hunting and trapping had dwindled and the main focus shifted to domestic animals and crops.

Children were not exempt from chores on our farm. My chores were mostly in the house under Mother's direction, but I often visited the barn during milking, and sometimes helped.

The milking area was on the lower level of a large wooden barn; above it was a hay mow and alongside were several concrete stave silos. When the doors were slid open from the barnyard, each cow knew where she was to go and they filed in to take their places in stanchions along the outer walls. In the winter you could see steam rising from their nostrils and backs.

Milking was done by machine, electrically powered, each with four stainless steel cups that were slipped over the cow's teats. The machines made a pulsating whoosh-swish sound as suction withdrew the milk and it was forced into a pipe. Over it all was music from a favorite radio station permanently tuned to German polka music. The milk machines sometimes seemed to keep time with the music, and at other times competed in an odd syncopation.

While the cows were being milked, they were also fed. Silage was their main diet. Made primarily from chopped green corn plants, silage was stored in the farm's silos where it fermented. It was fed to cattle as a supplement, or when pasture grazing was not available. In our barn, silo unloaders brought the silage to ground level where it was mixed with grist (ground corn) before being given to the animals.

Through the pungent smell of manure, the sharp odor of silage and the dusty smell of ground corn was the sweet scent of fresh milk.

Before milking system improvements piped milk directly from the cow to the milk house, milk machine tanks had to be emptied manually. A lid was removed from the milk collection tank and the milk was poured into a pail. Then the pail was hand carried into a milk house alongside the barn and dumped into a bulk tank. Once a day a big milk truck with "Borden" painted on the side would come to empty the bulk tank.

Milk inspectors paid unannounced visits to the farm, making certain that proper health standards were maintained. Everything had to be clean, all the time. Sometimes we children—cousins and siblings—were pressed into service, washing the milking machines in big, deep U-shaped stainless steel sinks, rinsing them with hoses like those found in commercial kitchens.

Most often, though, when I helped in the barn my job was to clean the barn floors. Cows are pretty much constant poopers, and cleaning up after them approaches full-time effort. My dad would yell, "Nancy, clean the floors," and I'd take a big, wide shovel and push it first down the middle of the aisle between the stanchions, then I'd clean the edges closer to the cows.

Of course we witnessed life and death on the farm, but oddly, my father never had me clean the cows' teats before milking nor would he let his children witness a calf being born. Even in my teen years he would tell us children, "Get out," or "Go to the steps," if a calf was on its way and we would dutifully retreat.

Our lives on the farm were busy, full and fulfilling. The members of our family supported each other through good times and bad, but they rarely showed much emotion. That just wasn't their way.

There were lots of cats on our farm and, for the most part, no one paid much attention to them. The adults tolerated them because they helped keep mice under control, but they weren't pets—with four exceptions.

I was nine or ten years old when someone gave my father an unwanted litter of four kittens. I suppose my father figured that with plentiful milk and mice, four more cats would easily mix in with the brood. But to me, these were different than the straggly, mixed-breed farm cats that lurked in the shadows of the barn. These kittens probably had angora ancestry because their fur was long and silky. Each of the kittens had comparable white underbellies and legs, but wore distinctly different colorations on their backs and heads. They were beautiful and I adopted them, making a special home for them in the hay mow of the barn. Unlike most of the other cats, I named these, choosing Muffin and Cupcake for two of the kittens—the other names escape me.

Every afternoon, when I got off the school bus, I'd quickly change clothes and grab a snack on my way outside, then run past Grandpa's house up the rise to the barn's hay mow. When I called, "Here kitty, kitty," the four kittens bounded toward me. Petting them was a joy. Their "motors" were going so loudly you could hear their purrs ten feet away. As they vied for a place on my lap, I experienced the unconditional love that only beloved pets provide.

My after-school routine continued for weeks. But one day, only three cats bounded toward me when I called. Muffin was missing. After calling and searching for her in the hay mow, I went downstairs into the milking area of the barn. The cows were still outside in the barnyard, so it was fairly quiet. My dad and my uncle were off somewhere tending to other farm duties before the nightly milking started.

I called, "Here kitty, kitty," and heard a faint cry. On the stone ledge that topped the barn's foundation was a small space and inside that space was Muffin. She was caked with manure and her left front leg was stiff—an unnatural boomerang shape. Somehow she must have been caught in the mechanism that cleared the barn gutter and her leg was broken.

I reached up carefully and grabbed Muffin by the scruff of the neck. Then I made a pocket in the front of my sweatshirt and cradled her there while I ran for help. Outside the barn, I saw a light at Grandpa's house. Surely he would know what to do.

Words were not needed; my tear-stained face and pleading eyes said it all. Grandpa gently took the cat from me, pulled keys from his pocket and drove away in his blue and white Buick.

I didn't know what was going to happen. Cats were a commodity. Veterinarians regularly came to the farm, but tending to a cat was never—I stress, never!—their duty. Half of me thought Grandpa would put the cat out of its misery, the other half hoped upon hope that he had taken Muffin to the veterinarian.

It seemed like an eternity, but finally the Buick returned. I met Grandpa at the driver's door and saw that he cradled Muffin in one arm while he drove with the other. Muffin's leg was now set in the right position, held in place with a thick elastic bandage. The bandage would need to stay on for three weeks, Grandpa told me.

To protect Muffin while she recovered, I built her a special pen using hay bales for walls. When my dad saw the bandaged kitten, he shook his head. To this day I don't know whether his amazement was over my grandfather's act of kindness or anticipation of the bill they would soon receive from the veterinarian.

Day by day Muffin improved and when the bandage was removed her leg looked fine. The limb strengthened, and as she aged, only a slight limp differentiated Muffin from her siblings.

As the days moved toward winter, my after-school routine was inhibited by cold and darkness. My special cats soon joined the throng of downstairs cats in the barn. Yet they always came running toward me enthusiastically whenever I ventured to the barn for a visit.

Love comes in unique packages. Animals give unconditional love. Yet, what I remember most of this event is Grandpa. Lots of hugs, kisses, and saying "I love you" were not part of my upbringing, yet there is no question that I was loved. My grandfather taking an injured cat to the veterinarian for his granddaughter said it all.

When we were very small, if Mother needed a break, she would take one of us to my father and we would ride on his lap while he drove tractor. My youngest brother, Dean, especially liked that. If the Luedtke men were working in the fields, or going back and forth on the farm, Dad would have Dean on his lap. It was good training. Dean and my cousin, Rick, now operate the farm.

That's how I learned to drive. At first I just enjoyed sitting on Dad's lap, then as I got bigger I rode on the fender while he drove (for safety reasons that's no longer recommended). Sometimes he let me steer, then I learned how to shift gears while he operated the clutch. By the age of ten I was tall enough, strong enough, and had the dexterity to operate the clutch myself. After that I was on my own and I drove tractor frequently, developing a wonderful farmer's tan outdoors in the sunlight.

One of my summer tasks was to help with haying, a task that was a multi-generational affair. Following the path of the cutter I drove a tractor attached to a piece of equipment called a rake that turned the hay into windrows.

Later I drove the tractor down the windrows, pulling a baler, while my dad stacked the rectangular hay bales on a wagon hitched behind the baler. For the first layer he laid the bales side by side across the wagon, on the second layer he positioned them end to end, and so on until bales were six layers deep. His careful crisscross stacking prevented the bales from toppling over when there was a bump in the field or when a corner was turned. Dad had the art of creating "steps" between layers so he could move up to stack bales on top. When there were only a couple spaces left

John Luedtke
(Brother)

"Nancy drove the tractor quite a bit in the summer. Baling hay means driving down row after row and it can be boring, so Nancy would sing and make up little songs."

where he could sit, we headed for the edge of the field where we unhitched the full wagon and exchanged it for an empty wagon. Someone on the unloading crew would take the full wagon to the barn for unloading and leave another empty wagon in its place.

At the barn my grandfather unloaded the bales (helped by my brother, John, and cousins when they were old enough) while Uncle Roy stacked the bales in the hay mow.

Most of the time, though, I helped in the house more than outside, learning from my mother how to do laundry, clean, cook, and tend a garden. She was a good teacher.

Ours was a small kitchen, but it was up to date for the era. The sink was located in a corner beneath windows that faced east and south. The kitchen had cabinets and counter tops on three walls, plus a peninsula. Our kitchen table was on the far side of the peninsula. Fuel for the kitchen stove

Dean Luedtke
(Brother)

"Today, there are four houses on the farm and all four are heated with wood using outdoor boilers. You have to clean up the fence lines and edges of the woods anyway, so you might as well burn the wood. All the houses have supplementary heat, but the wood is free."

was piped in from a big white liquid propane tank outside.

Our main heat came from coal and wood, but sometimes the furnace would go out at night and it would be cold in the morning. There were sliding doors between the kitchen and the back hall, and the kitchen and dining room, so Mother would close them and turn on the oven, leaving the oven door open to heat the room. She'd have our clothes in the kitchen and when it was time to get up for school, she'd tell us to run to the kitchen and get dressed.

Dad, Uncle Roy and Grandpa cut wood in the winter. When John and I were big enough to help, we threw wood down an outside chute into the basement. Coal was delivered, and also unloaded down the chute into the basement where it kicked up a lot of dust. That coal smelled, and the burning coal created a gray line along the heating vents.

A conventional forced-air furnace was installed when I was in junior high school, but to this day the house's heat is augmented by wood.

My mother baked bread on Fridays. There was nothing better than coming home from school to the smell of freshly baked bread, followed by a slice of bread covered with strawberry jam. After my brothers came along, Mom usually baked six loaves of bread each week. She'd freeze them in huge, thick plastic bags and pull one out as needed. We'd use those six loaves in a week's time.

⌦

White Bread or Rolls

3 pkgs. dry yeast
¾ cup lukewarm water
6 tsp. salt
6 tbsp. sugar
3 tbsp. shortening
6 cups scalded milk (or potato water)
18 cups flour
3 well-beaten eggs

Dissolve together yeast and lukewarm water. Put salt, sugar and shortening in bowl. Add scalded milk. Cool to lukewarm. Add 6 cups of flour and beat. Then add dissolved yeast and eggs. Beat well. Add flour to make stiff enough dough (approximately 12 more cups). Knead well. Let rise in greased pan or bowl until double in size. Punch dough down. Put into six loaf pans and let rise again. May also be made into finger rolls or dinner rolls. Bake at 400° F. until done.

⌦

Mom was a good cook then, and still is today. Since we raised cows, beef was often on the menu. Steak was not unusual and mashed potatoes, gravy and vegetables were routine fare. Mom's meals were always balanced and she was concerned about the color of the food. She wanted meals to be pleasing to the eye as well as the tongue.

When we were in school, my brothers and I often ate breakfast at a different time than our parents. Dad ate breakfast after he was done with milking. His breakfast was usually three eggs (and sometimes bacon), toast and cookies—always cookies. Then he'd head out to do chores. The biggest meal of the day was a mid-day meal that we called dinner. As a family we waited until we could all gather together after evening milking to eat what we called supper.

Mom made cakes, cookies and desserts every day, and her meals were heavy with carbohydrates. We had dessert with every meal. That may seem odd to many people, but the physical demands of farm life wore off a lot of calories. No one in our family was overweight in spite of the sweets and rich desserts we consumed every day. Even now, when I'm more concerned about health issues, I still love desserts and can hardly pass on a cookie.

For decades my mother was a member of the Winnebago County Homemakers Club which is sort of like a grown-up 4-H. Homemakers is administered by the University of Wisconsin Extension Service, the same organization that oversees the state's 4-H clubs (more about 4-H later). Homemakers Clubs are educational and social. They meet in members' homes and whenever it was Mother's turn to host the group, we cleaned especially well and got everything perfect. I remember for one meeting she made a pie with a graham cracker crust, vanilla pudding filling, and meringue topping. Delicious!

At Homemakers, Mom learned to make a maple pecan ring that became her specialty. The maple ring was made by rolling bread dough into a long rectangle and then topping it with a filling of brown sugar, hickory nuts that replaced the pecans in the original recipe, maple flavoring and butter. The dough was then rolled to encase the filling and circled into a ring. The top of the ring was snipped every inch or so and the dough given a little twist for effect.

I've made the maple ring several times, but have never been able to do it as well as my mother. At the point at which the ends of the dough meet, she can cut/twist, cut/twist and perfectly camouflage the seam. It is an art.

❧

Maple Pecan Ring
(Makes two coffee cakes)

5½ to 6½ cups unsifted flour
½ cup sugar
1½ tsp. salt
2 pkgs. dry yeast
½ cup (1 stick) softened butter
1½ cups very hot tap water
2 eggs at room temperature
¾ cup chopped pecans
⅓ cup firmly packed brown sugar
1 tsp. maple flavoring
Melted butter
Liquid peanut oil
Confectioners sugar frosting

In a large bowl thoroughly mix 2 cups flour, sugar, salt, and undissolved dry yeast. Add softened butter.

Gradually add very hot tap water to dry ingredients and beat two minutes at medium speed of electric mixer, scraping bowl occasionally. Add eggs and ½ cup flour, or enough flour to make a thick batter. Beat at high speed two minutes, scraping bowl occasionally. Stir in enough additional flour to make soft dough. Turn out onto lightly floured board; knead until smooth and elastic about 8 to 10 minutes. Cover with plastic wrap, then a towel; let rest 20 minutes.

Combine pecans, brown sugar and maple flavoring. Punch dough down; divide in half. On lightly floured board, roll half of the dough into a 16" x 18" rectangle. Brush with melted butter. Sprinkle half of the brown sugar mixture over dough. Roll up from long side to form a 16" roll. Pinch seam to seal. Place sealed edge down in circle on greased baking sheet. Seal ends together firmly. Cut two-thirds of the way into the ring with scissors at 1" intervals; turn each section on its side. Repeat with remaining half of dough and brown sugar mixture. Brush rings with peanut oil and cover loosely with plastic wrap. Refrigerate 2 to 24 hours.

When ready to bake, remove from refrigerator. Uncover the dough carefully. Let stand, uncovered, 10 minutes at room temperature.
Bake in moderate oven 375° F. about 20 to 25 minutes, or until done. Remove immediately from baking sheets and cool on wire racks. When cool, frost with confectioners sugar frosting. If desired, sprinkle with additional chopped pecans.

～

    I loved baking and still do. When I was eight years old, Mom began teaching me to bake and during the summers baking became my responsibility. There were few days during the summer when we didn't bake, but I do recall a couple of very hot Tuesdays (ironing day was always Tuesday) when the kitchen was so uncomfortable that we didn't bake that day.

    But I had other chores as well, and helping tend a vegetable garden was one of them. We grew sweet corn, green beans, carrots, peas, radishes, onions, tomatoes, and cucumbers—the staples of upper Midwest gardens. John and I were often assigned weeding duties. One day I suggested to Mother that we forget the weeding and plant two rows of flowers around the garden, then two rows of sweet corn behind them so no one would be able to see the rest of the garden. She didn't take me up on that.

    Although my mother is diplomatic and kind, she is calm, reserved and quiet as well. She is not given to telling jokes or spinning yarns. An extremely capable and resourceful woman, she prefers a background role to center stage. You could say she's a No Drama Mama.

My mother woke me around 6:30 one summer morning to help her pick strawberries before the heat rose. I was still half asleep, and I'm sure, less than enthusiastic. We were picking in silence, the only sounds were of our containers being pushed along the ground as we shuffled forward. But suddenly, without preamble, Mother said:

"Starkle, starkle little twink,

What the heck you am, I think.

Up above the sky so high,

What do you think I am—a flashlight?!"

Then she went silent again while I sat in shock. Then I stood up and laughed! It was so unlike her. I don't think Mother's little ditty was original—she had likely heard it somewhere—but it provided a rare glimpse into a zany corner of my mother's persona.

Melons were one of my dad's favorite foods and he planted a patch of watermelons and cantaloupe (we called them muskmelons) in a sandy part of one field. Melon-growing conditions there were perfect. The melons all tended to ripen at once, and for a short time every summer we feasted on them. There is nothing better than a home grown, freshly-picked cantaloupe, still warm from the sun.

We had a chest-type freezer in the utility room and a cool area in the basement where jars of canned vegetables and fruit were stored. I helped Mom with both canning and freezing. We froze beans and corn, but canned tomatoes, crab apples, applesauce and pickles—all kinds of pickles—one jar for every week of the year. Sometimes we also canned pears and peaches.

It was satisfying to see the results of our efforts. You knew you had done your job of canning well when you heard the pop created when cooling contents made a vacuum that sealed the jar's lid.

We also had flower gardens and I enjoyed tending them as well. I still love gardening and have a small vegetable garden plus flower gardens that surround our home. Other than maxing out on beef (we had it almost every day and I've had plenty, thanks) none of my assigned chores as a child made me loathe the activity as an adult. I still love baking. I still love gardening.

There were hickory trees along some of the fence lines and we picked nuts in the fall. There was also wild asparagus along the road and creamed asparagus on toast was a special late spring treat. We knew where the plants were, in fact, I could go directly to those spots today. Asparagus reseeds itself if you're careful not to pick all the shoots. But sometimes before we had a chance to pick, people from town (we always claimed they must be from the big cities of Oshkosh or Appleton since we didn't know them) would drive down our road and pick the asparagus. That made my dad angry. Even though it was wild asparagus, I guess he regarded it as ours since it grew in our ditch along our fence.

Life was not all work and no play, even for the adults.

Once a year my father's family held a reunion in Oshkosh along the shores of Lake Winnebago. We had a big picnic under the trees, and the adults made us children wait an hour after eating before we could go swimming. Even aside from reunions, we had a lot of picnics in the summer.

The little town of Fremont, Wisconsin, has a small beach along a canal of the Wolf River. We used to swim there; in fact, the Luedtke cousins all took swimming lessons at that beach. I learned how to float, kick and dog paddle. A woman in our church tried to take us beyond our basic lessons at Fremont. She taught swimming to a group of kids from St. Peter's at Lake Poygan about ten miles from home on the same lake where my grandfather had his fishing cottage. Although I enjoy swimming and do it year-round, I never did master the art of synchronizing breathing with swimming strokes, and I still don't consider myself a good swimmer.

We visited with other family and friends often. Sunday afternoons were a favorite time to socialize.

On my father's side of the family I had cousins to play with. On my mother's side it was different. She was an only child and her cousins were much younger. Their children were about ten years younger than I was. So, on that side of the family I was taught to play canasta and other card games at an early age, and I played alongside the adults.

I always enjoyed visiting with my mother's family. My mother's aunts were great home decorators—there were bows and candles like nothing we had at home—and I found their homes fascinating.

I learned how to ice skate on a shallow depression that filled with rainwater, then froze, in one of the fields on the farm. I remember that it wasn't very cold and that the ice was thin. I learned how to balance on the skate blades by holding onto a chair. (John learned that way, too.) Although I can't ice skate now, I still have my first skates and they hang on a hook in our garage as reminders of childhood fun.

Our lives were pretty normal—Norman Rockwell type stuff—nothing exciting, nothing abnormal, but nice for us.

I loved being outdoors and still do. There was a trickle-sized creek next to our house and I caught pollywogs there. Especially in the spring I spent lots of time in the woods by myself, looking for spring flowers like trilliums, mayflowers, and cowslips which are also called marsh marigolds.

Walking in the woods was wonderful. There were few paths in the woods, so I probably went into the woods more in search of flowers than anything else. As a teen I got a camera and started taking pictures, an interest that has remained with me to this day and that has blossomed into an interest in landscape quilting as well.

There was something, though, that made everyone for miles around—children and adults—reluctant to venture into the woods or outdoors alone. It came every spring for several years and we called it The Thing.

Some in our community thought it might be a cougar, but the common consensus was that The Thing was a bobcat. We were accustomed to the night sounds of cattle, owls, dogs barking, crickets and frogs, but this was different. This creature screamed and cried like a baby in the night, and the sound made the hair stand up on your arms. No one ever saw it, but it cried in the darkness and its unnerving cries followed a set path through our area.

Farmers worried about their calves; children worried about their pets; parents worried about their children.

I took piano lessons for several years and rode my bike through the woods to and from my teacher's home. Even in the daytime, whenever The Thing was around, I rode very fast, afraid that it might get me.

But mine wasn't just a childish reaction—my practical and loving, solid-as-a-rock father met me at the end of the driveway as I was driven home from baby sitting one evening. The Thing had been crying and he could not rest until I was safe at home. Like my grandfather, my father showed his love through his actions.

Life at home was happy, stable and secure. But life always gives us challenges, and they were waiting.

Chapter 3

~

The Bell's palsy that pressed the right side of my face didn't dampen my childish exuberance—not at first. Only fourteen months old when it happened, at that age children don't make the connection that something is different. But as time passes, awareness grows.

My family was very matter-of-fact about my condition, and treated me with no special accommodation. Privately my mother prayed that I would not become introverted. She told me a few years ago that what happened to me was her first major problem in life. The fact that she said it recently says something—it wasn't discussed much. We were a quiet family, not given to display of any kind, and my parents were pragmatic. They did what they needed to do for my care, were assured that in time I would outgrow the condition, and we went about living our lives. My family—immediate and extended—loved and nurtured me.

When I was a child, the condition was less obvious than it is today. My muscles were more taut, my skin smoother. But when Bell's palsy arrived in the night, it stole my smile along with muscle control on the right side of my face.

I came to know, "The Look."

"The Look" happens after someone's first glance. There's a certain tilt of the head, a slight opening of the mouth, and a puzzled stare that follows. It happens face-to-face and from a distance. As the person's gaze lingers longer than normal, one can almost see them trying to figure out what's wrong, trying to determine if my face truly is different on one side or if a trick of shadow may have obscured normal symmetry.

Barbara Luedtke Eckstein

"I remember people saying things like, 'Isn't that sad,' and 'Isn't that a shame,' about Nancy, right in front of me. But, if Nancy had remained a beautiful baby and had grown into a woman with a perfect smile, would she have pursued or tried as hard as she did? We'll never know..."

As a child, I clammed up. As an adult I get a feeling of, "Oh darn, here it comes."

Most people are polite; those who are not have been mercifully few and far between. Still, I know that they have seen me as different and unless they come to know me, that difference is their only perception of who I am.

Within the cloistered atmosphere of the farm, among people who loved me, none of that mattered. When I started school, though, my world—as it does for all children—changed.

Kindergarten began for me just after Labor Day in 1958. Today kindergarten is the norm and before they get there, many kindergarten children have already attended pre-school programs. But in the rural Wisconsin of that day, kindergarten was a fledgling concept. Mine was among the first kindergarten classes in that region.

There were ten to twelve students in my class. Most were farm kids and since our schedule was abbreviated to mornings only, we didn't ride the regular school bus. Instead a red station wagon made its way down the road to take us to Mathison, a one-room schoolhouse. My first childhood crush was on a boy who shared that red wagon ride.

I don't remember a lot about kindergarten at Mathison School. My class was there a full school year, then for first grade we moved to a school in the town of Winchester. Soon after, an addition to the Winchester school made room for kindergarten students to attend there and Mathison was abandoned.

Winchester was a kindergarten through sixth grade satellite school for the larger Winneconne Public School which included junior high and high school as well. The building was constructed in the post-World War II expansion to educate baby boomers, so it was fairly new when I was there. Today the Winchester school building still stands, but is no longer a school. A sprawling one-story building with lots of large windows, there were six classrooms, one for each grade, and all faced south. I remember a cafeteria and gym, and that the desks were metal with attached chairs. They had wood or plastic laminate lids that lifted on hinges for access to inner storage.

There were about twenty-five students in each class at Winchester and, as you might expect, we came to know each other very well. With only a couple exceptions, those who started grade school with me also graduated with me from high school.

Although I learned to read in first grade, and I enjoyed second grade, I wasn't the best student. For some reason my family tends toward being late academic bloomers. We just don't connect the dots as quickly as most do.

But third grade—gosh, what can I say?!—third grade was horrible.

It may be that our teacher didn't like teaching. She was very strict and had special little rules. Every morning we had to have a tissue or hankie on our desk, along with a comb. I remember that one of the boys whose parents didn't send tissues or hankies had a roll of toilet paper on his desk.

I'm an outdoors person at heart and always have been. I like light and I like windows. In every other grade except third our desks were positioned with the windows to our left. But in third grade, our backs were toward the window. That may seem like a small thing, but facing away from the windows made me feel closed in.

I was afraid of my third grade teacher. There were things that she thought I should have already known and I think that during one grading period I got a "D" in reading. Since my right eye watered slightly and I wasn't always aware of it, she always required me to have a hanky with me in reading circle.

When I first went to school, the teachers and other students had to get accustomed to my appearance. For the most part the kids in my class were good to me, but I remember one older boy who made fun of me. "Crooked Face" and "Dog" he called me, and made faces. Sometimes he pushed me.

Kids don't have the filters that adults have learned to employ; some of his comments hurt a lot. Sometimes I told my mother, but unless the comments were especially cutting, I didn't. Perhaps there were times when

I also was not kind to others, but I hope not. I don't remember that boy's name—that's probably a good thing—but he taught me something valuable. In the Golden Rule order of things, I didn't want to inflict pain on others.

When I was very young, my facial paralysis was much less obvious than it is today. Even so, it was in early grade school that I began sitting in profile for photos. Since the right side of my face draws down and is less mobile than the left, I have always regarded it as the "sad" side while the more expressive left is the "happy" side. But for me, trying to smile would be a competition that neither side wins, so I don't. Instead I make do with a pleasant expression. In grade school I began turning the "happy" side to the camera, and the world.

The cutoff line for the Winneconne school district was just feet from the Luedtke property and children living on the farm were its northernmost students.

On school days the bus came at 7:10 a.m., so wake up time was about 6:30. After dressing and eating breakfast, I watched for the school bus from my west-facing bedroom window and when it rounded the hill up the road by my uncle's place, I ran out to meet it.

Beth was my best friend in grade school and is still a good friend. She lived about a mile or so from me in Zittau, an unincorporated town that was home to a cheese factory, a church and a tavern—a typical combo for Wisconsin. The bus picked her up first and when I climbed aboard, Beth slid over so I could sit with her.

Beth's parents owned the Union Star Cheese Factory in Zittau and her family lived above the factory. Once there were thousands of small cheese factories around Wisconsin, but only a few remain today. Union Star Cheese Factory is a survivor. Founded by Beth's grandfather in 1911, since then four generations of her family have been involved in cheese making at Union Star. Starting in third or fourth grade, Beth and I began staying overnight in each other's homes. For me the farm was familiar and routine so that made it all the more exciting to stay with Beth. We had a great time.

Milk from our farm didn't go to Union Star; it was sold to Borden. Even so, I was fascinated by the cheese-making process. Maybe because I was around milk so much, I didn't notice the distinctive sour milk odor common to cheese factories. Beth and I ate delicious fresh cheese curds from the vat, explored the factory together and played.

Her parents were good to me. Once, when they went to Wisconsin Dells, a popular resort and amusement area about ninety miles away, I was invited along.

John Luedtke

"As far as Nancy's facial issues are concerned, the criticisms hurt, but she doesn't say much about it. Kids can be cruel. As a family it was not discussed, but when Nancy woke up that day with Bell's palsy, I know it really hurt Mom. As a child my ears stuck out more than they should have. Mom taped them back with tape and I looked like a monkey, but it worked."

I was quiet as a child, but even so I had nice girlfriends. At Winchester the students were similar in so many ways—from our agricultural backgrounds, to our German and Scandinavian ancestry, to our Lutheran faith. In our community, it usually wasn't a matter of what church you belonged to, but which Lutheran church you attended. There were at least seven Lutheran churches within a few miles of our home and none for other denominations.

Because of the facial paralysis, my right eye doesn't close completely, a situation that causes a number of challenges. As I mentioned earlier, that eye waters a lot so I am constantly touching a tissue to the edge of my eye. It also doesn't close when I sleep or when I yawn.

"Cover your whole face," Mother would tell me when I yawned or when I laughed. She wanted to save me the embarrassment of uncomfortable reactions from others.

Covering my whole face, especially when laughing, had a down side. Sure, it saved me from embarrassment, but most of the time the act of hiding my face had a far bigger negative effect than did the joy of laughter. My quiet nature became more withdrawn. The quieter I became the more others began to regard me as aloof, and their embracing smiles and laughter were extended less and less. My self-confidence, in all but the most familiar situations, sank.

When our tight-knit class from Winchester school—the satellite school in the district—merged into the Winneconne school for my junior

45

high years, I moved from a comfort zone to a terrified zone. The post-merger seventh grade class totaled around one hundred (seventy-five or so from Winneconne and twenty-five from Winchester.) For the Winneconne kids it was home base, for some of us newcomers it was intimidating.

At Winneconne we were split into four groups. Although it was never officially stated, those four divisions were based on intelligence—or rather, assumed intelligence. Beth and my other friends were assigned to the "smart" group and sent to different classes. In the worst way I wanted to be part of their group, not just because they were my friends, but because I wanted to be seen as bright. But, I struggled with my studies and we were separated.

The move to Winneconne shuffled the deck. I was assigned to Class 7C—"7" for the grade, and "C" for Mr. Christianson who was our home room teacher. In my class there was only one other girl from my past school, a girl who was not among my circle of friends.

For some reading this book, a class of one hundred students seems small. For me it was overwhelming. Middle school was seventh grade and eighth grade, so now there were seventy-five new people in my grade and one hundred students in eighth grade, all of whom had probably never seen someone with Bell's palsy. So, there were one hundred seventy-five opportunities for "The Look." Granted others had it worse. Victims of polio and those with what would now be labeled autism were also in a new environment and likely uncomfortable as well.

I'm sure I was not alone in my dread of going to school, but since I can only speak for myself, I can tell you it was a very difficult time. Initially not having a friend to walk with to and from classes, or sit beside during class, only made me more self-conscious. My old Winchester girlfriends didn't desert me, but our contact was very limited.

The first semester was devastating. My grades suffered, my confidence plummeted, I drew inside myself, and I tried to hide my face even more. Think about a kid walking alone with rounded shoulders, hugging her books to her chest and looking down without making eye contact—that was me.

In second grade I was the smallest girl in my class; by seventh grade

I was among the tallest and I felt gawky; then the onset of puberty was added to the mix. I felt sad much of the time and my seventh grade school year was my crying year. It was also a year of literal growing pains and often I was awakened in the night with severe cramps behind my knees.

In our school, delinquents and students with behavioral problems ended up in the guidance counselor's office. We knew who they were and the good kids stayed away from them. It was a mark of dishonor to be among the traffic that flowed in and out of the guidance counselor's office, but I was sent to her. Even today, when I think about that time in my life, the thought of her resurrects an old and deep dread.

I can see her sitting behind her desk. Her expression was always intense and like many teachers of that era, she maintained an authoritative presence. Her hair was black and tightly curled and she dressed nicely despite a physical deformity. Her smartly tailored suits accommodated a hunched back and impeccably fit her petite figure. In another time and place I would have admired her style.

She wanted to talk about my face.

To be truthful, I can't remember what she said, but as a tenderhearted seventh grader, being in her office was greater trauma than any other challenge in my life. I do remember that 'Get over it and get on with it' was her mantra, but instead of motivating me, her approach left me in shame and humiliation. Although I'm sure her desire was for my good, I always left her office crying. Maybe the crying was because her words had struck a nerve, identifying something I was already dealing with in secret. Maybe I was simply intimidated—I don't know—but she made me cry.

I was called to her office several times that first semester and off and on through the end of eighth grade. Each time I was an unwilling visitor, and a weeping escapee when dismissed. In the hallways I dodged her glances and ducked into bathrooms to avoid her. I felt singled out and not in a good way.

Eventually I did 'Get on with it' sometime during the second semester of my seventh grade year. I made new friends in my homeroom, including another Nancy who remains my friend today.

But, I needed more—I needed something to build confidence,

something that would brake my downward slide and affirm my worth.

That something came through 4-H membership and discovering my destiny in sewing.

Bless her heart—my mother is a giver. But she doesn't give, and walk away. No, she's the kind of person who offers a hand to help you stand, pushes in a nurturing way, then walks alongside until you're strong enough to make it on your own. That's one of her gifts and exercising that gift has allowed her children to discover their own.

When I was ten years old, I joined the Winchester 4-H Club. That same year my mother became a 4-H leader, a position she held for twenty-seven years—from my first year in 4-H through my sister, Gina's, last.

4-H Pledge

I pledge my head to clearer thinking, my heart to greater loyalty, my hands to larger service, and my health to better living, for my club, my community, my country, and my world.

As a youth organization 4-H has been around over one hundred years and its name represents four H's in the club pledge—head, heart, hands, and health. Although now there are 4-H clubs in cities, towns and rural areas, at first 4-H was primarily directed toward youth in rural, agricultural settings.

Its far-reaching goal is to help young people establish a foundation of skills and leadership abilities that will help them in their careers, families, and communities. That's a lofty goal; accomplishing it requires mentoring youth as they learn how to take the lead on their own projects, establish realistic goals, test their efforts against those of their peers, and articulate their efforts to others.

Our club was mostly farm kids. Our monthly meetings began after milking—around 8:00 p.m.—and were held in the basement fellowship hall of Grace Lutheran Church in Winchester, my mother's home church during her childhood. The room had a stage, and back then it seemed a huge room, but not long ago I was there for a family funeral, and now it seems very small.

There were about sixty in our club, quite large considering that Winchester's population, the year I joined 4-H (1963), was about three hundred, and nearby Larsen was only two hundred.

Young people ages ten through nineteen can participate in 4-H activities and the broad categories under which members develop their individual projects are relevant to their lives. When I started in 4-H, things were quite gender stereotyped. Girls usually took Sewing, Cooking and Home Furnishings; boys developed their interests in things like Woodworking, Electricity, Swine, Beef and Poultry.

4-H categories are divided into skill levels and members advance from one to the next. Since young people acquire the skills necessary to move from one level to the next from year to year, that means the ages of the students are about the same at each level, making for a more even playing field when it comes to 4-H competitions.

Our monthly club meetings were structured. Volunteer adult leaders provided guidance and, if needed, the last say. Youth elected to leadership roles ran the meetings using parliamentary procedure. We usually opened with the Pledge of Allegiance, a song, the 4-H Pledge, and then we got down to business. At our meetings, the macho guys always sat in the back of the room.

In our club, the head volunteer adult was Eugene Anderson, my mother's cousin. A man devoted to 4-H, he was an effective leader for many years. In addition to my mother, two or three other mothers were also adult leaders. Aside from monthly club meetings, we also had monthly meetings centered on the categories in which we had chosen to participate.

4-H members learn by doing. Of course, from the categories available I took Sewing, but over my years in 4-H, I also took Home Furnishings, Knitting, Junior Leadership and Conservation. Conservation was Mother's idea. We needed a wind break on the farm so Mother said, "We're planting trees. Sign up for Conservation." By then my brother, John, was also a 4-H member, and so we both signed up. I remember that John and I, along with Mother, planted two hundred Norway pines and fifty white pine trees then went for ice cream cones afterwards to celebrate. I'm amazed at how many of those trees lived, and amazed, too, at how huge they are today.

I took Sewing as my project the first year. Before then I never asked to sew and wasn't offered that option. My mother tells me that my grandmother, Georgina Larson, was an excellent seamstress, and although Mother didn't sew a lot as a child, Mother was also a 4-H member who participated in Sewing. In the first year that my parents were married, Mom got a Pfaff 130 sewing machine and after Grandma Georgina's death, she returned to sewing. She did a good job, too.

Mom's Pfaff was the machine I learned on and even after all these years and dozens of sewing machines later, my hand still holds the memory of its threading sequence. For Christmas in 2012, Mom gave me that sewing machine with the cabinet restored to its original blonde color.

There are judged competitions in 4-H. In the Sewing category, the big deal each July was the Dress Revue in which members modeled garments they made. Prizes in the form of ribbons—blue (first place), red (2nd place), white (3rd place), and pink (4th place)—were awarded for each age level. Top winners also advanced to the state fair style show competition. The garments could also be entered at the county fair competition.

First year participants in Sewing, all made the same project—a gathered skirt and fringed scarf. After that, they could branch out on their own.

My skirt and scarf were gold—cotton probably, although the fabric may have had some synthetic fibers. I think my mother may have already had the fabric because it was not my choice. Our family was very economical, conservative and frugal. We never wanted for food or clothing or safety or warmth, or any other necessity, but extras were carefully considered before purchase. For my first project I used what was on hand.

The pattern for the outfit came from a 4-H pamphlet for beginners in the Sewing category. I remember the goal was to stitch straight and close to the edge; then you had to pull threads to make the fringe for the scarf. With fringes on all four sides, the scarf was so outdated that I never wore it.

As was required of all members, I recorded activities and projects in a book for each 4-H category. Those records included descriptions of projects, costs, comments on what was learned in the process of completion, and whether or not my goals were achieved. Achievement certificates were awarded when requirements for each category were completed. Thanks to my mother's tendencies to save, I still have all my record books from my years in 4-H.

Mary Luedtke Rebman

"I hated that book. You had to write down everything in that book. Barbara was my 4-H leader and she probably ended up doing most of it for me."

The second year, I made a reversible jumper and a blouse with a bow—everyone in my age group made the same blouse. My jumper was broadcloth, a red, white, and blue plaid on one side and solid red on the other. That year (1965), I was able to move beyond fabric on hand and purchase the materials. My jumper fabric cost $5.04 and the blouse fabric was $2.07.

It wasn't until my third or fourth year in 4-H that I gave any thought to winning a prize at the annual Dress Revue. But as I got older, I moved from thinking about it, to planning to win.

Mention the word "demonstrations" in the same sentence as "1960s," and the mental images will be of protests and peace marches. But for those of us in 4-H, a demonstration was a presentation made with a goal of educating others as it showcased an individual member's skill in his or her project area.

Barbara Luedtke Eckstein

"Nancy's brothers hated the record books required for 4-H members. They managed to get through, but Nancy would work at hers diligently."

To my mother's credit she pushed me. She said, "Nancy, you need to do demonstrations." She knew how to put demonstrations together and I owe her a tremendous amount of gratitude.

My first demonstration in Sewing was, "How to put on a Waistband." With help from Mother, I broke the process down into various steps and created different samples showing each of those steps. There is no magic to a waistband, but when I stood before the judges of my club, demonstrating step-by-step how to prepare and attach a waistband, the girl who spoke was confident, articulate, and at home in herself.

Nothing else mattered—I had discovered where I belonged.

Chapter 4

∞

My 4-H involvement was both a confidence boost and a diversion from the school, farm, and church routines of my life.

I was ten the year I started 4-H. That was also the year my brother, Dean, was born. My brother, John, was a first grader. As a farm wife and mother, plus a volunteer 4-H leader, my mother worked hard to maintain all the responsibilities of her life.

After Dean was born, my mother got an automatic washer, but up until then she did laundry with a wringer washer and two rinse tubs. She did have an automatic dryer, given to her by Grandpa Larson soon after my birth. It helped handle my cloth diapers.

Mother was careful to run her home as economically as possible. Even though the electric clothes dryer saw use for diapers and on days when the weather didn't cooperate, most of the time laundry was hung to dry on clotheslines stretched behind the house. Free solar and wind power made the washing, and especially the bedding, smell wonderful fresh off the line. Clotheslines stretched in the basement helped finish drying if needed.

Since I was only fourteen months old when it happened, I don't remember the earache that preceded the onset of Bell's palsy. I also don't remember being sick much before or during my grade school years. There were the occasional colds, stomach bugs and things like measles, mumps and chicken pox that swept through the childhood populace, but nothing unusual. What I do remember is that if one of us children felt especially bad at night, Mother would sleep at the end of our bed, curled up with a blanket, right there in case we needed her. I remember how comforted I felt by her presence.

I remember Mother sitting in a child-sized rocker in my bedroom, reciting nursery rhymes to me. Every evening at bedtime there was prayer time as well and we drifted off to sleep in the assurance that God and our parents loved us.

Managing the household was Mother's job, and since most of our personal needs came through the home, it was Mother's example in handling money that I noticed first. To the uninitiated person driving past our farm, the buildings, land and cattle might prompt them to think we were doing quite well and they would be partly right. The farm had substantial assets, but cash was often limited. Mother carefully considered every need before spending.

Barbara Luedtke Eckstein

"We never felt poor. We just didn't have much money."

Each year our garden increased to help feed a growing family. The fruit cellar in the basement where we stored the vegetables and fruit we canned each summer was as large as my parents' bedroom. The chest freezer was kept stocked with vegetables and fruit, meat (hunted and farm-raised), plus a constantly revolving supply of baked goods—bread, rolls and cookies.

My mother is a woman who has lived her life by the Golden Rule—treat others as you want to be treated. She is fair, but diplomatic.

My father was more forthright than my mother. Like his father, Grandpa Luedtke, he wasn't given to hugs or verbal expressions of devotion. He frequently smiled at me, would ask, "How you doin', kid?" and sometimes squeezed my shoulder, but he usually shook hands with my brothers when congratulating them on special occasions. Yet, when we were little he gave us all "bear hugs," squeeze-tight hugs with accompanying funny noises.

He wasn't tough on me too often. But I remember one time, when he bellowed at me in anger.

Although I drove tractor around the farm, I took driver's education in high school and got my driver's license when I was sixteen. But we had only one car, so I didn't have access to driving too often.

One time, though, I drove too fast on a snowy road, lost control on a curve, and ploughed into a snow bank. I didn't damage the car—snow is very forgiving—but Dad had to come and pull me out. My father didn't get angry too often, and when he yelled at me, I felt like I wanted to die.

My parents worked well together as a team. If they ever argued, it was never in front of us children. Mother's perspective on marriage was mostly a Biblical one—she believed the husband was the head of the household. My brothers sometimes felt my father was tough on them, but even so, they knew he loved them.

Dad was also a frugal man. Until Grandpa Luedtke died, the farm supported three families. So as the demands of growing families increased, the dairy herd was expanded and more barns were added to accommodate larger dairy herds.

Dean Luedtke

"Growing up on a farm fosters a work ethic. If you don't do something you're responsible for doing, it won't get done; and if you do a lousy job, you're the one who pays. You see the trials and tribulations, but you also get to see the glory of God in how plants grow and calves are born, and how things fit together in this world."

In the 1960s through the 1980s, many farms erected low-oxygen silos, steel structures that sealed outside air away from the contents. The silos—most of them—were manufactured by Harvestore and are identifiable by their signature dark blue color. They promised higher quality silage and less decay and mold. But, they were also about three times more expensive than regular concrete stave silos constructed of small pre-cast concrete blocks that lock together and are circled by steel hoops (staves) for strength. As the Luedtke Farm grew, more silos were added to bring the total to four, but ours were always the traditional concrete stave silos.

A farm is a unique place to raise a family. The demands of farming give opportunity (and sometimes necessity) for farm children to help out. We were no exception. Working alongside our parents gave us a close relationship with them. By seeing them in family and work settings, we learned their character, were witness to those challenges that concerned them, and learned how to manage as adults by watching them.

My brother, John, remembers going with Dad and Uncle Roy

John Luedtke

"The things we got from Dad were his conservative values on money. I remember that we had been cutting hay with a simple six-foot sickle mower and Uncle Roy wanted to purchase a ten-foot Owatonna Haybine mower. My father was very conservative, while my uncle was more progressive. After much deliberation they purchased the mower. It represented a big investment at the time, but one that made much quicker work of haying. As conservative as Dad was, it sometimes was his best strength and his worst enemy, too."

to farm auctions, on the hunt for good used equipment. That was in the late 1960s and early 1970s, when many family farms, especially across the upper Midwest, were in crisis. There were lots of foreclosures and many farmers were selling out. There were also protests over government farm policies and even a tractor caravan to Washington, D.C., to draw attention to the needs of farmers. Although my father may have had some sympathy for fellow farmers, he never joined the organizations involved in public protests. Even though operating our farm wasn't always easy, he and my uncle worked hard to keep the debt load manageable.

I was away from home and married when Grandpa Larson died. There was a stipulation in his will that my mother could purchase the farm where she grew up at a price much lower than market value—forty thousand dollars for eighty acres. My parents decided to do it. John remembers that they made the payments on the Larson farm from our father's salary for a long time. Still, they were able to invest as well, and when my father died in 1997, our mother was financially secure.

Learning about handling money came through watching our parents. We were never officially taught how to budget money, but we watched, learned, and mainly listened. We never had too much, never had too little money or the things it could buy. With the exception of the purchase of Grandpa Larson's farm and some improvements for the Luedtke farm, our parents paid for things as they went along and their philosophy was not to purchase until they had the money.

I observed Mom, carefully evaluating the necessity of every

56

purchase. Extra purchases were rare, but the Luedtke family wasn't alone in their frugality. That was the case with most of my classmates and other relatives, so it didn't seem unusual. Being financially careful was the way everyone in our community operated.

Our financial routines didn't include allowances. We all received what was needed and I never felt I was lacking.

But, there was a brief time when I did receive an allowance of twenty-five cents a week. The reason was that I wanted to buy a ring. The jewelry department of Prange's Department Store in nearby Appleton was just inside the main entrance and shoppers had to pass its glass display cases on their way to other areas. Like most other farm families, my family shopped at Prange's for things we couldn't make at home, or for the supplies to make them ourselves—shoes, underwear, work jeans, fabric and patterns. On one of those shopping trips, I saw the ring—an adjust-to-fit band, with the initial "N" etched into a black background.

It had to be mine.

The price of the ring was $1.25, very little in today's marketplace, but I was a child with no money and it was the wrong time of year to ask for the ring as a birthday or Christmas gift. It seemed unattainable, but I asked for it anyway, and received the expected "no" in response. Still, every time we went into Prange's I stopped to admire it.

On the way home from one shopping trip in which I once again gazed longingly at the ring, I remember suggesting (timidly, I'm sure) that if I had an allowance I could save up to buy it. What followed was a rare negotiation in which Mother listed extra chores that I agreed to perform in exchange for twenty-five cents a week.

The weekly quarter went into a glass jar tucked away on the top shelf of my closet. After week five, that ring was mine. Funny thing about it, though—I remember the pursuit of the ring more than wearing it! After a short time, the "N" became scratched and the ring lost its appeal.

When I was thirteen years old, I took a Red Cross training course for baby sitters. The Immel family lived about a mile away and I started baby sitting for their children, Julie and Patrick, on Saturday nights and an occasional weeknight as well. That gave me a little more freedom in terms of spending money.

My best gift ever was one I received in junior high school when my Larson grandparents gave me an olive green sweater and matching skirt. It fit perfectly and was made of wool. The sweater was a pullover with a zipper in the back and the skirt was tweed. I didn't have a lot of personal belongings and that outfit made me feel pretty classy; I wore it with matching fishnet stockings and it remained a vital part of my wardrobe all the way through college until it got into the wrong batch of laundry and was ruined.

My father loved to fish and hunt. On rare occasions, Dad took a day off from farming to go deep water fishing in Lake Michigan, something he would have enjoyed doing more often. We all fished on local lakes in the summer, and even went ice fishing in the winter. As a supplement to farm-raised beef, pork and chicken, we ate fish, pheasant and venison.

Dean Luedtke

"We have deer stands in the woods and we hunt. Before the new highway came in we had one of the better stands in the area."

The men in the family put up several deer stands in the woods on the farm. Deer stands are like tree houses, but are usually supported by legs. They actually look like miniature versions of the old fire towers that can still be seen overlooking some forests. Built ten to twenty feet above ground level they provide a platform for viewing and shooting deer during the annual deer hunting season.

Several years ago a new highway went in about a mile north of the farm. Dad would have hated that in part because of what it meant to hunting and wildlife. There are no exits from the highway onto the land, but you can hear traffic. The wildlife can hear the traffic, too, and they move farther from the road.

Hunting and fishing not only provided food, but also provided an opportunity to be together outside of normal routines. All of us children learned how to fish, handle guns and hunt. I learned, too, and even went so far as to get a hunting license once, but never had the heart to shoot.

Multiple generations of Luedtke's hunt and fish, something that was part of our heritage long before my great-great grandfather's arrival on

Mary Luedtke Rebman

"Living on a farm was great. I love being outside and to this day I don't like being inside. After my mother died, being with my dad and my brothers was important. That's probably why I hunted and fished with them—I wanted to be with them. If you weren't with them, you stayed home."

the land that became our farm. Aunt Mary was already hunting with Grandpa Luedtke, Dad and Uncle Roy when she was barely a teenager and to this day she frequently goes on deer and elk hunting trips with family and friends. My brother, Dean, and his family are carrying on the tradition by hunting around home as well as traveling to Canada on family hunting and fishing trips.

My father played fast pitch softball during the summers on a team sponsored by Union Star Cheese, the cheese factory owned by my friend Beth's parents. A lot of the players were farmers so games were scheduled to start after evening milking. The whole family went to Winchester to watch him play. When John joined the team, Dad continued playing and played until he was about forty years old, becoming the senior member of the league.

John wasn't just interested in playing—it became a passion for him. And he was good. He played American Legion baseball in high school, and was a pitcher in college. He's still associated with baseball as a coach and head of the athletic department at a college in Arkansas.

Dean Luedtke

"Basketball was a winter sport and I played it in high school. Because games were often held at milking time, Dad couldn't make it to some of them."

Everyone in our family had responsibilities. Dad shouldered the major farm chores, and Mother anchored our home, of course. But as children, we also had assigned chores. Mine centered mostly on the house and assisting Mom, while John and Dean helped on the farm. My sister, Gina, is eighteen years younger than I am, but her chores also centered primarily on the home. None of us had chores to do before school. School was our prime responsibility and we were expected to have

Gina Luedtke Crispell

(Sister)

"Our parents instilled a legacy of hard work and kindness in us. They were good people and they expected us to be good at, and succeed in, whatever we chose to do. There was no time for failure."

homework done and everything organized the night before, to get up when called, dress, eat breakfast, and be out the door to meet the bus when it stopped at the end of the driveway.

We had our routines on Saturdays, too. No one slept in beyond 8:00 a.m. There might be church, 4-H, or school events to attend, but Saturday was not a day off.

Sundays, though, were a time to relax. We attended church in the morning—no options on that! There was still evening milking, but Sunday afternoons and evenings were family time. Sometimes we visited with relatives or friends, in our home or theirs. Sunday evenings after milking we often popped corn and sipped instant Tang, a breakfast drink, while watching a TV movie.

There wasn't a lot of sibling rivalry in our family. There were probably several reasons for the mostly harmonious atmosphere in our home. First, we were focused on the chores and responsibilities each of

John Luedtke

"There wasn't a lot of competition between siblings. But one time, Nancy got mad at me. She'd probably kill me for telling this, but she was standing at the mirror in her bedroom and she threw a dictionary at me. It hit near my eye and I have a scar there to this day."

us needed to finish and not on each other. Being busy reduced the boredom that often fuels childhood fights. Also, the spread of years between the children in our family put us at different maturity levels where there wasn't much point to petty conflict. Our parents wouldn't have put up with bickering and fighting either; they didn't argue in front of us and they kept us in order quite well. I have to say that they were very fair-minded people. They didn't play favorites, so we didn't either.

Still, there were times…

As I've already mentioned, there were (and still are) many Lutheran churches near

Dean Luedtke

"When I was in grade school, my place at the dinner table was across from Nancy. One of her major dislikes was her youngest brother chewing with his mouth open. She would say, 'Dean Charles Luedtke, eat with your mouth shut' and she would slam her fist down and the glasses on the table would jump."

where I grew up. The town of Winneconne where I attended middle school had a Presbyterian, Baptist and Catholic church in addition to Lutheran churches, but before middle school, I can't recall that any of the students in my class were anything other than Lutheran. There were, however, various denominations within Lutheranism.

The church we attended, St. Peter's, is part of the Wisconsin Evangelical Lutheran Synod, arguably the most conservative of all Lutheran denominations. Garrison Keillor is the founding talent behind the long-running radio variety program *A Prairie Home Companion*, produced by Minnesota Public Radio. In his monologues about the residents of mythical Lake Wobegon, he occasionally pokes gentle fun at a congregation of "sad Lutherans." I always smile knowingly when he says it. Although I now attend and teach third grade Sunday School in a Lutheran church Garrison might describe as a "smiley" church, at St. Peter's things were taken very seriously. We were taught traditional viewpoints of worship, instruction, relationships, and service.

Vacation Bible School was held at St. Peter's in the summer, and sometimes John and I rode our bikes the four miles to the church. The church is still there, and still has an active congregation. When I was a child, the congregation was small—about one hundred, at the most one hundred fifty. On Sundays, about sixty were in attendance.

St. Peter's Lutheran Church was not large enough to support a full time pastor, so our pastor's time was split between two churches. The tiny unincorporated town of Readfield, about eight miles north of the farm, had a tavern, a feed mill, a gas station, a few houses and Zion Lutheran Church—the second, and largest, church in our pastor's parish.

Confirmation is a rite of passage for children raised in the Lutheran faith, following a course of study designed to develop a mature understanding of the beliefs of the church. Starting at age nine and continuing to age thirteen, every Saturday morning from 9:00 a.m. to noon during the school year I attended Confirmation classes at Zion. There were four of us from St. Peter's—Marilyn, Katy, Kenny and me—and there were fifteen from Zion Lutheran. The young people from Zion were in a different school district so we didn't know them and, it seemed, they weren't interested in us. We sat with our own group and there was little communication between us.

The first two years classes were held in the church basement and were taught by a woman whose name I can't recall. However, I do remember that I dreaded the class. Not that I didn't want to learn, but the class was three hours long with only one fifteen-minute break. The teacher was not a gifted instructor and her lecture and our memorization were based around *Luther's Small Catechism*. Besides, it was Saturday morning—need I say more?

One thing I can say is that we were all well-behaved. When I think of the Sunday School class, I teach today and look back at our behavior then (wow!), there's a huge difference.

For the last two years of Confirmation classes, we moved from the church basement to an adjacent building which had once been a small, one-room schoolhouse. Except for what we wore and the fact that there were electric lights in the building, everything had the appearance of a bygone era. The only heat source was a potbelly stove. In the winter, we often shivered in our winter coats.

Earlier, I mentioned that my family tends toward being late bloomers academically. That was the case for me with Confirmation classes as well. I was overwhelmed with facts and stories, and couldn't seem to grasp the details. Still, I never questioned—questioning was foreign to me. My classmates often had better understandings of the material we were covering. For one assignment, I remember that we were to use descriptions in the Bible to draw what we thought the temple in Jerusalem looked like. I totally failed. I remember looking at Katy's drawing and thinking, 'Where did she read about that?!'

During my childhood, St. Peter's had three different pastors. Pastor

Stelter became our teacher for the last two years of Confirmation classes, and he's the pastor I remember best. He always wore a black suit and I remember him as a congenial man with a pleasant smile. When students in the class asked questions he couldn't answer, he'd pull out a small note pad from the inside breast pocket of his suit and say, "I don't know the answer. Let me write it down and ask God when I get to heaven."

I appreciated him a lot, especially his warmth and frankness. He stressed trusting God, but told us that as humans we couldn't always understand God's ways. Yet, he assured us, God would never let us down.

When it came time for our official Confirmation as members of a congregation, the members of our class went back to their home churches. The process and celebration of Confirmation took place at St. Peter's over three Sundays, the first being Examination Sunday. The four of us, the Confirmands, were seated in the front of the church facing the altar, our backs to the congregation. I'm sure there was a hymn or two, but in lieu of a traditional service, we were asked questions for an hour. Talk about stress! We had no idea which questions would be presented to us so we really studied our lists of Bible verses and knew the Catechism inside and out. If one of us didn't know an answer, the question passed to the next person.

To this day, when I think of Examination Sunday my palms sweat. But my brother, John, had it worse than I did. When John was confirmed, the students had to face the congregation, while the minister (Pastor Stelter had moved on by then) stood in the back of the church asking the questions.

The second Sunday, Confirmation Sunday, was a big deal. Mom made me a light blue jacket and skirt. Actually she made me two jackets and two skirts, since she originally intended to make the outfit reversible. But the fabric was too heavy for that, so I ended up with two outfits the same style. The duplicate skirt and jacket was a light blue plaid. Mom saved the light blue version and it hangs in the back of my closet. Confirmation was also the first time I wore nylons and "high heels," white pumps with one-inch heels.

A dinner for about twenty relatives was held after church. Mother had been planning the menu for weeks. Ham, green bean casserole, fruit salad and cake were served. Grandpa Luedtke brought baked beans; he started soaking beans and cooking his special recipe the Friday night before. And in a surprise for guests, Mom introduced an innovation to the meal—she served instant mashed potatoes for the first time in her life. She practiced making them several weeks in advance so they would turn out just right.

In the afternoon, great aunts and uncles were invited for coffee, dessert bars and cake. We took family pictures. Since my grandparents had been my sponsors when I was baptized as an infant, for one photo Grandpa Luedtke and Grandpa Larson stood on either side of me; they looked proud.

I received gifts, too. Great Aunt Alma made me pillowcases with beautifully crocheted edges. I still have the pillowcases and can't bring myself to use them in fear that I'll stain them with mascara remnants.

As for the Confirmation service at church, the most memorable part for me was that Pastor Stelter was almost late. He was always at church by 8:00 a.m., but that day he forgot that we had switched to daylight savings time overnight. We wondered if we were going to be left "standing at the altar," until he arrived in a flurry of confusion and apology a few minutes before church started at 9:00 a.m.

During the Confirmation service, members of the congregation were witnesses as we four Confirmands recited our vows and received a blessing. It was one of the most formal services in our church. The Sunday after Confirmation marked our First Communion as members of the church.

Several years ago, I stepped into an art gallery, and the painting of a simple, white, clapboard-sided country church caught my eye. It was so like St. Peter's that I was drawn to it. Without pausing to consider whether or not the purchase was practical, I bought it. The painting hangs in the hall of our home as a reminder that my faith is my foundation, and that St. Peter's is where it began.

When I was a teenager, my bedroom walls were painted lavender. A window faced west and was curtained with white sheers over a pull down shade. The bedspread on my twin bed was nubby chenille that left marks on your face if you slept on it. I had a little metal desk with two drawers on one side. Mounted on the walls were a big mirror and two paint-by-number pictures I painted—one of a mountain scene and the other of some ducks.

Today my mother uses my old bedroom as her sewing room, but when I was at home it was a good place to watch for the school bus, and a good place from which to monitor the weather. The upper Midwest has its share of tornadoes, and they usually travel from west to east. I can remember several occasions when we took shelter in the basement, though fortunately we never had serious damage from bad storms.

It's funny what you remember. That TV and radio warning that has a blaring horn and beeps followed by the announcement, "This is a test of the emergency broadcast system…" I hated that as a child and it still makes me cringe today.

We were farmers, so of course weather was a big concern. Spring planting could be delayed by excessive snow melt or rains. Too little summer rain could stunt crops; too much rain could damage hay and ruin harvests. Hail was bad anytime. Weather is the reigning factor in farming.

My worst childhood weather experience, though, occurred when I was fourteen. Mother had a cousin who lived in Brownsville, Texas, and the day after Christmas we left home to go visit their family. Because Dad needed to be back for milking and chores, it was rare for our family to go anywhere that required driving time of more than an hour or two. So, the trip to Texas was the first major family trip I can remember.

Wisconsin gets a lot of snow and by Christmas of that year there was a lot of it on the ground. The smallest breeze caused the snow to drift, but that's the way it was most winters. On the farm, my dad and my uncle kept our driveways open using a wide bucket mounted

John Luedtke

"I played baseball in high school, and I remember once not making it to a game because rain was threatening and we needed to get the hay in. We just had to do it and that was that. Each wagon held a hundred bales and a good day was ten wagons. Everyone worked hard and we had a good system going. We made it. The rain started as we were unloading the last wagon."

on the front of a tractor. Farm equipment had to move and the milk truck had to get in and out.

I remember stopping at Grandpa Luedtke's house to say goodbye before we packed ourselves into the car. We were still in high spirits several hours later when we crossed from Wisconsin into Iowa, the farthest I had ever been from home.

By the time we reached Brownsville, snowdrifts were far behind us. It seemed odd to step into weather so warm that we were comfortable without heavy coats or jackets.

We hadn't been there a day, though, when Uncle Roy called to tell my father that Grandpa Luedtke had suffered a stroke and the prognosis was not good. My father made quick arrangements and flew home, arriving just in time to say goodbye to his father. The rest of us remained in Texas—Mom, my brothers, John and Dean, (Dean was only four years old) and me.

John and I shared a room in my mother's cousin's home and I remember us clinging to each other in bed, crying because our grandpa had died. I remember feeling helpless and longing to be home.

Mom, of course, had to drive us home. The longest road trip of her life suddenly turned into the longest road trip of her life without another driver and three children in the car. Meanwhile, the entire upper Midwest was slammed with another snowstorm.

I don't know how the connection was made, but somehow Mother learned that another family from nearby Winchester, Wisconsin, was also in Texas visiting relatives. We waited until they were headed home and caravanned with them. There was comfort in knowing familiar help was only a few car lengths away.

The trip was mile after mile of wishing it would end. The closer to Wisconsin and home we drove, the deeper the snow, and the worse the roads became. Fortunately, my mother is experienced in driving on snow and ice and she brought us home safely. We stayed one night in a motel on the way home, but still, Mother must have been exhausted by the time we pulled into our driveway, almost seventeen hundred miles later.

So much snow had fallen while we were away that snowdrifts reached to the eaves of our house. Pathways between buildings were long trenches with high, cold, white walls and when I think about it, that image goes a long way toward describing my grief over losing my grandpa. We missed his funeral and when we drove into our driveway, there was a funeral bouquet in the snow outside our house. It felt like spring would never come again.

Chapter 5

~

Moving from middle school to high school was less difficult than the move from grade school to middle school. For one thing, we merely moved to the high school section of the Winneconne school, rather than to a bigger school. Our class size remained at about one hundred and with only a couple exceptions, the student populace held the same faces as in our seventh and eighth grade years. By my freshman year I had developed new friends and my grades were improving.

Almost every child questions their name at some point and longs for something else, an affectionate version of their real name that reflects their acceptance—a nickname that they can imagine their friends using. When I was in middle school, I wanted to be known as Nan, but everyone continued to call me Nancy. In high school I wanted to be called Nance, but no one did that either. No one ever called me anything but Nancy until Nancy's Notions was well established and a young man with a developmental disability came to work in our warehouse. "Hiya Nance!" he would call as I walked through. He was a trend of one. Nancy I am, and Nancy I will forever be.

Outside of school I was involved in 4-H and in a youth group made up of young people who had been confirmed into the Lutheran church about the same time I was. There were six to eight kids in that group and we did things together, like bowling and ice skating.

I suppose part of the reasoning behind the youth group was to keep boys and girls socializing with others of our own faith. Boyfriends, though, were not even on the radar for me. I saw myself as undesirable.

Of course, I had my share of romantic crushes. In grade school there was a red-haired boy I liked a lot and my dad teased me about him.

In middle school I was interested in a couple of boys, but by then I knew to keep my romantic interests to myself. One year in high school gym class we learned how to square dance. Boys and girls were lined up in rows and paired off by height. My partner was a basketball player and the exertion of square dancing wasn't the only thing that brought color to my cheeks. But he barely knew I existed, and I didn't know how to show him.

In my freshman year, one of my girlfriends had a boy/girl party. While excitedly voicing her party plans she told me that I wouldn't be invited because, "No one would want to be with you." She wasn't the only person who felt that way—I was convinced of the same.

I guarded myself from potential rejection by being quiet and my classmates saw me as aloof, a bit stuck up. More than anything, that was a shield of defense. All through high school I never had a date and never went to prom or homecoming. Whenever I tried to move out from behind my shield, the results were dismal.

Being a cheerleader was, of course, the pinnacle of high school acceptance, so I tried out for the squad. Tryouts were held in front of the student body. I was so self-conscious and when I assembled with the others who were trying out, I looked at their outfits and just knew I was dressed all wrong and that I had no business being a cheerleader. When my turn came to try out, I could hardly even find my voice to cheer loud enough to be heard. What a painful experience! I wanted to die.

Barbara Luedtke Eckstein

"Sometimes Nancy came home from school discouraged. One time in high school I felt so bad for her because she tried out to be school mascot—Willy the Wolf—where her costume would have completely covered her. She could have been carefree in that role, but she didn't get it. Her senior year she applied to do one of the graduation speeches, but she didn't get picked then either. 'Never got picked' was the story of her high school life."

My senior year, still craving companionship and team spirit, I tried out for team mascot, a role in which I would be costumed and anonymous. That didn't happen either.

I was so self conscious that I had a difficult time with things that for a more confident student might have been a minor incident. Also, I know that almost everyone has horror stories from high school, so I don't think my experience was dramatically worse than what other students went through.

In ninth grade, one of my teachers was a fiery little man, who coached football. Frequently he would stand on the waste basket in the classroom. My only guess about that is he was using it to show his authority in some sort of compensation for his stature.

We used to call him "Mr. Read Out Loud" because he had us do that, often. One day, he called on me and while I was reading, instead of forming the word "beast" as it appeared on the page, I said "breast." That was in 1967, and mentioning covered body parts wasn't socially acceptable. I was mortified at what had slipped from my mouth. My classmates started laughing, but the teacher started yelling, mocking what I had said, and accusing me of doing it on purpose. I felt myself shrinking under his onslaught. I collapsed back into my desk chair and prayed to be invisible. After that, I would sweat going into his class in fear that he might call on me.

But although some things were difficult, there were victories. In contrast with "Mr. Read Out Loud," that same year I had an English teacher, Mrs. Fawcett, who was a recent graduate of the University of Wisconsin at Oshkosh. Her job at Winneconne High School was the first of her career. She was also cute, petite and recently married; her husband was in the military, serving in Vietnam.

The four class divisions to which we were assigned in middle school were unofficially based on intelligence. Those divisions remained largely intact from middle school through high school. I had gained some ground academically, but things did not come easy for me and I studied hard.

Mrs. Fawcett delighted me, as a person and as a teacher. I worked especially hard in her class. One day, after a long string of "A" assignments, she pulled me aside and said, "You don't belong in this class. Come with me." She led me to the principal's office and I stood nervously next to her as she told the principal that I should be moved to the smart class. He listened, agreed, and I was moved to the "smart" division. What an adrenaline rush and boost to my confidence!

During high school, I participated in forensics, an extra-curricular public speaking program and contest. For a while, I was a member of Future Homemakers of America, a club for high school girls. I also played tenor saxophone in band, using an instrument rented from the school. Not surprisingly, I did very well in home economics. I liked chemistry, but I thoroughly enjoyed geometry—working with angles intrigued me then and still does today. The principles of geometry have proven invaluable, when creating and altering patterns for sewists, embroiderers, and quilters. But my best subject, thanks in no small part to Mrs. Fawcett and her belief in me, was English.

Just a few years ago, wanting to thank Mrs. Fawcett for what she had meant to me, I searched for her. First, I checked in my high school yearbook. Each teacher's alma mater was listed, so I e-mailed the college she had attended and they responded with a mailing address.

By then, Mrs. Fawcett and her husband had both retired; after decades as a teacher, she was enjoying time free from correcting student homework and tests. Her children—a son and a daughter—had given her five grandchildren.

Sometimes people fail to recognize how far a little encouragement can go. Mrs. Fawcett believed in me, and because she believed in me, I could believe in myself as well. I studied hard and gave my best effort. When final grades were announced just before graduation, I was ranked ninth out of the one hundred students in my class.

In high school, I received little recognition, but it was a different situation in 4-H.

As an organization, 4-H does an excellent job of preparing their members for roles in society. Requirements that must be completed for individual 4-H projects give young people an opportunity to exercise initiative and see projects through to completion—attributes that, as adults, make them valuable in the workplace. There are committees to serve on for various activities, so young people learn how to plan and work with others. Achievement is rewarded with recognition; promotion to higher levels of responsibility and service follow. Club structure also provides for elected youth to serve as leaders. Those elected by their peers conduct and keep records of club meetings and finances.

All local clubs had a president, vice-president, treasurer, secretary, and reporter. As 4-H clubs go, ours was very large, about sixty members when I was there. To be elected to a leadership position by one's peers was a validation. Since much of my life to that point had been in the shadows, when I was elected to serve as reporter at the age of fourteen, it felt to me like a stamp of approval and acceptance. The reporter's job was to prepare a news release about the club meeting and then submit it to the local newspaper, the Winneconne News, for publication. In our rural community, we faithfully read the published reports from 4-H clubs in addition to our own.

In my sophomore year of high school, I was elected secretary of our 4-H club and kept minutes of our 4-H club meetings. Until I graduated high school in 1971, I participated in Junior Leadership activities at the local and county levels, and for regional and state events.

We had monthly meetings for those involved in the various project categories. For example, those showing cattle met monthly to gain expertise in their area of interest. It was the same in project categories like Gardening, Knitting, Sewing and others. Junior Leadership was its own category and those enrolled met monthly as well, learning how to lead by example and service. We were given plenty of opportunity to exercise our abilities; adult leaders mentored us and critiqued our progress.

By my junior year in high school, I was serving as a Junior Leadership assistant to our sewing leader—my mother, who served in that role along with Mrs. Possett, another volunteer sewing leader.

My role was to help however needed, from moving supplies to serving as a tutor for others whose skills were less advanced. There were about ten girls enrolled in sewing, and I was frequently pressed into service as a tutor. 4-H gave me the opportunity to develop my teaching skills by doing demonstrations in front of groups, and by actual one-on-one teaching.

Junior Leadership participants also helped out at the county fair. We worked as assistants, helping with check-in and display of fair entries, serving as ushers for fair events and assisting in many ways. Working alongside adults and other 4-Hers provided great learning experiences in following directions and working with others.

One interesting thing—years later, when Sewing Weekend became a big event for Nancy's Notions, we started inviting well-known instructors to present seminars and workshops. Using the Junior Leadership model employed in 4-H we assigned each teacher a staff member or volunteer as an assistant. Now that Quilt Expo is attracting thousands every September, we've done something similar at that event. Each classroom is assigned a volunteer to help move supplies, usher instructors through crowds to their destination, assist in setting up materials, and stay nearby to lend a hand as needed. Teachers tell us how much they appreciate that help and many who teach at other events where that sort of assistance is lacking act as if the assistance we provide is something new, but I learned it in 4-H.

In my junior year in high school I participated in a statewide Junior Leadership event held one summer at the University of Wisconsin at Madison. More than nine hundred young people from all over the state were in attendance at the three-day event. We stayed in dorms on campus, ate in the cafeteria and walked to various buildings for workshops; it gave us a little taste of what college life would be like.

About that time I adopted a motto that I still use today—"If something is worthwhile you have to work for it." Achieving a goal, and doing a good job in the process, is not easy, but it is rewarding. That held true in 4-H and has held true since.

In addition to my project categories, I participated in other 4-H activities: eighth grade, singing in a Drama Night program; ninth grade, acting in a play and playing baseball on our club's baseball team; and in my tenth grade year I participated in a 4-H speaking contest.

The Winnebago County Fair was held every August and was huge for 4-H members. That's when the projects worked on by members during that year were judged. It was also when those who had animals showed them, and sold them as well, making money from their efforts.

Clubs in the county each had a booth along the perimeter of the big 4-H building at the fair and there was a competition for ribbons and prizes for best booth. Committees were formed in each club and went to work designing a model that interpreted an assigned theme. Booths were judged on creativity and presentation. Some of the booths were elaborately decorated. I helped with our booth several years and although we did receive recognition, we never attained top honors.

At the fair the 4-Hers always looked like they were having fun in their respective areas. My projects were in the 4-H building, a huge pole barn and I helped there as a junior leader as well. There were masses of tables covered with garden boxes, displays of woodworking and home furnishings projects, plus lots more. The work of hundreds of 4-H members was on display and each was judged against a standard for the category and level as well as against other projects on display. Along one side there were lots of clothes racks where garments made by 4-H members were hung in sections designated for the different levels in the Sewing category. It seemed that the hanging garments went on forever. Moving from one end of the row to the other, judges examined and critiqued every piece. Later the blue, red, green, or pink ribbons that signified first through fourth places were attached to the winners. Although we could watch the judging, I waited until later to see if what I had made had been accessorized by a ribbon.

I had fun, but it seemed that the kids with animals had the most fun. They hung out together in the barns and had a great time.

My brother, John, showed calves at the fair, so he went every day to care for his animals. John wore white pants and a white shirt because both he and the animal had to be kept clean and remain clean for judging. On the day of calf judging, we watched nervously as John and others led their calves around the arena.

John Luedtke

"One time I had a calf I was showing. It was clean and ready for the arena, when some horses almost trampled it. Both the calf and I were dirty. Mother and I cried."

Among the girls my age in 4-H, none of them showed animals. But Dean, John, and my little sister, Gina, all showed animals at the fair. Gina had pigs and cows she showed, and she won first place several times. I'm sure part of it had to do with her cute little pigtails; she got first place for looking so good.

"Nancy was never nervous before a 4-H demonstration. Once I watched while she did a sewing demonstration on a back neck closure and I thought, 'That was really good.' I also noticed that in sewing she was very particular about getting it right."

The county fair always included a carnival with amusement rides and was held Labor Day weekend. The new school year started the next day. I remember one time that Mother had given me $1.30 in advance for school lunch money. My friends, Sandy and Joanie, wanted to go on the rides, so I spent the money on tickets. I remember riding the Ferris wheel and feeling awful because I had spent my lunch money. When she found out, Mother's look was one of utter disappointment. I never wanted to disappoint my parents. She did give me lunch money for the next day, though.

Even though I participated in other project categories, Sewing was where the action centered for me. I was making my mark in sewing demonstrations and entered demonstration contests. My freshman year in high school I won first place for a sewing demonstration, "Tips for a Good Collar."

Most of my sewing skills were developed in 4-H. Even though our high school offered home economics classes (and they were mandatory for all girls), our teacher added nothing new to what I had already learned in 4-H.

Dean Luedtke

"In 4-H it seemed like a big vacation to spend time at the county fair with my friends. I did especially well in showmanship and with steers and heifers. I also had a couple of grand champion hogs."

I had taken to sewing like butter takes to corn-on-the-cob and was a voracious learner. Beginning at age ten, I made nearly all of my own clothes.

Before school ended each year I had already made pattern and fabric selections for the outfit I was going to sew for the annual county-wide 4-H Dress Revue Contest in July and for the county fair in August.

At the county fair, garments were judged "on the hanger"—modeling was not involved. But Dress Revue gave 4-Hers enrolled in Sewing a chance not only to exhibit their sewing skills, but to also model the garments they had made. There were two phases to judging at Dress Revue which was usually held at a high school. Garments on hangers were inspected by judges for construction quality and how appropriate the selected fabric was for the chosen pattern. Then Dress Revue participants appeared before the judges wearing their garments. At that appearance they were judged on fit and whether the garment was pleasing in appearance; contestants answered questions from the judges that ranged from why they made a certain fabric selection to the intricacies of the sewing methods they used.

Crowning the Dress Revue judging was a fashion show in which contestants modeled their garments. So, posture, grooming habits, poise and self image all played a strong part in the judging. After the fashion show, winners were announced, with two winners from the upper levels of Sewing advancing to the Wisconsin State Fair for competition with top winners from each county in the state. First and second alternates were announced in the event either winner was unavailable at fair time.

My first year I modeled the gathered gold skirt and fringed scarf

Barbara Luedtke Eckstein

"In high school Nancy was smart, but a slow starter. When 4-H came along it was a big, big help. She did so well in Sewing and it emotionally strengthened her. Some of the girls in 4-H tried hard to beat Nancy Luedtke."

that was made from a pattern used by all Sewing 1 participants. Although I'm sure I maintained a calm exterior, when I received a first place in my category, I was doing cartwheels inside. I had been singled out for first place honor.

That was the point I decided I liked winning and set my eye on top prizes.

The Dress Revue and county fair were two different events. Garments were modeled at the Dress Revue and only one ensemble was modeled by an entrant. The modeled garments were inspected closely by judges who also had an opportunity to ask the 4-H members questions about their work. The same garment that had been modeled at Dress Revue could also be entered into the county fair, along with others that had not been worn at Dress Revue. At the county fair, there was no interaction with judges; each garment stood on its own and was judged by construction and fashion standards.

A blouse and jumper I made the second year in 4-H Sewing earned first place at both the Dress Revue and county fair.

When I was twelve, I modeled a blouse at Dress Revue and won first; the same blouse later won a first at county fair. A dress I made that same year was awarded a second place ribbon at the fair.

I was gaining momentum by my fourth year in 4-H. That year a dress I modeled at Dress Revue won a first place there and a second place at county fair. A blouse earned fourth place (oh, the shame!), and a skirt a second place, both at the county fair.

You get the idea. By that time I'd been sewing for five years and the more I sewed, the better I liked it. As the years rolled by, I worked with increasingly challenging fabrics (that were also increasingly expensive), and with patterns that stretched my sewing skills.

I tackled my first coat in 1969, at the age of fifteen. The same year I made a wool dress and a dress and jacket combo—both were entered in the county fair.

Being a 4-H member helped me in so many ways. My family has always been supportive, and my faith is foundational, but it was in 4-H that I discovered I was truly good at something. Winning wasn't really about pride; I wasn't competing against others as much as I was working to do the best that I could possibly do. 4-H helped me develop a "can do" attitude. I know I'm not alone in that viewpoint because over the years I've talked with many, many former 4-H members who say the same thing.

For me, though, it went beyond a "can do" attitude. Since the standards of achievement for 4-H Sewing also aligned with my career purpose in life, my involvement helped me discover my identity and what I wanted to become.

The pinnacle of Dress Revue competition for me took place in early July of 1970. I had just turned seventeen. Months earlier, though, I started working toward the goal of winning. I knew I needed to choose the perfect fabric. Since all the previous winners had chosen wool, that's what I wanted as well.

When I saw a three-inch square of cream and olive hounds-tooth wool stapled to a fancy index card from a mail order fabric company, for weeks I dreamed about the end result. Finally my parents agreed that I could order yardage enough to make a Vogue pants suit. At forty-five dollars for wool and lining, it was the most expensive fabric that I (well, my parents) had purchased to that point. I spent many hot summer hours cutting out and sewing, making certain the loosely woven hounds-tooth design matched perfectly at the seams.

During the Dress Revue competition everything went well. I wanted so much to advance to the competition at the Wisconsin State Fair. When the scores were tallied and the winners announced, I was one of two named to represent Winnebago County at the state fair Dress Revue near Milwaukee.

But I would never make it.

Other than the onset of Bell's palsy when I was just fourteen months old, I had been a healthy and active child. At home we played strenuous games of softball and archery. In 4-H, I played on our club softball team and was quite athletic. Had there been girls' sports when I entered high school, I probably would have been all over that opportunity.

As I entered my teen years, the effects of Bell's palsy were becoming more obvious. My smile was crooked and the lower lid on my right eye drooped. In the summer between my freshman and sophomore years in high school, I underwent surgery that attempted to raise my lower right eyelid, but it didn't work. Afterwards, when I looked in a mirror for the first time, the face that looked back seemed even worse than before and I cried.

A second facial surgery that same

Barbara Luedtke Eckstein

"I regret not proceeding fast enough about the Bell's palsy. We were so young and so broke. Money was not plentiful and even for my parents it was a difficult time. When Nancy was in her teens we did the plastic surgery and she did [facial] exercises."

summer attempted to balance my smile. Three small muscles from the unaffected left side of my face were removed causing it to lower slightly. At the same time an incision was made on the affected right side of my face to create the appearance of a smile line. Since I referred to the Bell's palsy side of my face as my "sad" side, and the other side as "happy," I guess you could say that the surgery attempted to make the happy side sadder, and the sadder side happier.

Fortunately, that surgery was successful, but took a while to heal. When I started school in September, I looked like the victim of a serious accident.

Also fortunately, somewhere along the way my parents obtained health insurance. It would prove invaluable in the years to come.

My sophomore year marked the beginning of a physical down slide that continued for many years. Its effects ripple through my life to this day.

A physician once told me that children who grow exceptionally fast are susceptible to knee problems. While I don't know the science behind his statement, I may be evidence that supports his claim. Until about fourth grade, I was among the shortest in my class. But by the time I entered middle school three years later, I was almost to my full adult height of five feet, eight and one-half inches.

In my sophomore year, at the age of fifteen, I got pneumonia. It started with cold-like symptoms after Christmas. The cold turned into a very deep cough. We went to our family physician, a wonderful man named Dr. Haselow, who said I likely had a mild form of pneumonia—"walking pneumonia," he called it. He prescribed medication. For about two weeks I pushed myself to go to school. Since I had medication for the cough, I thought, and so did my parents, that I would eventually get better and that I could still go to school.

As the days went on I became weaker and weaker, especially my legs. I remember sitting in algebra class one day thinking that I wasn't going to be able to walk to the next class.

When I was done taking the medication, I was worse off than when I began. My mom took me back to Dr. Haselow who announced that I now had full-fledged pneumonia. He admitted me to Theda Clark Hospital in

Neenah, the same hospital where I was born. For nearly a week I was treated with medications and inhalation treatments. When I got out of bed, I had to hang onto things for support. All in all, I think I was out of school for two to three weeks.

Four muscles called the quadriceps femoris (known collectively as "quads" to fitness fans) control knee movements and are crucial in walking, running, jumping and squatting. One of the four, the vastus medialis, stabilizes the patella—the knee cap.

In my junior year, my knees started bothering me. My left knee was worse than the right, but both were almost constantly sore, and I experienced severe muscle spasms behind them.

Perhaps with the lingering effects of Bell's palsy in their minds, my parents were more aggressive in seeking treatment for the physical needs of my teen years. Dr. Haselow recommended exercises to strengthen my knees, but they didn't help. I tried hot packs and cold packs, exercise and rest, but there was no improvement. I struggled through the school year, but in 1970, during summer vacation between my junior and senior year in high school, I was in constant pain, especially in my left knee. I was referred to a specialist at the Mayo Clinic in Rochester, Minnesota, two hundred-fifty miles away. The verdict was that surgery was necessary and it was scheduled for a few weeks later.

Back at home I hobbled painfully from one room to another, but the greatest pain was that I was unable to participate in the Wisconsin State Fair 4-H Dress Revue. An alternate took my place. The lovely hounds-tooth wool suit I had made hung in the closet, a taunting reminder of thwarted dreams.

Almost every high school girl carefully plans what she will wear the first day of school. My outfit the first day of twelfth grade included a large ace bandage wrapped around my knee. Rather than confidently striding through the hallways, I hobbled from class to class. Only a few days later, my parents and I traveled to the Mayo Clinic where I underwent surgery to remove three, one-inch chips under my left kneecap. I returned home and went back to school on crutches sporting a big, zipper-like incision on my inner left knee.

My mother was with me during my first knee surgery. My brothers were seven and thirteen that year so I suppose she arranged for someone to help provide for them.

During that era there were very few hotels in Rochester, Minnesota. Near the Mayo Clinic and adjacent St. Mary's Hospital, was a boarding house that catered to those who needed to be near the medical facilities. Mother rented an upstairs bedroom with a shared bath there.

I was admitted to a five-bed ward at St. Mary's Hospital.

The surgery was conducted using a pre-arthroscopic technique—invasive, and with a hospital recovery time of about a week. That was followed by a week to two weeks of recovery at home. Also, the prescribed method to facilitate healing was to put the leg in a cast—a thigh to ankle cast, no less.

Once I returned home, my friend, Beth, and my cousin, Rosemarie, transported school assignments back and forth and I tried to catch up. About three weeks after surgery the cast was removed and I was encouraged to exercise that leg. In 1970, there was no physical therapy.

At a time when most teens are in the prime of their life, I was in pain. Recovering from the surgery was difficult enough, but my legs were still weak. In February of that same school year, while walking down a ramp that connected a new section of the high school with the original building, I fell, re-injuring my left knee. I can't tell you what was worse—the blazing pain in my knee, or the discouragement I felt. Any plan for going out in style my senior year in high school was now over. Mom, Dad and I headed back to Mayo Clinic.

When I was growing up, I never wanted to disappoint my parents. They were loving authorities in my life; I respected them and they were fair in their treatment of us children. For the most part I was compliant and eager to please.

When we arrived in Rochester, Minnesota, for another session with specialists at the Mayo Clinic, the white winter snow had turned to gray slush and skies were overcast. It all matched my mood when I learned that another surgery was necessary and scheduled for the following week.

On earlier visits, my parents had discovered an economical

Barbara Luedtke Eckstein

"About Nancy's knee surgeries—there was one time she got so frightened that she hyperventilated. It was not a good time. Getting through it took patience and perseverance and trust and work."

restaurant, a Swedish smorgasbord (buffet), and it was already a habit for us to eat there. My father stopped the car in front of the restaurant to let us out, and then he drove off to find a parking place.

Learning I was to undergo yet another surgery had put me under more stress than I had ever before experienced. That stress came to the surface as anger. Somehow I just wanted to hurt someone and the only person available was my mother. Mother removed her coat to hang it and she was wearing a dress with no waistline, a style she had been wearing for several weeks.

"Either you're pregnant or you had better lose some weight," I said.

Mother paused for a moment, her arm extended. She slowly lowered the coat hanger over the bar of the rack and without looking at me softly replied, "Yes, I am pregnant."

That was all she said.

I never talked to my parents that way—never!—and I instantly regretted it. I know it was my way of lashing out and my mother recognized that as well, but there was no excuse for what I said and how I said it. To this day I rank it as the worst thing I ever did as a child. Some time later—I can't remember how long—Mother told me that a new baby was due in August.

In pictures of my high school graduation, I'm wearing white boots and a white dress with a calf-length skirt, popularly known in the early 1970s as a middy skirt. The white polyester knit outfit had a long, button closure with navy blue topstitching, and a wide white belt. I made the dress and knew I was wearing the height of fashion for 1971. But my boots and skirt were more than fashion, they covered the long scar on my left knee.

Chapter 6

～

Throughout high school, I seriously considered what I would do once my diploma was in hand. For me, I knew that college was the way to go.

My grades were good, in spite of having missed a considerable amount of school for two surgeries. I still wasn't part of the popular crowd at school, but my achievements in 4-H had fostered a growing confidence and I was beginning to see myself as successful.

No doubt about it—I excelled in sewing. In high school our home economics teacher was a nice woman whose strengths were in cooking, not sewing, so most of what I learned came through 4-H. Although I enjoyed teaching through 4-H demonstrations, I couldn't see myself as a school teacher. Instead, I decided on a career in clothing and textiles. I started dreaming of turning my interest in sewing and fashion into a career that centered on the fashion industry—perhaps a job with a big pattern company like Simplicity, Butterick, McCall's or even Vogue.

Neither of my parents had attended a four-year college. In fact, I would be the first Luedtke in our family's known history to do so. But that wasn't a factor when I let it be known I intended to enroll in college. Both of my parents were supportive.

Let me step aside here to make a few comments about my parents. They wanted their children to find careers that they loved. When my dad was young, Grandpa Luedtke assumed that his two sons would operate the family farm, and they did. My father never complained or expressed that he desired anything else. My mother worked in a bank for a couple of years before marrying my father. Mother had been valedictorian of her high school class, but she chose to follow the norm for her generation. She concentrated on raising a family and being behind-the-scenes support for her husband instead of pursuing higher education and a career outside the home.

When it came to us children, we knew that our parents would support whatever career decisions we made. John's interests in baseball led him into a career as a coach and head of the athletic department at a college in Arkansas. Gina became a respiratory therapist. Dean went to Fox Valley Technical College in Oshkosh to prepare for his choice to remain on the family farm; today he and our cousin carry on the farming tradition as modern, educated businessmen. Our parents were happy for each of us and quietly proud.

So, when I started considering the 'what next?' of education, I narrowed a list of colleges to three, where I could get a home economics degree with an emphasis in clothing and textiles. The University of Wisconsin (UW) at Madison had the strongest program, followed by Stout State University in Menomonie, Wisconsin, and then, Wisconsin State University at Steven's Point.

It was the era of Vietnam war protests and of student unrest on campuses across the nation. Before I made my decision, on August 24, 1970, a bomb intended to destroy the Army Mathematics Research Center in Sterling Hall on the UW Madison campus exploded outside the building. One man was killed and several were injured.

"You're not going to Madison," my father announced. "Stout is good." End of conversation. I applied to Stout.

John Luedtke

"I loved baseball, but was content working as a carpenter after high school. By then Nancy had finished college and told me I was smart enough. So, Mom and I went to the University of Wisconsin at Oshkosh and I registered for classes. When I started college, Dad wrote me a letter that said, "Yes, you can do it." Mom and Dad didn't insist on any of us working the farm. For me, I didn't want the seven days a week. Farming is demanding. Thanks to encouragement from Mom, Dad and Nancy, I went to college."

Until I arrived for registration, I had never been to the campus at UW-Stout. (In 1971, Stout State University was renamed the University of Wisconsin-Stout—UW-Stout, for short.) But, the summer between, when I graduated high school and began college I received two scholarships. The first was a four-year academic scholarship. The second came to me through the Department of Rehabilitation. I was eligible for the second scholarship for two reasons: First, although my parents had considerable assets in land and equipment, their cash flow was not good; and second, the scholarship was available to me because of the knee surgeries I had undergone the previous year. So there was a silver lining to my physical suffering—it would help me go to college.

In spite of the surgeries, the summer after I graduated high school my knees were still bothering me and I hadn't recovered well from the second knee surgery. I tried every suggested knee strengthening exercise, but to no avail—it was back to the Mayo Clinic.

Mom was eight months pregnant, so Dad and I went without her. I remember it was a beautiful, warm July day and I should have enjoyed the lovely scenery we passed on the two hundred fifty mile drive across Wisconsin and into Minnesota. Instead, I felt only dread.

"This isn't going to get any better," the doctor told us, and added, "I want to do surgery tomorrow."

Neither Dad nor I had planned to stay overnight in Rochester, and I certainly hadn't envisioned having surgery the next day. We called Mom to tell her of the day's outcome, but there was no way that Dad could stay with me for the surgery. It was July. Hay needed to be baled, cows had to be milked, Mom was expecting a baby soon, and he was needed.

By the time I got through pre-surgery tests and procedures, and checked in to St. Mary's Hospital, it was well after dark. Since the surgery hadn't been planned, I was given a temporary, private room for just one night. There wasn't any hugging to say goodbye—that wasn't expected. Of course, Dad gave me words of encouragement, yet much is often conveyed without words. What I distinctly remember is my dad crying—walking away from me, crying. And more than forty years later, when I think of that moment, I do, too.

Sleep that night was fitful at best. It was lonely and frightening awaiting my third surgery in less than a year. I can only imagine that my father felt the same on his four-hour trip home.

As I awoke from surgery I remember swimming up through the anesthesia into nausea and pain. My left leg was encased in a plaster cast that extended from upper thigh to ankle. My kneecap had been removed. Today such surgery would only be performed in rare circumstances. The fluorescent lights in the hallways were bright so I closed my eyes and drifted in and out of sleep as I was wheeled on a gurney from post-surgical recovery to a five-bed ward.

As the anesthesia wore off and I started to become aware of my surroundings, I met the other women who shared the ward. Two of them, I learned, were there for an experimental hip replacement surgery. One of the two was from Hollywood, California, and like a glamorous movie star, she wore blue eye shadow, and even wore it into surgery.

Our hospital ward offered little in the way of diversion—no television, not even a radio. Occasionally the nurses brought books to patients, but the books were of their choice, not ours. There wasn't much to capture my attention or imagination and I felt alone and physically depleted. It was hard to hold onto an optimistic outlook.

My Aunt Mary helped. With Mother's pregnancy so close to full term, a visit from my parents was out of the question. Mary was twenty-six that year, married and with a young son, but she came the afternoon following my surgery and stayed for several days. Her presence both cheered and comforted me. She became my personal nurse, caring for me as I struggled with terrible pain.

Recovery is an interesting word that usually means restoration of well-being, at least as it applies in a medical sense. But after surgery, with my leg in a cast, I was confined to my bed and developed bed sores as the result of inactivity. Although I wasn't much inclined to using the slang of the day, the term "gross" certainly applied to those bed sores.

The tenth day after surgery I was finally allowed to be up and was given approval to ambulate, a fancy term for walking under my own steam.

So, I was ambulating in the halls of the Mayo Clinic, when my right knee gave out. The next day Leg Surgery Number Four was performed. This time the surgeon did not perform a patellectomy (knee cap removal) as he had on the other leg. Instead he diverted a tendon to keep the knee cap riding in the correct track.

This time, when I awoke from surgery, I discovered that I wore a matching pair of heavy plaster casts, thigh to ankle. Just a day earlier I had been looking forward to going home and getting ready for my move to Stout, but now it looked as though that plan had been kicked to the sidelines. My bed sores returned. The effects of anesthesia from two surgeries just ten days apart left me dazed and even when I tried to read, I couldn't focus.

This time Grandpa Larson and Grandma Evelyn came and stayed for a couple of days, but then they had to return home. Looking back on that time through the perspective of being a mother and grandmother, I can imagine how frustrated my parents must have been. They were concerned for my welfare, and probably felt helpless. Having their eldest child in a hospital far away likely also undermined their anticipation of the birth of a new baby. But my father employed some resourceful thinking. He thought he remembered that a distant relative lived in Rochester, Minnesota, so he called family to find out. The answer was yes—his first cousin's daughter lived there.

One day I looked up to see Karen, an attractive young woman, standing beside my bed. Her arms held wrapped presents and she was smiling as if she were my long-lost friend. I barely knew her. She re-introduced herself and explained. Dad had called and asked if she would visit me.

She came frequently during the final weeks of my month-long hospital stay, her visits both diversion and prevention. Not only did she bring the comfort of family connections, but her presence also helped me fight off the despair that threatened to overwhelm me.

I went home in August. Once again, the 4-H Dress Revue had gone on without me. My dream of going to the Wisconsin State Fair as a Dress Revue contestant would never happen.

Mother was eight and a half months pregnant. I needed help with everything, so to keep me centrally located the living room couch became my bed. The casts on my legs not only kept them straight and stiff, but the weight of them applied tremendous pressure on the incisions which caused me great pain while standing. Plus, my balance was so bad that I couldn't even stand without support. Dad had to carry me to the bathroom, a necessity, but for me at age eighteen, also humiliating. Those casts were destructive, too; I broke three toilet seats, when my casts struck them as I tried to maneuver into position.

With help I was able to go outside and it felt so good to be back in the sunlight again. But all I could do was sit. A photograph from that time shows me sitting in a lawn chair with my legs straight ahead of me propped on another lawn chair, and with a sad, sad look on my face.

Food gifts are normal fare for my family. If someone's sick we generally start making casseroles or baking quick breads, cakes and cookies. Thankfully, that was the case as well, when I was sporting two legs in casts and Mom was days away from giving birth.

It was a hot August day. I was on the couch and Mom was in the recliner. It was a toss up as to who was most miserable. In mid-morning there was a knock on the door followed by a female voice singing a friendly, "Hello!" Betty, my dad's cousin and our close neighbor, let herself in, holding a frosted chocolate cake.

It may seem like a small thing, but I'll never forget that cake and the welcome relief her visit brought us. Our moods lifted—Mother's and my own—while we savored Betty's cake and company. That experience taught me a lot about the gift of food. When you don't know how to help someone, get into the kitchen and bake!

Two weeks after my return home, and six weeks since I received the first one, my casts

Barbara Luedtke Eckstein

"Nancy had a hard time standing up and her balance was horrible. I was pregnant and I remember it was so hot the day I took the picture of her. That picture was taken at about the lowest point for Nancy. But I remember, too, when a cousin stopped by, bringing chocolate cake that we ate with glasses of cold milk."

were removed. My legs had been immobile for weeks and, as mentioned earlier, physical therapy was not available to help me regain mobility. The medical advice we were given involved having me sit on the end of a bed while someone pushed down on my legs to stretch the muscles and tendons. That sounds simple enough, but legs unaccustomed to moving resist movement and resistance brings pain. Not only that, but without a kneecap, the tendon that normally passes through the patella was cut and reconstructed and the pain was excruciating.

From my early days of 4-H, I remember giving a talk titled, "Aspirin: Do we really need it?" With the evangelism of the uninitiated, I opined that aspirin was abused and misused, often unnecessary when simple little adjustments would do as well. I called on my fellow 4-Hers to pause and consider whether aspirin was really necessary before they reached for the bottle, but aspirin didn't begin to touch what I felt in the bleak darkness of continual pain. I was on some powerful pain relievers.

My sister, Gina, was born August 16, 1971. Pain for me was a constant, especially at night. Sleep, if I could do it at all, was fitful. So, since I was up anyway, I took care of Gina at night. Rocking soothed my baby sister, but it also soothed me. Often while rocking and holding Gina on my chest, we both fell asleep.

Eighteen years separate my sister and I, but caring for her during those nights when I struggled against pain forged a bond between us that we, otherwise, may not have known. When Gina was three, she spent a weekend with me at college and was welcomed and pampered as the youngest girl in the dorm. She was the flower girl in my wedding. It would have been a

Barbara Luedtke Eckstein

"I hadn't planned to have another child with one about to start college. When we brought Gina home from the hospital it was a hot day and the baby was hot, too. Nancy said, 'What are we going to do with this little red thing?' Gina lived a completely different life from Nancy's. Gina had boyfriends, she was prom queen, and she didn't study as hard as Nancy, but Nancy watched Gina's life with enjoyment. They became best friends."

Gina Luedtke Crispell

"Since Nancy was much older, she could have been my mother. In the beginning ours was probably a more motherly relationship, but when I became a mother myself. we became closer. Our age difference is not a big deal."

pleasure to have been closer in age and to have grown up together, but a sister is a sister. She moved to Madison, Wisconsin, when she left home, got married and had a baby. Now she's even farther away. But recently, I made zucchini bread and chicken soup for a neighbor who wasn't feeling well. When I talked with Gina later that evening, she told me she had made zucchini bread and chicken soup for an ailing friend. We're alike in many ways; we even have the same walk.

With only weeks until college registration, it was obvious that I couldn't go to Stout. I still needed help and was on crutches. Menomonie, Wisconsin, where Stout is located, was over three hours away. So, at the last moment, I enrolled at the University of Wisconsin at Oshkosh, only thirty minutes away. I attended on Tuesdays and Thursdays, taking a sociology class in the mornings and a history class in the afternoons. Both were in the same building and a handicapped parking sticker gave me easy access. Between classes I rested at the Oshkosh home of one of my mother's friends.

Other than bonding with Gina, I remember that time as a very dark part of my life. I hobbled around on crutches and wore granny outfits and peasant-style dresses to cover the scars on my legs. Gradually I regained strength and began walking, but ever since those surgeries in the summer of 1971, there are a lot of things I can't do. I can't kneel, squat, run, ski or skate, but when stacked against challenges that a lot of people face, it could have been so much worse.

As the end of my first semester in college approached, I had improved. In January new students at Stout were required to be on campus for orientation three days before the beginning of second semester. I was determined to go and determined that going would mark a turning point in my life. Unlike my prior school experiences, I resolved to be outgoing and, above all, I was going to be included.

My parents drove me to Stout on a frigid January day. Icy winds whipped snow around us as we carried my things into Antrim Hall, the girls' dorm. I was assigned to Room 109, on the first floor a few doors down the hall from the lobby.

One of the first people I met was Barb, a stunningly beautiful girl with a black, Cleopatra hairstyle and makeup to match. My assigned roommate wasn't due back for several days, but Barb had a job that kept her on campus through the semester break. She invited me to lunch.

Yes! First day and already Barb (a junior in college, no less) and I were doing lunch. My plan for being accepted was starting well and Barb was giving me pointers that would help me get acclimated to college life.

Other girls in the dorm began arriving and as our paths crossed I would reach toward them, my hand extended to shake theirs, and introduce myself. "Hi, I'm Nancy Luedtke and I'm in Room 109." They would respond with their name and room number. It was easy.

When I saw a young woman leaving the shower room, I approached her, extended my hand and said, "Hi, I'm Nancy Luedtke and I'm in Room 109."

Her eyes widened, then she started laughing and she laughed until she doubled over. When she caught her breath and straightened up, she said, "Nancy, it's me, Barb." I hadn't recognized her without her Cleopatra wig.

Even though residents in the dorm were cordial, it was a challenge to enter school mid-year. Those who had been there already had their friends and their lunch parties. Their routines were established and they knew what was going on, and where. Fading back into the old familiar of quiet reserve would have been easy, but I didn't want that. As uncomfortable as it might be, I no longer wanted to be seen as aloof or shy.

By March I had developed new friends. We met for lunch and even studied together. I was doing well in classes and as the snow and ice melted from sidewalks and streets, my walking strength improved as the stiffness in my legs relaxed.

At first I thought the tightness in my left calf was a charley horse and I tried to walk it out. But as the hours passed, the tight feeling turned to pain and became more and more intense. Finally, I sought help at the college infirmary. Within minutes, I found myself in the emergency room of the Menomonie hospital and from there I was moved just as quickly to a hospital bed where my feet were elevated and my head lowered. A nurse probed for a vein and started an IV; heparin and Coumadin were added to the fluids. My surgeries and the inactivity that followed had taken their toll. I was being treated for a blood clot.

The hospital called my parents. I knew an unscheduled trip would be an inconvenience for them, so I tried to convince them not to come. They came anyway, but could only stay for one day; farming is a demanding life and Dad needed to be there to do his part. My brothers were in school and Gina was an infant; they needed my mother's presence. But my new friends at Stout came to visit frequently, bringing friendly chatter along with homework and treats. I remained in bed with my feet elevated and head lowered. When I was released a week later, I returned to Stout and began working hard to make up for lost time.

What I'm about to tell you can be open to many interpretations, including my own, so I am simply going to tell you what I experienced.

One morning, soon after I was released from the hospital, I was in my dorm room alone. I didn't feel well—I was extremely tired, a bit dizzy, my heart was racing, every little movement caused me to sweat. I was also coughing slightly and the sputum was tinged with pink. Perhaps, I thought, I'm coming down with a chest cold. Then suddenly there was a sharp, stabbing pain in my left lung and I could no longer breathe.

As I struggled for air, I fell to the floor and lay there, totally helpless, not able to take breath. "Okay, I'm dying," I thought, and it really did seem okay. There was no fear; in fact, there was only a curious detachment. There was no longer any pain, either.

Then it seemed I began to move, and replacing the view from my dorm room floor was an aerial view of buildings far below. I could see trees and cars and lakes. They flashed by beneath me as I moved faster and faster.

Then, a pain like nothing I had ever experienced hit me, exploding through my lungs and chest where the first pain had stabbed. And just as suddenly, I could breathe again. I gulped air until I was finally able to reach up from the floor to turn the door handle and I fell into the hall outside.

A fellow student, Darlene Peterson, was walking down the hall and called an ambulance. I was taken to the emergency room at the Menomonie hospital and then transferred, lights and sirens blazing, to the Mayo Clinic and admitted to St. Mary's Hospital.

The diagnosis was a pulmonary embolism, a potentially fatal situation in which a blood clot becomes lodged in the lungs, blocking an artery leading to the heart. Most are caused by clots that originate in the lower extremities—clots like I had experienced just over a week earlier. Even today, if untreated, about thirty percent of pulmonary embolisms result in death. Many victims who are hit with the first stabbing pain never experience the second pain that I felt when the blood clot burst, the artery opened, and I breathed again.

Back at St. Mary's Hospital in Rochester, it seemed I had been thrown back into a wrecked life. I don't recall how long I remained in the hospital. After everything I'd been through, my body was in bad shape. I do remember the agitation I felt when I realized that finishing the semester at Stout was out of the question. My parents returned to the campus, packed up my things and took them home.

Somehow, though, as I lay there, waiting for tests to reveal when I could leave, I came to the realization that all was not lost. I adopted a verse of scripture—Romans 8:31—as my own: *If God is for us, who can be against us?*

Then, and over the years of college that followed my time in that stark, unadorned hospital ward, I began to view myself differently. Bell's palsy, patched knees, whatever the problem—they are only a façade, a matter of packaging. I came to realize that those things are not who I am.

Chapter 7

❧

At Stout, campus life was moving on without me. Professors had already noted my absence and were not planning for my return. My parents had emptied my dorm room. My new friends were immersed in lives that had touched mine briefly, but were moving on without me.

When I was released from St. Mary's Hospital near the Mayo Clinic and returned home, things there had moved on as well. Gina had grown into a bubbly eight-month-old. With high school behind us, my friends were off in other places starting adult lives of their own. My last year of 4-H had ended with me in Rochester for back-to-back knee surgeries by a Mayo Clinic surgeon. Even though I could have remained in 4-H for one more year, it felt wrong to become involved again.

I was excluded—once again betrayed by a body that seemed determined to keep me isolated and unaccepted.

Medically my condition was fragile. Every day for several weeks I had to have blood drawn to monitor against the possibility of more blood clots. That meant a daily trip to Neenah, twenty miles away.

With everything that had happened to me, I was exhausted; my body and emotions needed time to heal.

I've always loved gardening. As a child I sometimes resisted the weeding essential to good vegetable gardening, but I never minded working with flowers. There is something so peaceful about tending a garden— something that restores well-being. With spring moving toward summer, I decided to plant flowers in a sunny area on the south side of our house.

The new flower bed had a significant slope, so I chose creeping moss roses as the main flower. To my great disappointment, I discovered

Barbara Luedtke Eckstein

"Nancy went to the Mayo Clinic twenty-one times in all. In her freshman year of college she had to come home because a blood clot moved from her leg into her lung. To keep her sanity, while she was home, she planted and tended a big flower garden in back of the house."

that moss roses are annual flowers that only bloom in the full sun and close when the weather is cool or cloudy. I anticipated mounds of color, but they provided only sporadic blooms.

Rather than planting all annuals, I knew enough about gardening to plant perennials, too. But, I was new to flower gardening endeavors, so I asked for assistance from a few of my aunts who graciously split some of their perennial flowers and shared them with me. As often happens with new gardeners, my "terraced" garden was planted in haphazard fashion—no terracing was evident since I hadn't planned for, and hadn't known, the expected heights of the perennials. Hills and valleys were the norm rather than a graceful slope. Still, it was a start.

From mid-April to the end of June, 1972, I recovered at home. My parents were never prone to coddle any of their children, nor did they allow place for self-pity. We were always expected to give our best effort, effort that came up to and pushed against the borders of our circumstances. I rested, hunted spring trilliums in the woods and wild asparagus along the roadsides, planned and planted a flower garden, helped around the house, and held Gina's hands as she began moving toward walking. And as I did those things, I became stronger.

My grades arrived from Stout in the mail and I was surprised to see that among the "Incompletes" I had expected was an unexpected "A" in English. Later I learned that the English professor, a first year instructor with a rogue personality, gave an "A" to everyone in his classes. He was released from his position soon after, but my unearned grade stuck! Not everything had been lost from my false start at Stout.

I wanted so much to return to college at UW-Stout. In anticipation of my physician's approval, I registered for summer session classes. Medical approval came just in time for me to move back to Stout before classes began. Not wanting to fall behind the friends I had made, I was determined to catch up so I could graduate with my class. That summer I took two classes, including a three-credit chemistry class. By the time other students returned in the fall, I had made up some ground, and would close the gap entirely within two semesters.

Barbara Luedtke Eckstein

"In college, Nancy made nice friends. When she went to college Nancy made up her mind that she was not going to be 'Poor Nancy' with no friends. In college she dated a couple fellas and she had nice girlfriend relationships."

From the very beginning my intention was to major in home economics with an emphasis on clothing and textiles. Of less certainty, though, was the choice of a minor. For some time I weighed the pros and cons of minors in business administration, accounting and journalism, but finally settled on journalism. Although I know now that business administration and accounting would have helped me in my career, I believe journalism has helped me more.

The classes I took to fulfill requirements for a minor in journalism, especially a technical writing class, have served me very well over the years. Writing instructions telling others how to do something is more difficult than it seems. And, since my inclinations have always been towards teaching, it seemed logical to prepare to also teach through written instructions. Over the years there have been dozens of books, pamphlets, brochures, catalogs, press releases, magazine articles and more. Even when my staff helps with writing projects, what I learned in journalism classes helps me review with an informed eye.

My sophomore year on campus, I took a work/study job with the university news bureau. My duties were to help prepare news releases and prepare materials for the media. I held that job about two years. It was only a few hours a week and paid minimum wage, in 1972, only $1.60 an hour. My parents also sent me five or ten dollars a week—whatever they could spare. Today it is common to hear the term 'income streams,' but at that time my streams were mere trickles. Still, I was accustomed to being frugal and I was able to buy fabric and an occasional roll of camera film from that budget.

When I attended UW-Stout, the student body numbered just over five thousand. Menomonie, Wisconsin, where the university is located, had a population of around twelve thousand. I didn't range off campus often. I didn't have a car, and I don't remember any bus system or cabs. There wasn't a lot to do in Menomonie, but I was also very busy. I carried a full load of classes and worked part-time as well.

Menomonie is located in the northwestern part of Wisconsin and was a cold place to attend college. The campus was divided into north and south sections with all academic buildings on the south campus. I am still thankful that my dorm was located on the south campus. The north campus students had to cross a footbridge to get to classes—they were a hardy, close-knit group.

Very few of my friends had cars, so we were all in the same situation. Occasionally someone with a car provided transportation for a shopping trip to "The Cities," conversational linked reference for Minneapolis and St. Paul, Minnesota, about sixty miles away. Since extra spending money was a rarity for me, I think I only went shopping in The Cities twice during my three and a half years at Stout.

One winter, I purchased a bright orange ski jacket. It had a little stand-up collar, no hood, and was cropped just below the waistline. I thought the jacket was totally fashionable and the color, so mod! It looked great, but was not warm. Still, putting fashion over comfort, I wore my fashion statement every day. What was I thinking?!

I lived in Antrim Hall, one of the dorms at Stout, the whole time I was there. My senior year I debated living off campus in a house with friends, but decided that Antrim's central location and easy access to classes was a better choice for me.

Another reason I remained in the dorm was because I was a PASS advisor during my junior and senior years at Stout. PASS stood for Peer Advisor for Stout Students. There were two PASS advisors for every curriculum major offered. Our responsibility was to help underclassmen schedule their classes and serve as mentors.

I don't remember being paid to be a PASS advisor, but there were perks. The main perk was that PASS advisors were the first to register for classes. College registration was pandemonium. Hundreds of card tables were set up in the gymnasium; each was manned by an attendant. Every single class, activity, dorm assignment, financial aid award—whatever a student would touch that semester that required college records—required a stop at one of those tables where lines of students inched forward.

My goal was to graduate in four years. Since upper level classes were sometimes difficult to access (time of day, number of students) being a PASS advisor was the ticket to the perfect class lineup. As I write this, it sounds very self-serving. Perhaps it was, but I also enjoyed working with underclassmen.

Antrim Hall, where I lived, was one of three dorms that were connected by a central lobby. Antrim, Froggatt and McCalmot Halls—AFM for short—were under the supervision of an adult dorm supervisor who lived in an apartment on the ground floor just off the lobby. She was a petite grandmother-looking woman (probably my age now!), who scurried around. Each floor in the dorms had a student resident advisor (RA) who monitored student activities on that floor, and who reported to the dorm supervisor. Resident advisors had private rooms, but the other rooms housed two students.

Two desks, two twin beds, two dressers and small closets were in each room. It was against the rules to move the furniture, create a loft area or have a refrigerator.

The iconic (or should I say ironic) piece of equipment that I used almost every day in college was my mother's manual typewriter. It had a black carrying case and had been her high school graduation gift. I thought nothing of using that typewriter; no one else did either. Imagine today a student taking a computer to college that one of their parents had used twenty years earlier. Not going to happen!

I made, and still have, great friends from college. Several resident advisors from the dorm were friends. Just recently one of them, Tracy Sporel, called to reconnect. We hadn't spoken in years, but it was as though we had never parted. There's something about maturing together, learning together, that bonds friends.

Beth, my roommate the first year, and Marla, my second year roommate are still friends today. Today Marla lives in Washington State. Since I travel extensively, I've been able to visit friends who have moved far away. Marla and I took time during one visit to shop at a Nordstrom department store. Lunch followed shopping, and during the meal I looked across the table at a mature Marla, but in my mind saw and heard the Marla of 1975. Giggles and laughter are cleansing—there was plenty of that during our time together.

Beth searched me out several years ago, too. She still lives in Wisconsin and we had a three-hour lunch that bridged time.

There were other good friends as well. Beep (her given name was Vera) was a precious friend, as was Darlene, the one who found me in the hallway and called an ambulance after a blood clot nearly took my life.

I learned so much from my friends. My childhood was spent within a sheltered community of like-minded people. College friends helped me expand in knowledge, understanding and acceptance of others.

My years at UW-Stout came near and followed the end of the United States' involvement in Vietnam. There were a number of veterans who attended Stout and most were part of a tight-knit group. A friend of mine dated one of those returning veterans and groups of us would hang out together, often on Friday nights, and just as often at beer bars. (In Wisconsin eighteen-year-olds could drink beer back then. Wisconsin and beer go hand in hand.)

I'll never forget Max, a tall, handsome guy with piercing blue eyes. Those eyes were with us physically, but not always in reality. In Max's head, he was often somewhere else. Max was the first person I personally knew who committed suicide. When I heard, it was shocking news, but not really a surprise (if that makes sense). At that time, it was a condition without an acronym. Post-traumatic stress disorder (PTSD) wasn't part of our vernacular, but we all knew what killed Max.

Menomonie was a four-hour ride from home. Without a car, I depended on the "Ride Share" board—a pre-technology, disorganized version of text messaging. Students with cars would post a notice on the bulletin board. Messages read something like this: "Going to Oshkosh this weekend, leaving Friday at noon, returning Sunday at 4:00. Call North Hall, extension 4111; ask for Greg."

That's how it worked. Sometimes I caught a ride all the way to home, but other times my parents would drive to meet my "taxi" in a nearby town. I didn't go home often. Besides holidays, I probably went home one time in the fall and another time in the spring.

Even so, I lament not keeping a journal of my rides home. Most were uneventful, but some weren't. My most memorable ride was in the back seat (or whatever the rear area is called) in a Volkswagen Bug, sharing the space with a St. Bernard dog. It's a good thing I was very thin in college and that I liked dogs.

Not surprisingly my best subjects at Stout were Textiles 101, 201 and 301. In those classes we learned the anatomy of fabric, manufacturing methods and care. Textiles classes were taught by Professor Erma Jean Jackle who took a liking to me and mentored me through the program. Miss Jackle ranks as the most significant of my college instructors for many reasons. She was extremely knowledgeable, unassuming and friendly. When I graduated from UW-Stout, she hosted a luncheon for me and one other student.

The summer between my sophomore and junior years at Stout, I, along with other home economics majors and graduate students, participated in a fourteen-day tour of textile mills and related businesses in South- and North Carolina.

That trip marked my first airplane ride. We flew out of St. Paul, Minnesota, changed planes in Atlanta, Georgia, and arrived in Greenville, South Carolina, to discover that our luggage had not made the Atlanta connection. It was a full day before we were reunited with our belongings.

These days flying on commercial airlines is so routine for me that it is scarcely worth mention. Over the years my luggage has been lost seven or eight times. I remember thinking that perhaps I had managed to get the lost luggage specter out of the way early, but it still happens now and then.

Along with the experience of that horizon-expanding trip, I also remember one that was etiquette expanding. Once a month the chancellor of the college, Dr. Swanson, held a dinner at his residence for a few students. During my senior year, our dorm supervisor invited me to accompany her to the dinner. I accepted and wore a garment I had designed in my class on flat pattern design methods. Serving the gourmet dinner were students in the hotel and restaurant program at the college; they wore tuxedoes.

The first course was soup. A linen napkin was placed on my lap by one of the student wait staff, and before beginning, I glanced at the dorm supervisor to make sure I was using the correct spoon. After taking the first spoonful of soup, I heard her say, "The ship sails away from the port, and then returns." She was discreetly trying to tell me how to properly consume soup: skim the top of the soup with the spoon away from yourself, and then lift it to your mouth. I hadn't a clue. That night I ate gingerly, watching first, eating second.

Living in a college dorm is a lesson in playing nice with others. As a textiles and clothing major, I had a sewing machine, scissors, pin cushions, thread, fabric, patterns, needles—all the materials, equipment and notions to make garments. I used them frequently, too. My sewing machine was ready at all times and I didn't just sew projects for my classes, but for myself as well.

When our sons were in college and had issues with roommates or other students living in the dorm, I often mentioned that dorm living should be a two-credit course, providing you make it through the first year intact. It is a great sociology/physiology learning experience, meeting and sharing space with strangers who, in some cases, become lifelong friends. I never had to share a room when I was living at home and I wasn't the most tidy of people—I'm still not. I firmly believe in the saying, "Cluttered desk equals a creative mind."

The clothing construction classes I took required lots of time and were a challenge to execute in the very small space of a dorm room. One of my roommates, Peggy (bless her heart), was a very neat person and I just about caused her panic attacks over all the stuff on my half of the room. Imagine trying to keep a sewing machine, ironing area, patterns, fabric, a dress form, typewriter—organized chaos!—on one side with a dietitian major living on the other. I remember cutting out garments in the commons area between the dorms, taking over the area late at night when no one else was using the space. The area had lots of tables and chairs; I pushed tables together to form a cutting table.

Textiles, clothing construction and sewing classes were my favorites at Stout and I excelled at them. I also did well in speech classes and learned a lot about structuring and delivering a good speech. I had been doing demonstrations and giving speeches in 4-H since the age of ten, but this— this was a step above.

Some of the core clothing and textiles major courses included Flat Pattern Design, Draping (designing on a personalized dress form—think *Project Runway*), Tailoring, and various classes on textiles. Flat Pattern Design was one of my favorite courses. In it, we made a "sloper"—basic pattern pieces made from our body measurements which included a bodice front, bodice back, skirt front, skirt back, and sleeve. From those five pieces, in theory, I could design anything. It was only one course, but that one course provided the knowledge that allowed me to present design concepts to The McCall Pattern Company.

The draping course was one I took during a summer school session between my sophomore and junior years at Stout. In the class, our first task was to make a dress form. We were given a dress form that was much smaller than our body measurements then shown how to pad and shape the form to meet our measurements. Talk about time consuming! We'd add layers of batting then hold them in place by wrapping thread around and around, up and down. Layer, wrap, repeat—we continued until the form looked and measured correctly. Then the form was covered with muslin, using the sloper that we'd made in Flat Pattern Design.

I used odds and ends of thread to wrap around the dress form. Most of the others used white or cream thread. After adding the muslin sloper, my threads showed through as if they were veins.

Unless I guard against it, even to this day when I'm working on a project I tend to give it my main focus and set everything else aside. In college, my friend, Tracy, brought it to my attention that when I was working away at a project or paper, I'd put all my energies into finishing. I turned down simple things, like going to dinner with her at the commons or taking time for a chat, preferring to focus on a project. I still have those tendencies; my husband and adult friends have accused me of the same thing, so I know it's true. But I have tried to be more moderate, and not shut people out for the sake of completion.

Dorm life was filled with drama, but also with great life experiences. Anyone who has ever lived in a dorm knows the highs and lows of eighteen- to twenty-year-old girls. Just say the words "dating," "finals," "term papers," "breakups," and "interviews," and they will bring to mind comparable scenes whether from the 1970s or the current century. Sure, there are different nuances, but emotions and learning curves are the same.

I made a lot of mistakes and did things I regret, but what college student hasn't? One of the more stupid things I did was to make fun of the Greek organizations. During the first semester of my sophomore year, many of the girls on my floor were pledging to a sorority. Deep down, I also wanted to pledge, but there were costs involved, and that wasn't part of my budget.

I had a yellow T-shirt; so did one of my friends. One night during pledge week, when a number of our dorm-mates were wearing "I am a Tri Sig Pledge" T-shirts, my friend and I printed "Lemon Pledge" signs and pinned them to our yellow shirts. I apologize to all sorority/fraternity members for what I thought was rather clever. Our little statement was not received with humor, but disgust. But, it still makes me chuckle today.

Back in high school I started dreaming of a career with a major garment pattern company. Classes at Stout were teaching me how to create patterns and construct garments. I felt prepared to step into a career in a high-profile garment-related business.

I had my chance my senior year when I landed an interview with Simplicity Patterns. So, during spring break I went to New York City with a college friend, Riona Nebel. A native of New York City, Riona was a lovely young woman. No doubt about it, I was a country girl in the city for the first time. Everything was unfamiliar, fast-paced and incredibly urbane. Back in Wisconsin, the wardrobe I made for myself was admired for its style, fit, and versatility, but suddenly in that realm I felt dowdy. And it wasn't just clothing; there was a different mind set that seemed arrogant at worst and condescending at best.

I interviewed with Simplicity and the interview went smoothly enough, but I didn't get the job. My dream hadn't come true—not yet, at least. Over the years since then I came to realize that I wasn't ready. While my education was solid, I was too naïve for the New York fashion industry at that time; landing the job would not have been good for me.

Excerpt from letter home, May 13, 1975

"This is it, the last letter from me at Stout— hardly seems possible… Saying good-bye to friends must be the hardest part of leaving. Many of these people have been so influential in my life that the thought of never seeing or speaking to them again saddens me."

On May 10, 1975, wearing a royal blue gown and mortar board cap, I joined my classmates as we filed across a platform at UW-Stout's Johnson Fieldhouse to receive our diplomas. College life was over. As I hugged friends and told professors goodbye, I knew that what I had come there to achieve was mine.

In four years, I had transformed from being a teenager, who was never picked, into a young woman with good friends who accepted me and included me in their plans. My grades were good, my achievements noteworthy. My physical challenges were manageable. I had a solid foundation on which to build the future I wanted.

Between diploma and realization of a dream, lies a broad expanse of reality that all but the luckiest college grads must trudge through.

The job market in 1975 was bleak. I didn't have a degree in education so I couldn't step into a school system as a teacher. I had definite ideas and was driven to succeed but, for that era, I was unrealistic in my occupational goals. It would be some years until my education began to serve me well and it has done so ever since.

I moved back home after graduation and began looking for work. In my job search I came across an ad for the Sew/Fit Company. Started by Ruth Oblander, the company's focus was to teach women to make money on their own by offering sewing seminars to others.

In the women's movement that began in earnest in the 1970s, Ruth Oblander's feet were planted on both sides of the feminist fence. As an entrepreneur she led her own company, made her own decisions, wrote books, and traveled to lecture across the country. She was financially independent. She had cerebral palsy and walked with a limp, but didn't let that stop her. Her subject, though, was sewing—traditional women's work as ever was.

What Ruth's seminars offered was a new way of looking at sewing, a focus on quicker, easier, simpler sewing methods that recognized the value of a woman's time and gave her the impetus to spend that extra time however she pleased, and be dressed well as she did it.

Her training sessions gave women an opportunity to be independent as well by becoming freelance sewing instructors who taught her methods and materials. The fee for the training was three hundred dollars. When I talked with Ruth by phone, she offered to let me stay at her suburban Chicago home while I went through the four weeks of training. My parents thought it sounded good and they paid the fees.

Ruth's intention was to mold me into a strong, powerful and dynamic person.

"I decided that I am going to change you," she told me.

Even though I'm mostly quiet, my resolve is an inner rod of steel and I let her know that I might not want to be changed, but I came back day after day. I think part of the reason Ruth came to appreciate me is because I did stand up to her.

I was nearly done with the training when I saw an ad for home economists in a Chicago newspaper. Minnesota Fabrics was seeking college graduates to teach sewing classes in their chain of stores. When I stacked the possibility of full-time employment against the uncertainties of independent work, I decided to apply.

The position of home economist was a new one within the organization so my interview was with the regional manager for Minnesota Fabrics. Sitting in on that interview was the manager of a Minnesota Fabrics store in Homewood, Illinois, where the winning candidate would likely be placed.

I remember the regional manager talking about career opportunities within the company. "Why, some women even make a five-digit salary," he told me. As for me, when the job was offered, it was at an annual salary of six thousand dollars. Later I learned that there was a woman store manager in the Chicago area who made more than ten thousand dollars, but she was a token, the only one in a male-dominated management staff.

Minnesota Fabrics actively recruited employees who were from rural areas in the upper Midwest. Apparently top management had discovered that young people from that background generally had a good work ethic and were honest. Just to be sure, every candidate to whom they offered a job had to first take a lie detector test. I don't remember everything that was asked, but I do remember the question, "Have you stolen anything?" About a year after I was hired, requiring lie detector tests as a condition of employment became illegal and Minnesota Fabrics ended the practice. But, I passed the test and was offered the job.

Just before I left college, like other seniors, I was called to the financial aid office. I had received two scholarships that helped fund my education. One covered tuition and books while the other covered a portion of room and board. My parents helped some, but I also took out student loans that eventually totaled nine thousand dollars. In the financial aid office, a clerk moved her finger as she talked, pointing out numbers in various columns. "This is what you owe," she told me, "and this is your interest rate. Starting in nine months, this will be your monthly payment amount."

To help me save on interest, Grandpa Larson paid off my student loans, but I was expected to pay him back. I had obligations and needed to be frugal.

A search for an apartment finally landed me in Crete, Illinois, about twenty minutes from my job in Homewood. In those days, Crete seemed more like a modest-sized town than a suburb of Chicago and the neighborhood seemed safe. I found an apartment in a building with ten apartments arranged motel-style on a second floor above a self-serve laundry and dentist office. An outside stairway of twenty-three steps (yes, I counted them!) led to a concrete walkway spanning the width of the building. Doors to all ten one-bedroom apartments opened off that walkway. Mine was Number 8. The rent was one hundred sixty-five dollars a month.

At home in Wisconsin I loaded my personal items into a 1971 Ford LTD my grandfather helped me purchase and headed south toward Chicago and a new phase of my life.

A few days later Dad drove down from Wisconsin in a yellow pickup. He brought a few pieces of furniture—a bed and dresser, a castoff chair, a black and white TV that had been Grandpa Luedtke's, a desk that had belonged to Grandma Evelyn, and my parent's old 1950s-era table with a yellow Formica top and chrome legs. He also brought my mother and Gina who stayed several days after he returned home to help me settle in.

My apartment was tiny. Mother cheered the living room with a coat of yellow paint. She also put everything away for me and it was weeks before I found where some of my essentials were stored. To call my first apartment's décor "eclectic," is probably the kindest way to describe it. I found another chair at a garage sale, and an end table, but that apartment was never pretty. It was purely functional.

My first day of work was scheduled to begin at noon, so I arrived in plenty of time and pulled into the space closest to the customer entrance at the front of the store. Oops, that wasn't a good impression on my first day; I was told to park farther away from the front door the next day, leaving the prime spaces free for customers.

I was shown around the store and eventually ended up in the back storage area where I once again met the store manager, the one who had been present when the district manager interviewed me. A nice looking, tall, dark-haired young man sporting the mutton-chop sideburns fashionable in the mid-70s, welcomed me to the store and expressed his hope that I would enjoy my employment there.

His name, he reminded me as we shook hands, was Richard Zieman.

Chapter 8

Rich Zieman
(Husband)

"As far as the job was concerned, Nancy was qualified. There were three or four other candidates, but I thought Nancy would do the best job. My boss felt so, too. He said, 'You know, I really like Nancy Luedtke. I think she has talent, but did you notice something about her face?' I said I had noticed, but that I didn't think it would affect her public speaking. I sensed right away that her face wasn't what Nancy was all about."

Minnesota Fabrics expected a lot of their management staff, and as a home economist, I was considered management.

The normal work week was fifty hours. On Sundays the store was closed, but I worked every other Saturday and one or two nights each week. My schedule varied. Some days I worked 8:00 a.m. to 5:00 p.m., and other days noon to 9:00 p.m. One day a week I worked twelve hours. At the time I didn't think too much about the hours; I was just glad to have a job in my profession.

Every week for six to eight weeks during the spring and fall, home economists prepared and presented seminars on a new topic. Each week's seminar was presented three times on Thursdays—10:00 a.m., 2:00 p.m. and 7:00 p.m. In addition to presenting, it was also my responsibility to—along with other management staff—move the "stand-ups" of fabric where bolts are stored, and set up and take down tables plus thirty chairs before and after each session. If customers had questions after the session, I talked with them first before moving furniture. By the time Thursday was over, I could hardly walk and talk.

Minnesota Fabrics sold fabric and notions, but oddly, there was no in-store sewing machine on which I could make samples or demonstrate techniques. So, even though the fabric for samples was free, I had to make them at home on my own time. The job was all-consuming and at night, I fell into bed exhausted.

My colleagues were very kind to me. Most were women in their thirties and forties. They were helpful, lending a hand at seminars when they could and even occasionally making things that they lent for use as seminar samples before reclaiming them for their personal use.

One time I remember that I prepared a seminar on quilting. That was probably in 1976, and quilting was experiencing a resurgence of interest fueled by the United States' Bi-centennial celebration. One of the women staff members wanted a quilt. It was a very simple block pattern, machine pieced and double-bed sized. She did most of the work to make it, but let me use it for teaching. I remember thinking to myself that quilting would be a short-lived phase. I couldn't have been more wrong—it's bigger than ever.

Minnesota Fabrics sold primarily fashion and upholstery fabrics. Quilting was a small part of sewing in the 70s, but eventually became part of the inventory. Patterns were a big part of fabric chain stores at the time. The full lines of McCall's, Vogue, Butterick, Simplicity, and Kwik Sew patterns were carried. Thread and buttons were, of course, available in every size and color. The full offering of notions was there, but compared to today's selection, the options were quite limited.

Double knits were a hot commodity in the late 70s. A full-page ad ran every Sunday in *The Chicago Tribune* and suburban papers. Monday morning there would be lines and lines of women waiting to shop, especially for the dollar a yard double knits. I'm sure much of that yardage is still buried at the bottom of fabric stashes. Often customers would purchase fourteen to twenty pieces at one time. How they could sew it all was beyond me.

Four large tables were pushed together. The double knit fabric was not on bolts, but baled together with string. In the early morning, the fabric was neatly stacked. Within minutes of the store's opening on sale day, a swarm of eager shoppers tore through the once orderly stacks of fabrics to find their bargains. It was bedlam. To replenish inventory, sometimes managers just threw the bales onto the tables without cutting the strings. They knew the women would pull and tug on the fabric to separate the pieces. It was crazy, yet fun to watch the excitement.

Preparing for seminars kept me on my toes. For example, one week the topic was sewing with suede fabrics (Ultrasuede®), followed the next week with how to sew swimwear. Those topics were so different and also new to me. I was only one step ahead of the learning curve for most of the customers. (At least I hoped I was ahead!)

There were ten to twelve Minnesota Fabrics stores in the Chicago area. Once, due to the illness of another store's home economist, I was asked to be the replacement. While giving the seminar on swimwear to about a hundred people in a store in the northern suburbs, someone asked if the swimsuit I had made could be passed around. So, I handed out the yellow one-piece tank style suit.

All was going well until a hand went up in the back and someone asked, "Why do you have the stretch of the fabric going up and down?" She stood up and showed everyone that the garment wouldn't stretch crosswise, but lengthwise.

That was a major mistake. Without crosswise stretch, the garment could not expand to slip over the curves of the body. Until that moment I hadn't known I had cut the pieces wrong.

There was no choice—I admitted my mistake and asked my audience to cut the fabric as I instructed, not as I had done it. I'm sure my words stumbled and my face showed my mortification, but I had to carry on. For the remaining two seminars that day the swimsuit was not available for touch and feel. That was my first lesson in how to admit a mistake in public.

When not giving seminars, I was responsible for some management duties. I believe that once or twice a week I opened or closed the store. I was responsible for securing or releasing the money for the cash registers and for other duties along that line. It was my responsibility to assign

Rich Zieman

"Company policy was that if there was a fabric with a flaw or other similar issue, the sales person could not automatically give the customer a price reduction—the store manager had to work it out. But I let Nancy do that—I gave responsibility to the person who knew how best to work through it with the customer. At one point I asked my supervisor why the manager had to approve and he said 'because we've always done it that way.'"

construction of display and model garments. When a new fabric line came in, I was helpful in merchandising it—displaying it in a prominent location. Besides that, I spent a lot of time behind the pattern counter, answering questions.

Life for me was centered on work, but I craved contact with people outside of work as well. While I was at Stout, on Sunday mornings I frequently attended a nearby Lutheran church where student services were held at 11:00 a.m. In my new job outside Chicago, I looked for and found a Lutheran church just a few blocks away from my apartment. I began attending, but soon just to have a sense of belonging, I joined the choir.

I made it to as many choir practices as my schedule would allow and was there on Sunday mornings. One Sunday after the service the choir director became very angry with us; he felt we had not performed to his expectations. With his yells still ringing in my ears I left that church and never returned there again. Being reprimanded wasn't why I had joined the choir. Confrontation is something I've always avoided and I did so then, too. When I moved from my apartment in Crete, I threw away the choir music folder, something I still feel guilty about doing, but I didn't have the courage to return it to the church.

The district manager who was the first to interview me for a job at Minnesota Fabrics asked me one day how I was able to manage having an apartment on my own on the salary I made. Most of the other home economists had roommates, he said. Today I would think he should have followed his comments with a raise, but the truth was that my parents had taught us how to be frugal and their training was paying off.

My '71 Ford LTD got about ten miles per gallon and gasoline at that time cost about sixty cents a gallon. At that time I was making about $2.30 an hour. My commute was forty miles round trip, so gasoline costs ate up more than an hour's worth of pay each day. Before taxes my pay was only one hundred fifteen dollars per week so to pay my one hundred sixty-five dollar rent and my student loan, I had to be very careful.

Eating out? Never! I cooked for myself in my apartment and packed lunches for work. One time I remember making tuna salad using a recipe I had made while living with my parents. Unfortunately, it never dawned on me to scale back the proportions. I ate tuna salad for days and days and was so sick of it that I've had a hard time eating it since.

Work was hard, but it seemed I was learning. Some days, I wondered if I would ever truly feel comfortable in my job. I guess you could say I was not confident. For example, there was one way of dealing with customers, another with fellow staff members. Where customers could hear us, the staff addressed each other formally—I was Miss Luedtke there. In the office, however, we called each other by our first names.

When our store manager invited me to lunch one day at a nearby Walgreen's diner, I thought maybe I had done something wrong. Mr. Zieman—Rich—seemed to be a very kind and polite man, so, I reasoned, perhaps he was taking me away from the building in order to politely reprimand or (please, no!) fire me outside the earshot of colleagues.

But he didn't. He chatted about his life, asked me about mine, laughed, and even joked a little. Our lunch passed without trauma, in spite of my nervous responses to his conversation.

On our way back from lunch he asked, "So, would you like to go out for pizza tonight?" Leftover insecurities—romantic and professional—had blunted my awareness. I suddenly realized that the handsome young man walking next to me liked me and that his interest was more than professional. I was being asked out on a date.

That evening, when the pizza arrived at our table it was steaming hot. Rich took a piece and blew on it aggressively. Without thinking I said, "If you blow a little harder you'll cool mine off, too." He often tells that story (Rich loves to tell stories). At the time I was somewhat surprised by my comment, but followed my surprise with the thought that (oh, well)

Rich Zieman

"My interest in Nancy happened very slowly. I wasn't looking for anything serious, but marriages that last do so because you were friends first."

Earl Zieman

(Father-in-law)
"I knew Rich couldn't farm because the dust bothered him. He drove truck hauling peas to earn money for college, but when it was dry weather, the dust was a problem. So I really didn't want him to farm—too hard a life. He had too good a mind and I knew he could do something else. After graduation from college he went to work right away for Minnesota Fabrics. I think he enjoyed the work."

he'd need to get to know the real me sooner or later.

Although we were allowed to address each other by our first names while in the store office, out where customers could hear we were to use more formal address—Mr. Zieman, Miss Luedtke.

The truth is that Rich and I had a lot in common. We were both from east central Wisconsin where we grew up on farms located about seventy miles apart. Rich's father, Earl Zieman, had given up dairy cattle, though, in favor of cash crops. Both of us had answered the same ad for Minnesota Fabrics, a company that actively recruited people with our backgrounds. We held similar values and, once I relaxed, we worked well together.

Rich had attended Carroll College, a small Presbyterian-affiliated college in Waukesha, Wisconsin, near Milwaukee. By 1972, when he graduated with a degree in business and economics, he already had a job waiting with Minnesota Fabrics.

Minnesota Fabrics was opening so many new stores at that time that in order to get store managers into positions rapidly, they compressed their normal three-month training period into just three weeks. He was assigned to the Chicago area where he worked for a year and a half as assistant manager at the Northbrook store before being transferred to Homewood where he was responsible for setting up a new store and hiring staff. That's where we met.

He had been working at the

Rich Zieman

"When I introduced Nancy to two college friends, I told them she was from the Oshkosh area. 'We know where that is,' they responded. Nancy said, 'Well, I went to high school in Winneconne,' and one of them nodded while the other said, 'I've heard of Winneconne.' The next time when I introduced Nancy, I said that she lived near Oshkosh, Wisconsin, but went to school in Winneconne. She responded, 'Well, actually, our post office is in Larsen.' The fourth time I introduced her, I said that she grew up near Oshkosh, went to high school in Winneconne, but lived closer to Larsen. Nancy responded, 'Well, actually I'm from Zittau.' Somehow I knew that was the end of the road."

Homewood, Illinois, Minnesota Fabrics store for about a year when we started dating; I'd been there about three months.

Actually, I was always aware of Rich. He was my boss, so I naturally wanted to please him. But I'd also been watching him, and was impressed with how he handled the many responsibilities of his job. He was fair, capable, and definitely in charge. He respected people—customers and staff—so, in return, they respected him.

When Rich transferred to the Homewood store, he purchased a four-bedroom house in Park Forest. Gene Sekel, a close friend from his childhood and college years, worked for a car dealership in the area so Rich rented rooms to Gene, and two other men. The rent from others covered Rich's mortgage payments; they split the phone bill and utilities.

My old black and white television had given out so I had nothing to watch and couldn't afford to buy a new TV. After Rich and I started dating and I met his roommates, one of them had an old black and white portable television that he sold me for fifty dollars. He asked Rich to deliver it to my apartment. I was watching for Rich and saw him drive up, so I stood in my doorway so he'd know which apartment was mine. But when he was carrying the television up the cement steps toward the landing that led to my apartment, the handle broke and that TV went 'chink, chink, chink' all the way down the stairs. That was the end of that! I helped him toss the pieces into a dumpster.

Rich Zieman

"We got snowed in one Thanksgiving and the day after. Nancy had planned to drive to her parent's home for the holiday, but cancelled her trip because of the storm. My parents were coming to visit me and made it to my home the day before Thanksgiving. Since Nancy was in town, she came for Thanksgiving. It was our first Thanksgiving together and everything just clicked."

Rich had just purchased a new color TV so he invited me to his house to watch. To this day, a couple of his friends accuse him of breaking the TV on purpose so I'd have to go to his house to watch.

As Thanksgiving 1975 approached, I made plans to go to Wisconsin for the holiday, my first trip since taking the job at Minnesota Fabrics. I was looking forward to it, but then a snowstorm forced me to cancel my plans.

Rich's parents stopped at Minnesota Fabrics around noon the day before Thanksgiving. He had told me they would stop before going on to his house, but not much more. When a woman walked into the store, I knew immediately she was Rich's mom. Mother and son shared the same blue eyes. I was briefly introduced to his parents, then Earl said, "It's really snowing outside, I don't think you'll be able to drive home."

I was scheduled to work until 9:00 p.m., and had planned to leave for Wisconsin afterwards, but the snow was coming down hard. Rich's father was right; there would be no Thanksgiving trip to Wisconsin for me. Rich and his parents invited me to Thanksgiving dinner.

The store closed early that evening because of the snowstorm, and by then the roads were almost impassable. Rich suggested that instead of going to my apartment that I drive to his home. When I arrived, Rich, his parents, and Grandma Zieman were drinking vodka gimlets and eating appetizers of smoked oysters on Ritz crackers. 'Beats going home to my apartment,' I thought.

With the weather so bad outside, even though I didn't have a change of clothes or even a toothbrush, I camped out on the couch that night. The next day we were snowed in, but the fixings for Thanksgiving

Earl Zieman

"We first met Nancy when she and Rich lived in the Chicago area. She said she was from up Winneconne way and that her folks were farmers. I told my wife that we should drive up there to see where she was from, so we did. I could see a big farm off to the right. Sure enough, that was it. I didn't have the nerve to stop that first time, so we didn't talk to her family on that first trip up there."

Viv Sekel

(Friend)

"The first time I met Nancy she had an Afro hairstyle—a frizzy, round Afro. I commented on her style and she said, 'Oh no, they made a mistake. It's not supposed to be this way.' It was a perm gone bad."

were already set. Elaine, Rich's mother, had prepared everything in advance.

In the afternoon Rich's mother suddenly announced, "I think we should wash the downstairs bedroom walls!" Then she jumped out of her chair and prepared a bucket of water for the task. I was surprised at the announcement. I don't remember ever washing walls at home, especially not on Thanksgiving. It wasn't until later that I witnessed Elaine's immaculate housekeeping standards. In the meantime, I pitched in and scrubbed down a few walls, too. I haven't washed walls since.

I liked his parents immediately and we spent the day eating, playing games and getting to know each other. Like their son they were interesting, kind, and solid. I had no idea how vitally important they were to become to me.

It was mostly through work and Rich that I developed friends. Rich had introduced his friend and roommate, Gene Sekel, to a woman Rich knew from college, and they began dating. Viv (short for Vivian) became a good friend of mine and still is today. When Viv landed a job in the business department of the Marshall Field Company in nearby Orland Park, she moved in with me, becoming the roommate that finally helped me achieve a measure of financial breathing space. The district manager for Minnesota Fabrics was right in his presumptions—it was difficult to live without a roommate on my salary.

Rich and I double-dated with Gene and Viv, plus others as well. As couples we played a

Rich Zieman

"Nancy and I decided to take five or six days and drive leisurely from Chicago to visit friends in Madison, Wisconsin, then go on to my parents' home, then her parents' home. I think she expected that somewhere along the way we would get engaged. That was my plan, too. We got along well and I wanted to marry her.

So, we stopped for a picnic by a lake. I started breathing rather heavily and stammering around. My proposal went something like, 'Well, I suppose… Well, I suppose we should…'

Nancy said, 'We should what?' and I said, 'I suppose we should get married. Isn't that kind of the next step?'

'Well, I SUPPOSE!?!' Nancy said (she always over dramatizes that part and how heavily I was breathing). We agreed that we were going to get married, then drove on to stop and tell my parents and then her parents. That was in October and we set a wedding date for January."

lot of cards and made dinners together. Since Rich had a house, we held parties there—relatively mild parties for the mid-1970s. Although that was the era of experimentation with drugs, drugs were not something we did.

I lost my roommate when Viv and Gene married in 1976. By then Rich and I were very serious about each other. The district manager talked with Rich and asked if it might not be easier if I were transferred to another store. Rich thought things were working out just fine; he said that I was doing a good job and that our personal relationship would not interfere with work. His supervisor felt otherwise. I was transferred without being asked for my opinion or being consulted in any way. When I think back to that time, I realize that I was very compliant; that sort of thing would never happen now. I was transferred to a Minnesota Fabrics store in Tinley Park, about twenty miles north of where I lived in Crete.

I'd been on the job over a year by that time. The autumn series of seminars was winding down, and it was time to take a vacation.

I knew Rich was the right person for me. Our backgrounds were the same, our likes were similar, and we had fun together. That was the main thing; I liked being with him.

Our sons, one married and the

other recently engaged, proposed with style. Ted handed Ali a card and carried flowers in the other hand. The card had only two words, "Will You" … Ted supplied the other two, "Marry Me?" He had the ring in his pocket.

Tom proposed to Katelyn on bended knee on a suspension bridge with the night skyline of Minneapolis behind him. He asked the full question, "Will you marry me?" and like his brother, had the ring in his pocket.

I guess they learned from their father what not to do.

Rich's proposal was weak at best. "Well, I suppose…" That's how it started. I didn't know if he was trying to say something like, "Well, I suppose we should have lunch," or, "Well, I suppose we should get on the road." Not, "Well I suppose we should get married."

He was nervous, breathing as if he were going to make a terrible confession instead of a marriage proposal. No, there wasn't a ring either. I was happy, but thought, 'Is this the best he can do?'

In Rich's defense, he has redeemed himself from his engagement blunders. He's given me many gifts through the years that were unexpected, undeserved and quite lavish. To his credit he takes the kidding I've given him about the, "Well, I suppose…" very well.

For those involved in agriculture, a wedding in January is logical. The intensity of farm life is at its lowest ebb then—the fall harvest is finished, spring planting is months away, and there is undistracted time for celebration. We contacted the pastor of my home church, St. Peter's Lutheran, booked his time and the church for a wedding date of January 29, 1977.

From October to the end of January isn't a lot of time to plan a wedding. That wasn't all. I changed jobs during that time as well, moving from Minnesota Fabrics to a sales position with a Bernina Sewing machine distributor who owned nine stores in the Chicago area.

I have a confession to make: I really wanted to purchase my wedding dress. At a bridal shop I fell in love with a simple white dress, but at three hundred dollars for something I would wear only once, my practical side just couldn't justify the cost. Not only that, but when sewing is your business, it seems like some sort of betrayal to go with an off-the-rack garment. So, to borrow a phrase from today's television, I didn't 'Say yes to the dress.'

For months at Minnesota Fabrics I had been fingering bolts of Qiana knit—a fabric relatively new to the market. As I ran my hand under the fabric, it slipped across my skin like warm liquid. I knew it would drape beautifully. The fabric I chose for my dress was classic white and the dress design was very simple. Sleeves were long and full, gathered into buttoned cuffs. From a high collar there was one graceful A-line sweep that gently hugged curves before flaring out from the hip line. Everything I wore—from veil to hemline—cost fifty-five dollars.

When it came to the wedding party, there really was only one choice for my personal attendant, my close-as-a-sister aunt, Mary Luedtke Rebman. Viv Sekel, who had married Rich's best friend several months earlier and Mary Jo Zieman Check, Rich's sister, were bridesmaids. My six-year-old sister, Gina, was flower girl. Their dresses were a rose hue of the same Qiana knit.

Mary Luedtke Rebman

"I sewed my own dress and was still sewing it the day before Nancy's wedding. It held together, though. I did a lot of dancing at the reception and gave it a workout."

Mother made Gina's dress, Mary made her own, Viv's mother made hers, and I made Mary Jo's. Their dresses also had long, full sleeves and were softly draped A-lines.

My mother knew a photographer and booked his services for the wedding day. On one day in November we went shopping and selected the flowers, wedding cake and invitations. Mother and I made reservations at a hotel along the Wolf River not far from Zittau for a family dinner following the wedding rehearsal. We booked a supper club along Lake Winnebago for a reception after the wedding.

As I mentioned, January is a good time for farm families to celebrate a wedding. It is not, however, the best time of year to expect cooperation from Wisconsin's weather. The day before our wedding rehearsal a snowstorm roared through dumping inches of snow. As the storm ended, temperatures plummeted to far below zero and high winds began blowing the snow around, making for poor visibility and treacherous

Rich Zieman

"Several of our friends from the Chicago area didn't make it to the wedding because of the storm. I made it to the wedding rehearsal and our dinner afterwards then managed to make it across the bridge on my way back to Beaver Dam before it was closed again. The next morning the storm was over and it was bright and beautiful. The church where we got married is a little white country church, and on our wedding day it was a beautiful, serene scene—at thirty degrees below zero!"

Gina Luedtke Crispell

"I was the flower girl in Nancy's wedding. I was maybe five or six years old and I wet my pants at the altar and ran out."

road conditions.

I was already at my parents' home, but Rich drove from the Chicago area to his parents' home outside Beaver Dam, Wisconsin, through that snowstorm. The drive from Beaver Dam to the church and my parents' farm crosses the Butte des Morts Bridge over a broad expanse of water in Oshkosh. The morning of our rehearsal, officials closed that bridge because of dangerous conditions, and announced that if conditions permitted, they would open it again from 4:00 to 9:00 p.m.

Rehearsal went smoothly. My little brother, Dean, pretended to light candles; my brother, John, practiced escorting guests to their seats; bridesmaids, flower girl and groomsmen practiced their entrances while the organist played; the pastor reviewed how the wedding would progress. After rehearsal we bundled into warm coats and boots for a short trip to the rehearsal dinner.

Rich's friend, Jeff Trader, was in the wedding party. After the rehearsal dinner, Rich left so he could get across the bridge by Oshkosh before it closed. Jeff had relatives in Neenah, about twenty miles away, so he took me back to the farm. It was so snowy. When Jeff backed out of our driveway, he went too far and ended up in the ditch on the other side. It was 9:30 at night, dark, cold and windy. It would have been too difficult to dig the car out that night, so my father loaned Jeff his car. In the morning, Dad dug Jeff's car out of the snow and drove us to the church in it. Rich remembers my father saying,

Wedding Day observations

"I never thought I would end up taking my daughter to her wedding in someone else's car."

The weather wasn't the only challenge for people coming to our wedding. Tucked into wedding invitations were directions on how to get to the church located on County Road KK. But, the Wednesday before the wedding, the Winnebago County roads department erected new signs that reflected renaming of some county roads. Overnight County Road KK disappeared and County Road F took its place. Of course the locals knew where the church was, but Rich's family and out-of-town guests didn't. Quickly, Dad lettered some cardboard signs "Old KK" and somehow (in the cold) attached them to the new road signs.

My whole family was baptized and confirmed at St. Peter's Lutheran Church, but Aunt Mary and I were the only ones married there—both, ironically, to men named Richard.

Our wedding was a simple little ceremony held at 3:00 p.m., on Saturday, January 29, 1977. A strict code of conduct frowned on kissing in church so there was no "You may kiss your bride" permission granted to Rich. We turned to face the congregation as the pastor introduced us as Mr. and Mrs. Richard Zieman.

We danced the evening away at our wedding reception then slipped out. Our honeymoon was spent in the warmth of Corpus Christi, Texas, far, far from frozen Wisconsin.

Chapter 9

❧

Rich and I returned from our honeymoon to the house he owned in Park Forest. His roommates had moved out and we began settling in to married life.

Not long before Rich and I were married, I left my job with Minnesota Fabrics for a position with a Bernina sewing machine distributor who owned nine stores in the Chicago area. I had been transferred to another store without so much as being asked my opinion on the matter and the experience had left me open to the possibility of moving on. Minnesota Fabrics paid home economists a dismal wage and I knew I would earn little more over time. Bottom line: I felt it was time to try something else.

That "something else" was not a good fit for me. Underlying everything else in my job description was the responsibility for selling sewing machines. Service with the sale included lessons that taught sewing machine purchasers how to use their new equipment.

In truth, much of the difficulty I had in that position stemmed from my background. Growing up on the farm I learned to be frugal because we had to be frugal. I learned to make do with what I had because 'buy new' wasn't usually an option. I had a sewing machine, a perfectly good basic model Kenmore that served me well. The machines I was expected to sell, though, were newer models with gadgets and gizmos that I thought were impractical.

I remember thinking: "No one needs these things. I have a straight stitch, a zigzag stitch and a buttonhole stitch. Put in a stretch needle and I can sew knits—what else could I need?"

For me, sewing was a necessity. I did it not only because I liked sewing, but also because on my income I couldn't afford to purchase the same level of quality that I could create. But, I was wrong to believe that the features on more advanced sewing machines were something too good for customers. In reality, what I didn't understand was the concept of discretionary income.

For me, there wasn't much left over for spending, investing (impossible!) or saving (also difficult) after taxes and personal necessities were paid, but others had financial resources that I didn't have. They wanted the gadgets and gizmos and were willing to pay for them. It was short-sighted of me to assume that others were in the same position as I was. My short-sightedness lasted a long time. Even years later, when Nancy's Notions was gaining momentum, I tended to make product decisions excluding items that were expensive. It took me a long time before I finally stopped making decisions about other people's purchases based on my own assumptions.

That was the core of my challenge in selling sewing machines. I was so uncomfortable that after three months, when I was offered a manager's job at a Bernina store in Ford City, Illinois, I turned it down.

Two years earlier I had walked away from Ruth Oblander and my Sew/Fit training, lured by the security of a full-time job. Now I returned. Ruth hired me to help her write instructional books and teach seminars. There were three of us in Ruth's LaGrange, Illinois, office. After my first task, I booked seminars and traveled with Ruth.

That first task was to help write a book that explained Ruth's fitting and construction techniques. *The Sew/Fit Manual: A Guide to Making Patterns Fit by Pivoting and Sliding* was published in 1978 by the Sew/Fit Company. Authors were Ruth Oblander, Doris Ekern, and Nancy Luedtke Zieman. Doris was the third person in our office. A 450-page, 8½" x 11" black and white instructional manual with a color cover and a plastic ring binder spine, the manual became the flagship publication for Sew/Fit. Over the years it was reprinted time and time again.

Years earlier Ruth had promised to make me a success, and she had not forgotten her promise. She took me under her wing and taught me the process of selling.

We went to fabric stores—places like Cloth World and Northwest Fabrics. The store paid three hundred dollars for a seminar, but customers attended free. We taught three seminars in one day. The trunk of our car was loaded with books, and after each seminar we sold copies of Sew/Fit pamphlets for three dollars each and *The Sew/Fit Manual* for twenty-four dollars—and we made money! It was amazing.

Once I learned the process, I did seminars by myself. An artist designed some ads (embarrassing looking things!) that served the purpose of announcing where free Sew/Fit seminars were going to be held.

Hosting seminars was good for a fabric store because they pulled in customers who were eager to purchase supplies to try the new techniques they'd learned. I gave three seminars a day and there were fifty to one hundred people at each session. Afterwards I sold books and manuals.

Ruth ranged much farther than I did and was gone from the office a month or two at a stretch. Rich and I were newly married, though, and I stayed closer to home. Even so, I was often gone for a week or more, driving my own car, shifting books in and out of stores, carrying the money for book sales. Seminars were scheduled for 10:00 a.m., 1:00 p.m. and 7:00 p.m. After selling books and packing up, I'd head back to a motel room, sleep a little, and get up to do it again in a different location the next day.

By the winter of 1978, I was traveling extensively presenting Sew/Fit seminars. Irene James (an independent Sew/Fit contractor in Pennsylvania) and I had both taught at a conference for home economics teachers held at a downtown hotel in Washington, D.C. The conference was just about over when a snowstorm moved in, depositing twenty-four inches of heavy wet snow. Everything came to a stop. Nothing moved on the streets—no cabs, no people. Airlines were not flying, and there was no way to get to the airport if they were. We were snowbound. Several conference attendees who hadn't left before the storm were also stranded as was most of the hotel's staff.

There was a buffet-style restaurant in the hotel, but after several days of eating there, the thrill was gone. So one night I, along with three others—Irene and two teachers from Florida—trudged out into the snow. Our destination was a Chinese restaurant a few blocks away. I remember that the women from Florida were impressed with the sheer depth of the snow.

When we stepped inside the restaurant, a man that we took to be the owner scooted behind us, locked the door, and put up the "closed" sign. We made our way to one of the empty booths, slipped in and waited. And waited. And waited.

Now and then the man re-appeared carrying food, but it was obvious that, like us, many others were not being served. Equally obvious was the fact that the restaurant was short-staffed. So we offered to help. The man accepted our offer and we went to work.

On a white takeout bag he wrote three options that we could offer customers—a chicken dish, a beef dish, and a vegetarian dish. So, carrying our "menus," we went table to table taking orders and serving beverages. When the food was ready, we served that, too. Finally, we ordered for ourselves because we were the last ones in the restaurant. When we were done eating, we were politely presented with a bill, just like everyone else. So much for appreciation!

We paid for our meal, and when we had stepped outside and heard the door lock behind us, we started laughing. We laughed until our sides hurt over having paid for the privilege of brief careers as waitresses in a Chinese restaurant. Then we turned toward the hotel.

There's a magical moment after snow has stopped falling. It happens just before people start dressing for the battle of snow removal and arming themselves with shovels. Sounds are hushed by snow and everything is white and clean and somehow innocent.

We were in the capitol of the United States, governing seat of the most powerful country in the world, where decisions that affected the lives of people across the globe were commonplace and political maneuverings were expected. But on that night, we were caught in the moment, and when I spread my arms and fell backwards onto the snow, the other three did the same, and we made snow angels.

Rich has an entrepreneur's heart and a business instinct. Although his parents farmed, his mother had attended a business college and for many years supplemented the farm income by working as a secretary for a canning company. When Rich was in his teens, his mother and her friend, Ruth, opened a consignment shop where they sold used clothing. Rich watched his parents handle farm and business finances. He held jobs assisting the grounds keeper at a cemetery, waiting on customers at a Dog 'n Suds, and selling stereos, radios and televisions at an RCA store. His work ethic was strong, his education solid, and he had achieved success as a manager for Minnesota Fabrics. After our marriage he was eager for something of his own—a business he could help grow.

In 1978, Rich left Minnesota Fabrics and joined an upstart company called KoverKraft. The company designed and manufactured furniture, but not run-of-the-mill stuff. This unique line of furniture was designed to serve a young, mobile population. Pieces could be knocked down and moved easily. To allow for personal expression, upholstered pieces could have different covers.

The man who started KoverKraft was brilliant and Rich saw incredible potential for the business. But the man was also an alcoholic, who would call at 3:00 a.m. to talk excitedly about a great idea he'd just had, then as quickly would veer off to something else.

By then we had sold the house and moved closer to our jobs. We rented an upstairs flat directly across from the Burlington Northern train tracks in LaGrange, Illinois. The tracks not only served as an avenue for bringing freight in and out of the city, but were one of Chicago's main commuter train corridors as well. There were three sets of tracks in front of us and the apartment shook when two or three trains passed at the same time.

I was working, and Rich was making a salary, but his salary was barely enough to keep the rent paid. Times were tough for us then. We were still adjusting to marriage. Perhaps if we had waited a year longer to get married our adjustments would have been milder, but the reality is that I couldn't afford to live on my own. Besides, life is often tough financially for young people. Whatever our circumstances, I could not then, or now, imagine being married to anyone but Rich.

Rich struggled to keep KoverKraft afloat, believing that if a stable person were at the helm the business could succeed. But Rich wasn't at the helm—the owner was—and he was not a stable man. Things were gradually falling apart. Something needed to change for us.

In the late 1970s, Herberger's department stores dotted the upper Midwest. Most of the stores were in Minnesota, but adjacent states had several as well.

Before Herberger's was purchased by a larger company in the 1990s, they had fabric departments and one of my Sew/Fit accounts was with a Herberger's store. One weekend Rich and I drove to visit his family in Beaver Dam, Wisconsin, and there, in the middle of a cornfield, I saw a sign that read: Coming Soon—Herberger's. I jotted down the phone number listed on the sign. He made contact, interviewed with the company, and was hired as a management-level employee. Our hope was that we would end up in Beaver Dam which is where Rich grew up. That would put us near his parents and close to my family.

Rich was assigned to a training period at a Herberger's store in Virginia, Minnesota, 'way up in northern Minnesota on the Mesabi Iron Range. Major employers in the region were the iron mines, and businesses that moved and processed iron ore.

Virginia, Minnesota, is not only a mining community, but it is also located on the Laurentian Divide, a high point from which water flows either north to the Arctic Sea, or south and east to the Atlantic Ocean. Rich moved there a couple of months before I did and rented a two-bedroom apartment.

The prospect of moving to Virginia, Minnesota, presented something of a divide for me as well. Should I look for a job, or should I put my efforts into becoming a freelance home economist? We wanted to start a family at some point so another question revolved around how I could be a traveling teacher with a family? On the other hand, Rich's job would mean a move from Virginia to another Herberger's location when his training was over. If I got a job, I would need to quit when that happened.

Independence seemed the way to go. Before moving to Virginia,

Mary Luedtke Rebman

"When Nancy worked for Ruth Oblander, she assisted with a book, and she gave me a copy of that book. That was my first real awakening to what Nancy was doing, and that was before she even moved to Virginia, Minnesota. I don't think she got very much credit for the book."

Rich Zieman

"What Nancy was doing was an extension of what both of us had done at Minnesota Fabrics. I knew what she could do and was supportive."

I made arrangements with Ruth Oblander and went out on my own as a freelance home economist giving Sew/Fit seminars. I purchased the manuals from Sew/Fit at a wholesale price, and resold them at retail. It didn't matter that I was listed as one of the authors on the manual—I paid the same wholesale price as anyone else.

After the move, my first Sew/Fit seminar was held in the Herberger's store where Rich was the assistant manager. More than fifty women attended seminars that I presented three times a day for two days and the store's management was thrilled. Then I landed contracts for seminars with all of the Herberger's stores which at that time numbered a dozen or more, mostly in Minnesota, Wisconsin, and South Dakota.

When I became an independent contractor, before moving to Minnesota to join Rich, it seemed to me that being independent was key to accommodating the inevitable transfers that would come in Rich's career. As long as I had contacts in the sewing business I could book seminars, and as long as my car and health held up, I could get there.

Looking back from the perspective of what has happened in the four decades since that time, I realize now that what I was doing was a rarity. Today, there are many careers in which people commute to work from home offices, making proximity to a workplace of less importance than a good internet connection. In 1979, though, computers were in their infancy and cell phones were props for science fiction movies.

Although I had to put lots of miles on a car, I could work from an office almost anywhere. When I joined Rich in Minnesota, our second bedroom became that office. I invested in letterhead stationery and business cards that carried my name and identified me as a "Freelance Home Economist." I also bought a metal file cabinet, and set the portable typewriter that my mother had received as a high school graduation gift on a desk. I was in business.

As I traveled from town to town giving seminars, often women would ask, "Where did you get that?" They meant the tools I used—notions—that helped streamline the tasks of cutting, fitting and sewing.

My travels took me through larger cities where I could purchase supplies easily at large fabric stores, but in rural areas many who sewed didn't have access to big stores. For a while I simply told seminar participants where I had purchased my notions, but soon I realized that simply telling them wasn't helpful if they had no way to get there.

So, I decided to invest in some of the notions I used, make up a flyer and distribute the flyers at seminars. My first flyer offered a gauge to help space buttonholes with accuracy, a fiber iron cover that enabled ironing without scorching on any fabric and a hem gauge that aided in making pattern alterations and hems. I also offered several booklets on sewing and fitting techniques. The reverse side had our address in Virginia, and an order form.

Before I printed and distributed a flyer, though, I needed to name and register my little business. Rich suggested Sew Sensational. I opted for Nancy's Notions.

In addition to Herberger's, I scheduled seminars through county extension services and community colleges. I broke through my reticence about the necessity of gadgets and gizmos to purchase a top of the line Bernina sewing machine and, in doing so, depleted a savings account.

As 1980 began, I was traveling a lot. I still sold books that I carried in the trunk of my car and my biceps were well-shaped from hefting boxes of books. After selling books at seminars, it sometimes bothered me to carry the money with me, so I tucked it into sanitary napkin bags and hid it in my luggage, hoping that potential thieves still allowed some measure of dignity.

When I began distributing flyers for notions, orders started coming in. The bedroom that I used as an office was soon overrun with supplies.

While we lived in Virginia I decided to do my first mailing for Nancy's Notions. I had the raw materials for a mailing since I had been collecting names and addresses of seminar participants for a long time. Using my mother's typewriter, I typed names and addresses on mailing labels. Then I did "peel and stick" transfers to flyers. In order to get bulk postage rates at the post office, I had to sort the mailing. My first sort was by state (mostly South Dakota, Minnesota and Wisconsin), then by zip code within each state. I had piles on the couch, the chair, the table—all over our apartment.

While I was away teaching, Rich filled orders for me. After working all day, filling orders at night wasn't his preference and for a while he struggled with resentment, even to the point of seeming to pout when I returned home.

I remember saying, "This is my job. Are you going to be angry every time I return?" In time he got past his feelings. Apparently, like me, and like the town of Virginia's perch on the Laurentian Divide, he came to accept that the flow of my career was on the side of the divide that included travel.

As orders for Nancy's Notions came in, shipping them out became an issue. At first they went via the Virginia post office, but soon it became apparent that other arrangements were necessary.

I had seen a United Parcel Service (UPS) truck around town, but didn't know where the distribution center was located. So, one day I waited in my car for the truck's appearance. When I saw it, I started my car and followed, stopping and starting as the driver made deliveries, until we finally arrived back at the UPS distribution center.

That probably was the only time that anyone could accuse me of stalking, but I was doing it for good reason.

With our current awareness of the implications of shadowing another vehicle, I might not have done it. But today, I wouldn't have needed to—a quick cell phone check would give me the location.

It makes me think that following a UPS truck would make a great skit.

Mary Mulari has been my friend since 1980, when we both lived in Northern Minnesota. Together we've done many things—professionally and as friends. Mary's been a frequent guest on *Sewing With Nancy*, and over the years we have discovered the zany side of our characters. Several years ago she joined me for a Wisconsin Public Television fund-raising episode that we called, "Kick it Up a Stitch." It was anything but serious.

What if when I was sitting there, waiting for a uniformed UPS driver to return to his vehicle—what if, there had been a knock on my window.

It might go something like this:

Officer: Ma'am, I'd like to see your license, vehicle registration and proof of insurance, please.

Nancy: (startled, fumbles for purse) Officer, what have I done?

Officer: License, vehicle registration and proof of insurance, please ma'am.

Nancy: Here. (She hands documents to him; officer inspects)

Officer: Ma'am, it has been reported that you are following a UPS truck around town. Is that correct?

Nancy: Yes, sir. But you see I have this box here... (reaches for box)

Officer: (sharply) Hands on the wheel, ma'am! Don't make any sudden moves.

Nancy: But officer, it's just notions.

Officer: Notions? What do you mean, notions?

Nancy: I mean notions—supplies for sewing.

Officer: And you're following a UPS truck because you have notions to follow a UPS truck?

Nancy: No. I'm following because I need to ship notions.

Officer: Ship notions? Lady, you're stalking—stalking a UPS driver! I have a notion to write you a citation.

Nancy: A citation? For what?

Officer: A citation for stalking.

Nancy: Stalking? But I need to ship...

Officer: Okay, the charge is Stalking with Intent to Ship.

Nancy: Excuse me...

Officer: No excuses lady, I'm writing you up…
  (Dissolve to black)

Of course, that never happened. I followed that brown truck with gold lettering to the UPS distribution center, parked, and shipped my packages. But that day marked the beginning of a relationship with UPS, that endured for decades. In the 1980s, 90s and into the 2000s, we no longer had to look for UPS shipment centers—they came to us. Those brown vehicles backed up to loading docks at Nancy's Notions every day, delivering product and accepting shipments of orders that sometimes nearly filled their trucks.

Rich and I lived in Virginia, Minnesota, from September 1979 to January 1981, when he was offered the position of assistant manager at the new Herberger's store in Beaver Dam. We were going home.

Chapter 10

❧

Beaver Dam, Wisconsin, is a picturesque city whose population today numbers about sixteen thousand. Its name was a founding-fathers' nod to the furry creatures that were busy building dams along streams in the region when the first settlers arrived in 1841. The city is located along the south shore of Beaver Dam Lake, a large, shallow body of water created not by the dedication of dam-building beavers, but by a man-made dam on the Beaver Dam River that was built to provide power for a sawmill and later a flour mill as well.

A large spring in the area was considered sacred by Native Americans who lived in the region. After Native Americans were relocated to other areas of Wisconsin, the spring continued as a destination for those convinced of the healing reputation of its waters. Today, a pavilion marking the spring's location is located in Swan Park, a large green space in the center of town where community celebrations are held.

The city claims as its native son actor, Fred MacMurray, whose most famous role was as Steve Douglas, father in the popular *My Three Sons* television series that ran from 1960 to 1972.

Located about an hour's drive from Wisconsin's capitol city of Madison, Beaver Dam businesses are a mix of industrial and agricultural. As in the area where I grew up, the majority of the residents are descendants of German and Scandinavian immigrants. It is a clean community of busy, productive people who work hard and live quietly. It is a wonderful place for families.

Beaver Dam was where Rich grew up. It has been our home since January of 1981, when we moved there so Rich could become assistant

Earl Zieman

manager of a new Herberger's store in town.

Rich's childhood was spent on a farm a few miles outside Beaver Dam. His grandparents owned the land first, and they worked it as a dairy farm until after Rich's father, Earl Zieman, returned from World War II and took over.

Earl was dating another woman when he met her friend, Elaine, and saw in her the wisdom of a new direction. They married in 1946 and settled into the house his father had built on the Zieman farm. Their daughter, Mary Jo, one of my attendants in our wedding, was born in 1947. Rich followed in 1950.

Rich was three years old when Earl and Elaine sold their dairy cattle, purchased additional land, and focused on growing cash crops like field corn, sweet corn and peas—"cash crops" being a term used to define crops grown specifically for sale rather than for feed. They did, however, continue to raise chickens now and then.

Everyone knew Rich would not take over the family farm. He had severe allergies that were aggravated by dust, and farming always kicks up dust. Once, when he was about seven years old, he and a cousin were helping Earl as he loaded corncobs into a wagon. Rich started sneezing and couldn't stop. He sneezed all the way to the house and once inside, continued sneezing until his mother called the doctor in desperation, asking what to do. The doctor recommended cold compresses to Rich's head and nose, but still he sneezed on for six hours after they were applied. Gradually, Rich grew out of the worst of his allergies, but farming would never be his calling.

He attended a one-room school to start, then went to a small country school for grade school before moving to larger school buildings in Beaver Dam for middle and high school.

Rich came from a background similar to my own. His work ethic was strong. His first job at age fourteen was mowing a cemetery, but in high school he also held jobs as a cook at a Dog 'n Suds, and as a salesman of electronics equipment and appliances at an RCA store. He was raised and trained with honest values as a foundation, and he had an ability to develop rapport with people.

Rich's grandparents, Mary and Otto Zieman, built a house in town after Rich's parents, Earl and Elaine, married and took over the farming operation. After Rich's Grandpa Zieman died, his grandmother continued to live there. Her house was near the high school, and often Rich went there for lunch, sometimes taking a friend with him. His grandmother looked forward to his visits, fed him well as a reward, and kept an eye on the clock while he catnapped for a few minutes before heading back to school.

Rich Zieman
"In Beaver Dam the first house we lived in was a two-bedroom house with a basement. My grandmother had lived there, but she was in a nursing home. We rented it for one and a half years, then bought the house."

Rich's family—both immediate and extended—was smaller than mine, but everyone got along well, and it felt good to be moving near them.

Moving from northern Minnesota to Beaver Dam was somewhat more involved than the previous move had been. We had Nancy's Notions supplies to transport this time. By the time of our move to Wisconsin, the second bedroom in our apartment in Virginia, Minnesota, was full and overflowing with boxes of products, packaging supplies for shipping, mailing labels and the like.

In Beaver Dam we stashed everything into the second bedroom again, but it was obvious that wasn't going to last long. Before we got our own belongings unpacked and settled in, we were already eyeing the basement as a possible home for Nancy's Notions.

My business stationery declared that I was a freelance home economist who did sewing workshops, Sew/Fit method alterations, and store promotions. I traveled a lot—by road or air—to give seminars. Not only did I work in the upper Midwest, but I also did a lot of seminars for county extension services in the Northeast—Pennsylvania, New Jersey, Delaware and Rhode Island.

Together with Irene James, another freelance home economist who taught Sew/Fit methods, I developed products called Sew•Paks. Although a very limited product line, each pack was basically a kit, developed because we saw a need for something and couldn't readily find it. The Sew•Pak seamless slip, for example, included patterns for two slip variations, enough nylon tricot fabric to make one slip, elastic for the waist, and lace for edging. Other Sew•Paks offered a buttonhole foot for sewing machines, tailoring supplies and a kit to do screen printing.

By then I had also started writing brochures that explained and illustrated techniques perfected during seminars. For my early flyers and brochures, I did the layout and design work myself. This was in the era before the advent of desktop publishing. I cut and pasted elements, then took them to a printer for duplication. Everything was printed using black ink; I often printed on colored paper, but printing in color was too expensive for me.

Since the beginning of my career as a freelance home economist and teacher, I had kept the names and addresses of those attending my seminars. I transferred the names and addresses to index cards and they became the basis of a mailing list for product flyers.

Rich settled in to his job at Herberger's. The new store was very nice and the challenge of getting a retail establishment up and running was something he enjoyed. Although his schedule was more predictable than mine, he was a busy man. With spring approaching, despite a history of allergies, he was also considering working with his father on growing crops.

Before moving to Beaver Dam, I asked my father-in-law, Earl, to secure a post office box for Nancy's Notions. New flyers were designed prior to our move so that when we arrived in Beaver Dam, I could hit the ground running.

There wasn't much time for Nancy's Notions, but as I presented seminars in various places, I saw the need for more products, not less. By that time we had a modest flow of cash from Nancy's Notions, and really didn't want to give that up. As we added new products, we realized the spare bedroom wouldn't work, so we took half of the basement, hung a curtain to hide the washer and dryer area, and put the supplies down there. But finding storage space was only part of our need, we needed help with processing orders and maintaining records.

Rich Zieman
"Nancy really got to know my parents. At family gatherings Nancy and Mom would talk, talk, talk, talk."

My mother-in-law had a gift for keeping an office as efficiently organized as she kept her immaculate home. From the first time I met Elaine, I liked her, and my regard for her and my father-in-law, Earl, deepened into love and respect as the years passed. Although there are those who would cry, "You're asking for trouble if you hire a relative!" I hired Elaine to help with orders. It was one of the best things I ever did.

Elaine took charge and put everything in order. She sorted, arranged and quickly had things running with the efficiency of a time-management expert. While working, she identified what could be done to increase efficiency.

Earl, Rich's father, was incredibly capable as well. As farmers have to do, he became adept at adapting. Need something built? Earl could build it. Not sure what would really fit the bill? Earl could figure it out. Need an item repurposed? No problem. Give Earl a concept and he was on it.

Our basement was just a basement—cement walls and floor, exposed floor joists above, plumbing pipes, furnace, open wooden steps—the usual stuff. Sometimes it got a bit wet down there when we had a heavy rain or sudden snow melt. Wielding saw and hammer, Earl built bins for products and benches where shipments could be prepared. He was the engineer and carpenter who did most of the work, with a little help from others.

John Luedtke
"I remember helping to build bins and benches for Nancy's Notions at their house in Beaver Dam."

At that time Nancy's Notions carried three books from the Sew/Fit Company, pattern weights called Weight Mates, a washable marking pen (something new in the early 80s), a collar point and tube turner, Grabbit (a magnetic pincushion), Seams Great (a bias cut tricot seam finish—something that is no longer a viable product because serging quickly and neatly finishes seams), Hem Gauge, Simplex Gauge (for measuring and spacing buttons and buttonholes), and then the Sew•Pak kits.

Earl helped check in products and ship orders as well. It wasn't long after Elaine started that Earl was also employed by Nancy's Notions, both of them part-time to start.

That year, 1981, was a year of major changes. Bookings for seminars were keeping me on the road much of the time. Help was needed, not just with filling orders, but I needed a secretary as well. Earl's handiwork included not only bins, but a partition in the basement where we put an office, and I hired Betty Dye as my first secretary. She not only worked with me, but with Nancy's Notions as well and was our first non-family employee.

Rich Zieman

"The little house in Beaver Dam was in a residential area not zoned for commercial use. Sometimes we'd notice a car driving by slowly then it would turn around and go past again. Once in a while someone would stop. We really didn't want deliveries or customers coming to the residential area. None of the neighbors ever complained, but we didn't want them to, so we shipped packages from my parents' farm."

The flyers I handed out at seminars and mailed out to a growing list of people who had attended seminars, had a post office box address. Delivery trucks came to the house to drop off shipments of products, but every now and then, people passing through town found our location by checking the phone book (there were only two Ziemans) and stopped in to purchase items.

When Elaine and Earl had a number of packages to ship, Earl carried them upstairs and took them to the farm. He had a signal system for UPS. Whenever a shipment was ready to go, he set out a triangular red flag to notify the UPS driver to stop.

I turned twenty-eight that year— 1981—and I had much to be thankful for, both personally and professionally.

On the professional side, everything I had done to that point seemed to fit into what I was doing. Early 4-H demonstrations were great training for teaching sewing techniques. Physical adversities had taught me perseverance. The knowledge I'd gained at college absolutely fit with my career. The experience of working in the retail setting of Minnesota Fabrics not only helped me understand the motivations of those who sewed, but gave me customer relations training as well. As an independent home economist, I was learning how to handle myself as a business woman. Nancy's Notions was still small, but growing.

Each flyer for Nancy's Notions carried more products. We had expanded from a single 8½" x 11" flyer, to an 8½" x 14" flyer, then on to multiple-page catalogs.

As Christmas of 1981 approached, I decided to add even more pages for a holiday catalog. With an artist from the nearby town of Waupun, I put a catalog together. It was printed on Christmas green paper and had a line drawing of a Christmas stocking with the heading, "The Gift of Sewing."

By then, our mailing list was around ten thousand names and addresses. Labels were printed and applied to the catalogs. Clear tabs were added to the edges to keep the stapled, multiple-page catalog from flopping open in the mail. We started to sort the mailing when suddenly I screamed. I had noticed that the Nancy's Notions address had the wrong zip code. Instead of Beaver Dam's 53916 zip code, the zip code listed on both the order form and return address was 53963, that of Waupun, Wisconsin, 15 miles away—the zip code of my artist.

It was too late to reprint, and too costly as well, so every catalog needed to be manually corrected. That meant two changes per catalog— twenty thousand changes!—one on the order form and the second on the return address. I put out a call (a scream may have been more like it!) for help.

"The pen is mightier than the sword," goes an old saying. A small elite force of pen-wielding soldiers came to my aid—Elaine and Earl, Betty, my mother, and Aunt Mildred (my mother's aunt) worked crossing out the wrong zip and writing in the correct one until our arms ached from the effort.

That catalog became the stuff of legends for Nancy's Notions, recounted over and over again since then with great drama. For that reason alone the episode was almost (not quite, but almost) worth it.

As I traveled giving sewing seminars, I came in contact with Dave Larson, a man who owned several sewing machine stores in Milwaukee. He asked me if I would be a guest instructor on his cable television program called *Sew Video*. Initially, Dave's videos had started as sewing machine lessons. Rather than store personnel giving basic lessons, he recorded them and showed them to customers so they could learn the basics of using their new purchase. It was a completely revolutionary method of relaying information.

Gradually those lessons morphed into a television program. When cable television became available, he began airing programs hosted by his wife, Kate, in the Milwaukee area on the Satellite Program Network.

In 1981, cable television was in its infancy. In fact, if you mentioned the words cable and television in the same sentence, most people at that time would have thought you were referring to the wire that connected the television set to the antenna on the roof. Unlike today, there weren't numerous cable television networks with budgets for quality production. Cable TV was low-budget, mostly local and sparsely viewed. In fact, I didn't know anyone who had cable television.

But, television carries a mystique. The idea was exciting, but suddenly I remembered my face. The realization was almost a jolt—a jerk back into reality from a brief, but vivid dream. 'I can't do TV with my face,' I thought. 'I'm not television material.'

There was also a matter of confidence. I dealt with that by reminding myself that I was a sewing teacher; appearing on television would merely mean that I was teaching in front of several hundred people instead of thirty to sixty seminar attendees.

Finally, I convinced myself to say yes; a guest appearance is no big deal.

We taped in the Larson's dining room. There was only one camera and Dave ran it. Even though I knew next to nothing about television production, it was evident that he knew little more than I did. But when we were done, Dave asked if I would like my own show.

Issues of my face aside, I didn't understand the economics involved so I asked.

"How are we going to make money?"

"Don't worry," he replied.

But I persisted, I wanted to know how things worked because the concept of a television show and what it would mean financially just wasn't "jelling" in my mind. His offer simply was that I would develop topics and appear on camera; he would handle production. Even though I didn't have specific answers to my questions, I agreed.

Sewing With Nancy was born.

Chapter 11

❦

Just like that, I had my own television program. What to do with it was another question.

I've always seen myself as a teacher. As far back as my early 4-H days, I grasped the concept of teaching visually, using samples to illustrate techniques and progress. Those skills were honed while teaching at Minnesota Fabrics, and refined further while teaching sewing seminars as an independent home economist. My students related well to me and told me I made the complex simple to understand. Teaching on television was just another classroom, I told myself, just another classroom.

To be truthful about it, I didn't expect much of television. My face was the main reason. Even though I had made huge strides in confidence since my teen years, I was still very aware that my face was flawed. The people I saw on television were photogenic and symmetrical. I was not. To compensate for the effects of Bell's palsy, I always tried to turn the unaffected "happy" side of my face toward my audience, and led with my left side while talking. Would that work on TV? Although I wasn't going to be doing a Hollywood production, I feared that people would change channels from my program based on my appearance.

Still, opportunities shouldn't be dismissed on the basis of fear. Advantages of having a television program were that I could promote Nancy's Notions on air during the six, one-minute commercial slots in each program. Also, Rich and I wanted to have children; I was feeling that I shouldn't be traveling as much as I had been.

Even though I didn't understand all the financial nuances of having my own television program, I decided to give it a try. Rich agreed.

Early in 1982, we moved video taping to our home in Beaver Dam. The "set" was the small dining room area off our kitchen.

The first show we taped took thirteen hours to complete! There was only one television camera and it had to be repositioned for different angles, and lighting had to be repositioned as well. Today, *Sewing With Nancy* is taped using three or four cameras. After a run through—our term for a practice run—of each segment, we roll tape and the segment is recorded. If there is a blunder, we do it again. Most times, the switching between wide shots and tight shots tells the story. It is rare for recording of a half-hour show to take more than three hours. Then its onto the next segment of the episode; there are usually four to five segments per show. But back at the beginning, after recording, during the editing process, each tight shot or close up snippet was laboriously inserted to tell the story.

Rich Zieman

"The film crew arrived in the morning and was still there at 10:00 p.m. It took forever. Nancy was getting burned from the lights and our house was lit up. I went outside to get some air.

All of our draperies were closed and our neighbors were gathered around. They asked what was going on."

That's not all. There's a reason why television studios are cavernous spaces. Cameras on wheeled bases need room for maneuvering. Heavy television lights hang from high ceilings where they're angled for careful illumination, making what appears on a viewer's television screen look natural. And—very important!—in the "heat rises" principle of physics, height is needed to keep heat generated by the lights bearable.

In our small house, ceilings were low and I got "sunburned" from the lights. When taping ended that first day, I turned to look at Rich and my face was tomato red on the "happy" side and a rosy "cream of tomato soup" color on the "sad" side.

In all, we taped eleven episodes of *Sewing With Nancy* in our home. While we managed to shorten the length of tapings, the lights were still hot. Sometimes we taped into the evening.

Sewing With Nancy aired on the Satellite Program Network (SPN) on Thursday afternoons. SPN reached three million households in 1982, a small number in relation to national television today. I'm not even sure where it aired. We did get orders as a result of advertising Nancy's Notions on air, but they were a trickle, not a rush. It wasn't much for Nancy's Notions to grow on.

But something else was growing, I was pregnant. Rich and I were expecting a baby in mid-December.

Like my mother, I am long-waisted and slim so it hardly looked like I was pregnant. As my pregnancy advanced I wore shifts. Tables and my sewing machine were positioned carefully and the camera strategically angled to avoid showing my pregnancy. These days female TV and movie celebrities wear form-fitting dresses and tops that proudly show a "baby bump," but that wasn't acceptable in 1982.

Between tapings for *Sewing With Nancy*, I had been traveling a lot that year. Rich's job at Herberger's kept him busy and he was working with his father planting and tending crops. We were under a lot of stress. As my pregnancy progressed, I wondered how I was going to manage a baby and a business. Rich wondered, too.

Meanwhile, as more episodes of *Sewing With Nancy* aired, orders for Nancy's Notions began to increase. Elaine and Earl kept things organized and moving in and out of our basement. We decided to make arrangements with MasterCard so customers could pay for orders with a credit card. The first credit card orders began rolling in that fall.

That year was also the first time that we came up against a very old, very established mind set.

We needed a small loan—about five thousand dollars—and I applied at the bank where we had an account for Nancy's Notions. The request was denied.

Both Rich and I had been very responsible with money. We paid bills on time, and by that point in our marriage had even reimbursed Grandpa Larson who had paid off my student loans. At that time I was earning a respectable income from teaching seminars, Rich was earning a salary at Herberger's. The Zieman family was known and respected in Beaver Dam, and (not that we were counting on family connections for a loan) Earl and Elaine had banked at that bank for years. Then there was

Nancy's Notions which was growing, earning a tidy amount above expenses.

But they turned us down. I was surprised, but Elaine was furious. She could be a formidable woman when the occasion called for strength. She marched into the bank and confronted the loan officer. Had they even bothered to check what Nancy's Notions was depositing in their bank each week, she asked. No, they hadn't. Was the problem a credit rating? No, of course not. Was income adequate for repayment? Yes, it seemed so. Was the issue one of a woman's name being on the business? We were given the loan.

On November 10, 1982, family and friends held a baby shower for me. It was a lovely event, a great time with people who meant much to me, and the baby received some wonderful gifts. Rich and I were looking forward to being parents, and that day made it seem more real.

That day was a milestone in another way as well. November 10, 1982, was when that day's orders coming in to Nancy's Notions topped a thousand dollars for the first time.

Just a few days later I negotiated my first distributor buying terms. Prior to that time I had ordered products from vendors at the standard discount for retail stores. Those discounts were adequate when selling product directly to consumers, but retail stores wanted to be able to purchase from Nancy's Notions as well. Buying product at a steeper discount allowed that to happen.

Rich and I signed up for Lamaze classes. The first class was held in mid-November, but I was out of town teaching that evening. So, Rich attended without me. It was an interesting sight, I'm sure—a long, lanky man sitting cross-legged on the floor, alone, watching while other expectant couples went through their first breathing exercises. I didn't learn anything, but Rich learned how to do a very impressive cleansing breath.

As for me, a visit to my doctor that week had revealed the baby's head was not yet in position for birth. But with my due date several weeks away, there was time yet for Baby Zieman to make a move.

What was I thinking? My mother had me early and it seemed this baby was going to keep to a family tradition. I didn't make it to a single Lamaze class. On November 20, 1982, Theodore Loyall Zieman was born by Caesarean section, necessary because he was in a breech position.

We called him Teddy, and when he grew out of that, Ted.

Because I'd had surgery, Teddy and I remained in the hospital for five days. I hadn't taken the time to teach anyone else how to process credit card orders, so in my absence, orders piled up. Once I returned home, it was difficult to make my way up and down the basement steps.

Teddy immediately became the center of our attention. What can I say? He was a beautiful baby! Early on his physical characteristics resembled the Luedtke side, thirty years later he definitely looks like Rich.

We were overwhelmed as are all first-time parents. Teddy was a colicky baby and our family doctor suggested a unique home remedy—place him in an infant seat atop a running clothes dryer. We tried it and found that the combination of warmth and vibration magically turned an inconsolable baby into a sleeping child—that is, as long as we remembered to advance the timer before the buzzer went off!

My mother stayed with us a few days after I came home from the hospital—her presence gave me some needed rest and her experience helped us adjust to parenthood.

After a few weeks, it was difficult to remember what life was like before Teddy's birth. He was the essence of what life is about.

Having an office in my home was a big advantage at that time. Between baths and feedings and "baby time," we set up a baby swing in the office area downstairs and Ted went to work with me. Of course, his Zieman grandparents loved that! He was the first grandchild for both Rich's parents and mine. At times I almost had to fight to hold my own child.

Elaine didn't approve of disposable diapers. Cloth diapers had been good enough for her children and should be good enough for her grandchildren, too. Our washer and dryer were directly behind my desk, separated by a thin curtain from the desk where I conducted business. I wasn't too keen on having smelly diapers in the vicinity, or of hearing the washer and dryer spinning and thumping while I worked. I was also busy and was looking for ways to save time, so I purchased disposable diapers for Teddy. One day I left Teddy with Elaine for a while and came back to find her trying to wash out a disposable diaper. She got the hang of using disposables after a little tutoring, but I'm not sure she ever totally approved.

I made arrangements for someone to come to our home and provide day care several hours a week, but they cancelled just before they were scheduled to start. I didn't know what to do. Soon it would be time to tape more *Sewing With Nancy* programs, and a number of seminars were on my calendar.

Most mornings I take a few minutes and spend it in quiet reading, reflection and prayer. That habit has always settled me and given me the peace and focus to move forward through whatever the day brings. With a newborn and responsibilities piling up, I don't recall having time to say much more than, "Help!"

Joan Woods
(Child Caregiver)
"Not long before meeting Nancy, my husband and I had gone through losing two children. They were both stillborn. After that I needed to do something so I had a couple Avon territories.

When I rang the doorbell, Nancy looked so frazzled and tired. I offered to come back another time, but she said, 'No.' When she said she was looking for a child care provider for her baby, I said 'Me!' God put Rich and Nancy and Ted in my path to help me heal. I truly believe that."

It was winter and snow covered the ground. That day I had tried to work, but Teddy was fussy and I had about given up. Then the doorbell rang. I opened it to find a woman who identified herself as an Avon representative and asked if I was interested in looking at a catalog.

I wasn't, but I didn't want to seem rude, so I invited her inside.

"Joan," she said. "My name is Joan Woods." While I glanced through the catalog, Joan held Teddy and talked to him. He calmed in her arms. We chatted a little. She had a daughter, she told me, a girl about thirteen years old. Joan lived nearby, just a couple blocks away. We were neighbors.

She held Teddy while I ordered lipstick and nail polish, and when I held out my arms, she seemed reluctant to hand him back.

I said, "I'm looking for someone to watch Teddy several hours a week while I…"

"Me!" she said. "I'll do it," and for nearly twenty years and through two children, she has.

Joan started working mornings three days a week, moved to four days after a while and then came five days a week, full time. She nurtured Ted as much as any mother could and she made it possible for me to work. With my office downstairs, I could pop up the stairs for feedings, playtime and, of course, meals.

On Sunday afternoon, December 12, 1982, I was feeding Teddy when the phone rang. It was David Larson, the one producing *Sewing With Nancy*.

"This arrangement isn't working for me," he said by way of announcing an end to our television production. He was pulling out. "Go ahead and do it yourself," he said.

We had recorded only eleven programs. Dave did it all, both production and editing. The production and editing crews worked under contract to him. The contract with the Satellite Program Network held his signature, not mine. Without him I felt there could be no *Sewing With Nancy*, and if it wasn't profitable for Dave, how could it be for me. That was it. My television career was over.

A couple of nights later I awakened in the middle of the night in a sweat, something that had never happened before. As I bolted upright in bed, the thought came to me and wouldn't leave: 'If you don't do this now, you will never have another opportunity.'

In the morning I began making phone calls to see if I could produce *Sewing With Nancy* on my own.

The airtime on the Satellite Program Network cost about five hundred dollars per week. That was a substantial figure, but over the months orders generated from exposure on the network had brought increased revenue to Nancy's Notions. The extra revenues were covering the airtime.

I made a trip to the offices of the Satellite Program Network and negotiated a three-month contract for airtime. Part of that agreement included moving *Sewing With Nancy* to a Saturday morning timeslot. The reason I didn't negotiate a longer contract was because I didn't know if I'd have the money to continue beyond that point.

Then I had to find a video crew and production company. I located

Barbara Luedtke Eckstein

"I remember Nancy sitting with Ralph, her dad, one day telling him about taking over the sewing programs. She and her father were talking business. Ralph told her, 'Go for it.'"

Rich Zieman

"Nancy and I expected honesty. Our ethical background came from our parents. Both sets of parents would never tell a lie and we didn't have that gray area in the middle where you're not lying, but not telling the truth either. We couldn't work with someone who lied."

a video crew in Milwaukee. They used two cameras (twice as good as before!). The studio they worked from was in someone's basement and although they didn't edit the video tape, they had a production arrangement with another studio. I had no idea what production costs should be, so when the man who owned the video company said he would merely pass on what he was charged for production costs, I agreed.

We began video taping episodes. At that time I was the only person on camera. I didn't think about having guests; I was still feeling my way along.

The production crew did much better than the crew that video taped in our house. One day while video taping, the director let it slip that the man with whom I had made production arrangements was charging me double the normal costs. I was angry.

I don't like confrontation and avoid it whenever possible. But if I need to feel strong enough to confront something, I stand and put my hand on my backbone and tell myself I can do it. I called a meeting with him and asked if he had lied to me. When I knew for sure that he had, I fired him.

I needed new video and production crews. Finances were tight, so instead of trying to pay for everything myself, I decided to ask companies to underwrite production costs in exchange for on-air advertising.

I contacted the sewing machine manufacturer, Bernina, and presented a proposal outlining what it would take to underwrite production costs. They flatly turned me down. Some years later when *Sewing With Nancy* was more successful, the president of Bernina approached me at a trade show and admitted that his decision against underwriting *Sewing With Nancy* was short-sighted. They could have had a lot of exposure that would have had a positive impact on their sales.

After rejection by Bernina, I contacted Pfaff, also a manufacturer of sewing machines with headquarters in Germany. I was referred to their advertising agency in New Jersey. At that time Pfaff's United States' division had a new president, a man named Rainer Moser who was fresh to the States from Germany. When the ad agency presented him my proposal for underwriting *Sewing With Nancy,* he said, "Why not, she has a German last name."

When he and I met for the first time, he asked why the Ziemans dropped the last "n" from their name (apparently in Germany, the name is spelled Ziemann). My reply was that I had nothing to do with that, after all, it was my husband's name. A charming little conversation about my name started a wonderful, long relationship with Pfaff that would endure from 1983 through 2002. Several years later, Pfaff was sold to a larger company. I eventually lost contact with those I knew initially, but the company remained a faithful underwriter.

Sewing With Nancy started in 1982. At first everything was one hundred percent me. I was negotiating contracts and working with independent production companies. Each time I started with a new production company I had to coach them on how to tape when sewing machines were being used. Camera angles are an issue. The camera couldn't be at the back of the machine because viewers wouldn't be able to see the person seated at the machine. The angle needed to include enough of the sewing machine to make it look plausible, but still allow for me to talk to the audience. The solution is an awkward angle for the sewing machine, one that somehow looks reasonable when viewed on a television screen. Normal sewists would never sit the way I have to sit while recording and because of the odd angle, what I sew on *Sewing With Nancy* is never my best.

I've learned a lot over the years, though. Whether on *Sewing With Nancy* or at a seminar, I assume that the audience is blind. I never assume their knowledge. Instead, I describe and show every step. For example, I say, "To add the facing to the garment, pin the right sides together and stitch." I

Barbara Luedtke Eckstein

"Elaine Zieman was the first employee for Nancy's Notions. One time Elaine, Nancy and I went to Neenah for lunch and Nancy left us to pick up some boxes. Elaine looked at me and said, 'I foresee great things for this business.' 'Really?' I thought. 'Maybe.'"

show a sample of the same thing. Actually, I talk in technical writing style.

Through teaching seminars I have also learned that not everyone is watching me. Instead, they may be madly taking notes. So, sometimes I'll say, "Put your paper down and watch this. I'll do it again, but first see it." It works.

With the Satellite Program Network airing *Sewing With Nancy* on Saturday mornings, viewers increased, and along with more viewers came increased orders for Nancy's Notions products. Bins were crowding every available space in the basement, and orders were flying out the door. Nancy's Notions was growing rapidly.

As we neared the midpoint of 1983, Rich, Ted and I were trying to live in a home that housed my freelance home economist business, *Sewing With Nancy* headquarters, and Nancy's Notions. It was also a day care center for Ted, and the place where we fell into bed for a few hours' sleep every night. It was obvious that something had to give, and when the solution was presented, it was something to cluck about.

Chapter 12

❧

Sewing With Nancy's **first broadcast** was on September 2, 1982. Using the six, one-minute commercial slots in the program, I offered a free catalog in exchange for the postage to mail it. "Send three first class stamps to receive your copy of Nancy's Notions Sewing Catalog," I told the camera, and out there, in living rooms and homes where I couldn't see them, viewers began to respond. Requests for the catalog more than tripled.

Now, lest you think that we're talking thousands here, keep in mind that back then Nancy's Notions was just getting started. At first, catalog requests probably jumped from five to fifteen a day. But every time the program aired, the mail brought more requests—all accompanied by three, first class stamps.

Ted Zieman
(Son)

"I started a stamp collection from mail orders and it's probably in my parents' house somewhere. Grandpa Earl and I would go through the envelopes looking for cool stamps and we would clip them out."

When sending a single catalog, we used those stamps. But, if the catalog request came when we were about to do a large bulk mailing of catalogs, we shipped it as part of that mailing. The United States Postal Service required a bulk postage permit with accompanying imprint on the mailing piece. These mailings were paid by check so we always had more stamps on hand than we needed.

I'm getting 'way ahead of myself here, but I just want to mention that stamps became something of interest for young Teddy a few years later. He and Earl developed quite a collection and enjoyed themselves doing it. And,

157

as for those three, first class stamps—for the many years that I made that on-air offer, no one ever had to ask, "Do you have a stamp?"

My early *Sewing With Nancy* programs were not polished productions. Sometimes I even held a script above the camera shot, referred to it while talking, and demonstrated with my free hand. Commercials for Nancy's Notions were equally crude. Even so, requests for catalogs came in, followed by orders from the catalogs.

Encouraged, we added more products and increased the size of the catalog, which, in turn, increased orders. We were rapidly outgrowing the basement. Bins and products crowded the space.

There was only one real consideration when choosing products for Nancy's Notions to offer—they were products that I found useful. I consider myself a rather mainstream sewist. If I used or liked a product, perhaps others would, too. I never used focus groups to help make decisions, just basic common sense. I also used products offered by Nancy's Notions on TV, which showcased their convenience and usefulness—soft selling at its best.

There were products that bombed. We had several boxes of wooden purse handles that were designed for button-on, custom sewn bags. The handles were cumbersome and the bag section too small. We lost on that inventory, eventually selling it way below cost.

We also tried to sell upholstery notions in one or two flyers and catalogs. Rich's job with KoverKraft had piqued his interest in offering a book and notions used exclusively by upholsterers. Garment sewists or quilters rarely upholster—at least not the people on the Nancy's Notions mailing list. A few years ago I found a box of upholstery springs in our basement—so much for inventory control!

Jed Schroeder, the salesman from

Note

The term "sewist" is relatively new, but it is one I wholeheartedly embrace. Unlike *seamstress* which has gender associations, and *sewer* with its smelly overtones, *sewist* elevates interest to the realm of skill.

Sewing throughout history has been mostly assigned to women, and in the tendency to dismiss women's work as less important and therefore less artistic, it is time to break out!

W.H. Collins, often joked with me that I sold more button elevators (a two dollar product used to provide space between the button and fabric) than any other company. So, I took that lead to ask for better pricing. I told Jed that I should become a distributor so I could sell the button elevators, and possibly other W.H. Collins products, to the retailers I met while lecturing at their stores. I must have been convincing because I was granted distributor status and the accompanying discount on product purchases.

After being granted my first distributor account with W.H. Collins, I was then able to use that accreditation to buy supplies from other larger vendors such as June Tailor, Prym Dritz and Swiss Metrosene. I contacted smaller independent manufacturers by phone or mail; they were all anxious to sell product to me. In those days we were all hungry for business.

In 1983, Earl saw that there were too many orders coming in for the basement to handle, so he came to us with a suggestion. There was a building on the Zieman farm, a long, single story, one thousand square-foot structure with a simple roofline. It was where Earl and Elaine had raised chickens.

Quick! Before you start thinking, "A chicken coop?!" with accompanying mental flashes of old gray wood and flimsy walls with holes big enough to let marauding foxes slip through, stop! This was a chicken house, not a dirty old coop. Its walls, floor and ceiling were insulated against Wisconsin's frigid winters. There were windows and solid doors. Separate nesting boxes lined the walls, and Earl had kept the place clean. It was now empty and he wanted to turn it into a warehouse for Nancy's Notions.

Moving Nancy's Notions to the farm was a good idea for several reasons. First, we needed to be able to live in our own home. Since our home was not zoned for commercial use, we wanted to avoid having deliveries coming and going. That had already been partially addressed by Earl taking shipments to the farm for UPS pickup, but having Nancy's Notions at the farm would put shipping and product in the same location. Very logical!

Earl went to work paneling the building, building storage bins and shelves for products and installing a heating system and air conditioning units. He even carpeted the floors. There was no running water in the

Earl Zieman

"In town, I partitioned the basement and made things in the basement, and then had to do it again when we moved to the chicken house. When we got in that place I thought, 'What do we do with all this room?' but it wasn't long before Nancy's Notions was outrunning that space, then we had to move out of there."

building and, therefore, no bathroom; people working in the warehouse had to trek across the yard to Earl and Elaine's house for those comforts.

Supplies were still ordered from the office in our basement; mail was sorted and orders were opened there. But products and shipping were moved to the farm on July 1, 1983, and remained there for over a year.

We felt like we could breathe again. With Nancy's Notions products and shipping benches gone from our basement, I set up a sewing studio there—a place where I made samples for *Sewing With Nancy* and sewed my own clothes. Not long afterwards, though, we had a rainstorm and the basement flooded.

Our basement frequently had water leakage in the spring. The area where the house was built had been a marsh until landfill made housing development possible. Unfortunately, the home building methods employed in the 1940s, when the house was built, included cement block foundations that weren't up to the task of keeping torrential spring rains at bay. But then, our basement, which even included a fruit cellar, was intended as a place for storage and laundry, not an office.

Our makeshift office had indoor/outdoor carpeting. But since we knew the building's propensity for water seepage, it was not glued to the basement floor. Often in the spring, we would roll up the carpeting, move desks, and sweep the trickle of water toward a drain.

One year in the mid-80s, we had days of rain, including one middle of the night downpour. The trickle of water turned into a river in the basement. In pajamas and boots, Rich and I frantically moved desks, sewing machines, cabinets, ironing boards, and fabric—lots and lots of fabric—plus sewing samples from past TV shows. To keep things away from the widening river, we stacked items and boxes on top of each other in a very haphazard way while working feverishly to save our stuff.

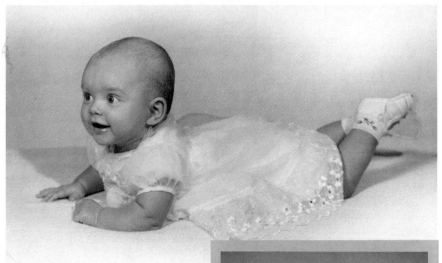

"She was a baby about as beautiful as anything."
—Nancy's Mom

Mary Luedtke, Hazel Luedtke, Nancy, Georgina Larson,
Back row: Leonard Luedtke and Loyall Larson

With my parents, Barbara and Ralph Luedtke, '56

Gina, Dean, John, and Nancy

Modeling one of my favorite
4-H dress projects, '69

4-H Record Book

Difficult times with both legs in casts.

4-H Girls Go to State Fair
Top Winnebago County dress revue winners, announced at Winneconne Central School Thursday
night, who will represent the county at the state
fair, are, front row, Nancy Luedtke, left, Winchester 4-H Club, and Bonnie Ross, Zion 3-C 4-H, both

modeling pants-suits they made; and alternates, back
row, Debbie Retzlaff, Poygan Go-Getters, party
dress, and Mary Jo Harvey, Rt. 1, Oshkosh, Mikes-
ville 4-H, wool dress.   —Northwestern photo.

4-H girls selected for state fair.
Look at how those plaids match!

First press photo, '79

Press shot, '83

Nancy with "new" type of sewing machine,
a serger, circa 1985

Press shot, '85

Baby Ted
Makes Three, '82

Adoption or "Gotcha" Day—Adoption of Tom, '91

Sewing with Tommy

Our family,
'99

Labeling a mailing at my kitchen table, '80

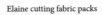

Elaine cutting fabric packs

Basement sewing room
and warehouse with
Donna Fenske

Basement picking and packing

Once a Chicken House,
now Nancy's Notions, '83

Chicken House picking
and packing area

Earl with packages at the
Chicken House

Delivery of 30,000
Catalogs, a big
day, '85

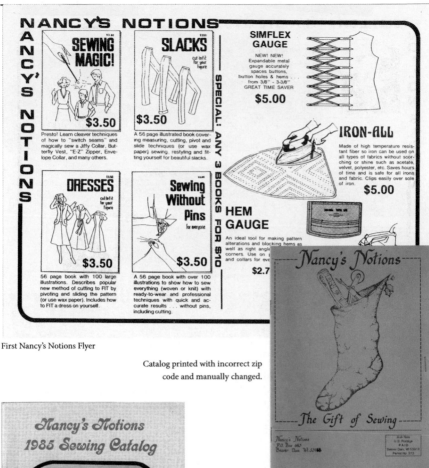

First Nancy's Notions Flyer

Catalog printed with incorrect zip
code and manually changed.

First catalog with a color cover!

The "Video Club" begins, '87

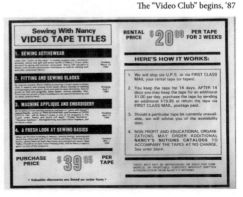

First building purchase,
DeClark Street, (before) '84

DeClark Street office &
warehouse, (after) '85

Building a building within a
building at DeClark Street

Grand Opening at DeClark
Street. I'm wearing the skirt
without Ted's "pocket", '85

Earl and Ted moving into
DeClark Street warehouse, '85

Warehouse at DeClark Street,
with John Nickel, '85

Sewing is her fabric

By Jocelyn Riley
Writes for The State Journal

Publicity from '85

First retail store at DeClark
Street. Lois Levenhagen and
Donna Fenske, '85.

First location shoot, '84

First location shoot, remote truck, '84

Taping at WKOW, '85

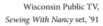

Wisconsin Public TV,
Sewing With Nancy set, '91

Earl and Nancy at a consumer show

Sewing Weekend Flyer, '91

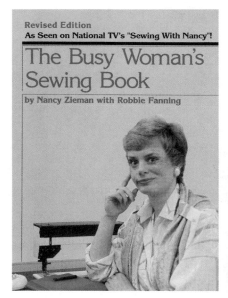

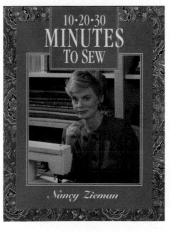

Do you have these books in your library?

Building 333 Beichl Avenue, '87

Rich on move-in day, '87

Inside the new
warehouse

Nancy's Notions
Family, '87

New retail
addition, '90

10th Anniversary Quilt, gift from co-workers, '89

Named Entrepreneur of the Year in
Wisconsin Women Magazine, '88

I'm a designer for McCall's, Wow! '89

With our parents at the Entrepreneur of the Year
Award Banquet. Elaine and Earl Zieman, me, Rich,
Barbara and Ralph Luedtke.

Gail Hamilton, The McCall
Pattern Co., models and
me, '87

With Gail Brown, '00

Kick it Up A Stitch
with Mary Mulari,
'10

With Natalie Sewell, '97

With Eileen Roche, '09

This is how the close-ups are shot.

All cameras on deck

The full *Sewing With Nancy* set

When you see me, this is how I see you!

Sewing with Nancy team
Pat Hahn,
Kate Bashynski,
Diane Dhein,
me,
Diane Sperling,
Laura Noe,
Donna Fenske,
Erica MacDonald

Giggles after taping SWN
30th Anniversary Special

Guests Donna Fenske,
Gail Brown, Mary Mulari,
Pat Hahn,
Director Laurie Gorman,
me, Guests Natalie Sewell,
Eileen Roche

Sewing With Nancy crew for the 30th Anniversary Special, '12

It is one thing to move things and quite another to return them to their rightful locations after the rains subsided. Plus we had to buy dehumidifiers to get rid of the damp smell.

Back before the office moved out of the basement of our home, a freelance writer for the *Milwaukee Journal* newspaper was given the assignment to interview me for a feature story. I was slightly embarrassed to have her come to the basement. After all, my desk was next to the washer and dryer—not at all a high-brow corporate location!

Bonnie Arndt

(Friend)

"I empathized with Nancy and Richard's grass roots cottage industry since I was also a product of a 'mom and pop' business family. My husband and I were also small business owners."

She made her way down the steps and I remember sitting across from her thinking, "I need to get to know her!" Moving to Beaver Dam had been lonely at first. I worked out of my home so I had little contact with people of my own age or interests. Rich's parents and their friends were our social contacts during the first year. They were very nice people, but I was starved for personal friends.

Her name was Bonnie Arndt and she was both a writer and photographer. After the interview, I asked where she lived and was surprised to learn that she, her husband, and two daughters lived just a few blocks from our house. I made it a point to cultivate the relationship and we're still friends today.

Throughout the thirty-year history of *Sewing With Nancy*, the television program and Nancy's Notions have maintained a relationship almost like that of a marriage. One supports the other. Each has different roles, but they are a team in many ways, even when one of the partners is silent.

In its infancy, *Sewing With Nancy* aired on television where I could use my six, one-minute commercial slots to promote Nancy's Notions, or mention an underwriter's support. With Pfaff as an underwriter, I used a Pfaff sewing machine on camera, and I used products available through Nancy's Notions, often mentioning them by name.

By the time the summer of 1983, rolled around, the post office was

Rich Zieman

"It was a good time for
Dad to sell out then
because he could get
rid of all the equipment,
tools and supplies he
had in storage. It also
gave my parents some
cash and got them out
of the routine of always
having to prepare for
the next year's crops."

handing us trays of mail and most of the mail
was orders.

When we moved to Beaver Dam, Earl
still had his farm equipment and he and Rich
did a bit of crop farming. But we were so busy
with Nancy's Notions, that the men decided
not to continue farming. Earl and Elaine had an
auction and sold the equipment.

Rich had been with Herberger's for
more than two years at that point. He enjoyed
his work and had hoped someday to be named
manager of the Beaver Dam store, but another
manager with more experience was awarded
the position. Rich liked the man and wished
him well, but realized that if, in the future, he were to be offered a store
manager's position with Herberger's, it would very likely require a move to
another community.

We both liked Beaver Dam. I liked Rich's family; he liked mine. We
saw Earl and Elaine almost daily, and weren't far from my family.

Rich Zieman

"It is very difficult
for a business to stay
where it is. Either it's
going to grow or die.
Nancy needed to focus
on marketing and
videos. I had a business
background. We were
young enough to take a
risk. We agreed that we
needed to work together
on Nancy's Notions."

Teddy was growing up with the
benefits of having grandparents and extended
family nearby. We were becoming a part of the
community, were developing friends and had
joined a Lutheran church in town. Joan—what
can I say about Joan except to claim her as a
childcare godsend!

Teddy was only nine months old when
Rich and I stepped outside into our backyard
and sat down at the picnic table to talk. On the
agenda was whether or not he should resign
from Herberger's to start working full-time with
Nancy's Notions.

We stood up from our first board
meeting with a decision. Rich would

leave Herberger's to join me in Nancy's Notions. He would devote his education, experience and energies to the operational side of things, while I concentrated on marketing.

With Rich joining the business, the legal implications changed as well, and we incorporated the business as Nancy's Notions Ltd. I was named president; Rich was vice-president. Legally we also needed a secretary and treasurer, so I became secretary, and Rich treasurer.

Rich gave notice at Herberger's and left there on very good terms. Stepping into his new role with Nancy's Notions was almost seamless. With the office for Nancy's Notions in the basement, Rich was working for the company long before it was made official.

While it may seem that the addition of a full-time person would make a huge difference to the work load, in reality, it did not. Rich began handling more and more business matters and freed me from some of those responsibilities, but he had already been heavily involved in helping to fill orders for Nancy's Notions so he couldn't replace himself. From an order fulfillment standpoint we were still short-staffed.

Chris Stam

(Colleague)

"Richard hired me. He interviewed me in town, but told me I'd be working mostly out at the farm. I didn't know what to expect. When I pulled up to the chicken house on the farm, I thought, 'Okay, so this is where I work,' but they made me feel like part of the family."

By then there were three facets of my work. I still gave seminars and lectures. I was the producer and on-air presence for *Sewing With Nancy.* Then there was Nancy's Notions. Although intertwined, the three were separate endeavors.

Nancy's Notions orders were pouring in, so while I was out of town at a speaking engagement, Rich hired Chris Stam to help part-time with filling orders. Within six months she was working full time and we had hired two others.

Filling orders was a process we called "pick and pack"—pick because an item is picked out of a bin or from a shelf and pack because that's what is done with it; it is packed for shipment.

Chris Stam

"With Rich and Nancy away on a family vacation, I got the mail from the post office every day, took it to Nancy and Rich's home, sorted orders, then took the orders to the farm where I picked and packed them and sent them off. It made me feel good that they were confident enough in me to take a vacation."

Rich Zieman

"By the time I joined Nancy's Notions there were trays of orders coming in. There was so much going on in my mind that one morning I left Teddy in the back seat of the car. He was okay, and I didn't leave him there very long, but that shook me."

Chris had attended college for three years where she was majoring in art, but she never finished her formal education. Thinking she might have to help with a family business, she had taken a few accounting classes. Her youngest child had just started kindergarten when she came to us and she's still with Nancy's Notions today. Over the years she's risen from part-time pick and pack help to vice-president of merchandising. Chris grew with the company and is a perfect example of a steadfast and loyal co-worker.

By Christmas of 1983, about two months after Chris joined Nancy's Notions, Rich and I desperately needed a vacation. Earl and Elaine needed one, too, and proposed taking their adult family—Rich's sister, Mary Jo Zieman Check, Rich and me—to the Bahamas between Christmas and New Years. Teddy could stay with my mother. We asked Chris if she could handle things while we were gone for a week and she did. Beautifully.

Our catalog had grown from a single sheet flyer in 1980 to a multiple page catalog. By the end of 1983, it had grown to so many pages and I needed help with layout and design. Two of my younger cousins—Rhonda, a graphic arts student, and Amy, a photography student—laid out the catalog for us. The catalog's finished dimensions were 5½" x 8", but I knew little about printing requirements. Today, I know that printers generally print in "signatures"— a group of sixteen pages printed on both sides of one sheet of paper, then folded and trimmed. Because of that, the number of pages needed to be multiples of sixteen. Naïvely I decided on a thirty-page catalog, so when customers paged through their catalogs, they probably wondered why the fronts and backs of two pages were blank.

There were definite advantages to Rich working with Nancy's Notions. As the parents of a baby, we were so grateful that Joan was there to make certain that Teddy's needs were met. But for us, it also meant that we could see him frequently—much more frequently than if we were working parents who disappeared every day to another location. Joan's hours increased as time went on, but there were days when Teddy played alongside the desk while I worked, or rode with Rich when he was on the go for business needs. We were busy, to be sure, but Teddy was right there in the mix.

I needed help. Betty Dye was already my secretary by then, but I needed someone to help sew samples and prepare kits for sale through Nancy's Notions. A woman who lived near Earl and Elaine heard that Nancy's Notions needed help. She told her twin sister, who was looking for work and Donna stopped by to talk with Elaine.

Donna knows sewing. In 1984, she had already taught classes at a local sewing store. She knew free-motion embroidery and enjoyed doll making, heirloom sewing, garment sewing, quilting and appliqué. She didn't fill out an application; she really didn't need to. Elaine was on the phone quickly, telling me, "You need to talk to Donna Fenske."

I called Donna, arranged an interview, and hired her. At first Donna divided her time between helping to pick and pack at the warehouse in the mornings, and sewing teaching samples and preparing kits for me in the afternoons. Twenty-nine years later she and I are still working together on samples for *Sewing With Nancy*. Still an employee of Nancy's Notions, she is now the vice-president of television production.

Donna's presence eased things a bit at the warehouse, but as floods of orders threatened to overwhelm us, we needed still more help.

Rich has a nice singing voice and he plays piano beautifully, too. Music soothes him, so despite a busy schedule (or maybe because of it) he joined the choir at church. Sitting alongside Rich was a young man named Scott Stanton. Scott had a degree in accounting, although he admits that his graduating class was the last before computers were incorporated into instruction, and he calls his a "dinosaur degree." He was on a sanitation crew, working third shift at a Kraft facility, when he met Rich and was hired to help pick and pack at the chicken house.

Like Chris and Donna, Scott is still with Nancy's Notions. He's now vice-president of administration and he's gone from a "dinosaur degree" with no computer knowledge to being the "go-to" guy for anything connected by wire or signal to a network. In 2000, Scott made another significant connection when he married Lois, also a Nancy's Notions employee.

The Chicken House group became a cohesive unit. Earl checked stock when it came in, and kept track as it went out. He was in charge in the warehouse and he was an easy man to be around. Everyone worked hard, but they had fun, too.

Ted Zieman

"I was still very young at that point, but I have memories of the chicken house. I was always playing on the farm. It was very nice. Grandma and Grandpa worked out there quite a bit and I remember helping to package samples."

There were so many orders to be shipped that the red flag Earl put up near the mailbox as a signal that UPS was to stop stayed up all the time. In fact, the UPS driver on that route timed his stop at the farm so he could enjoy eating his lunch with the crew.

Teddy was there a lot, too. He'd beg to go. Before he learned how to walk, he was climbing, and some of his favorite climbing was on the bins and shelves in the warehouse.

Things were moving so fast that it was difficult to keep up.

In 1981, I had been a guest on someone else's sewing program then suddenly I had my own program. In January 1983, I negotiated a contract with a cable television network and hired my first production crew. By year's end I had fired that production crew because the head of the group had lied to me about production fees. With a baby on my hip and a phone to my ear I had negotiated a contract with Pfaff, the first underwriter for *Sewing With Nancy.*

On the home front Rich and I were new parents. We had barely finished moving Nancy's Notions products to the chicken house on the farm when Rich left his job at Herberger's to work with the company.

As 1984 began, I was looking for a new production crew and studio for *Sewing With Nancy*. I wanted both to be in Madison, closer to Beaver Dam and an easier drive than going to Milwaukee. I found what I was looking for in WKOW, an ABC-affiliate television station in Madison.

There were several advantages to working with WKOW. First of all, the crew was professional. Unlike the hours and hours of taping we went through in my home and even at the Milwaukee studio where we recorded for a while, these people knew what they were doing and had the equipment to do it. We would also be recording at their studio; no more basements or living rooms. WKOW owned several television stations throughout Wisconsin. A huge advantage to going with them was that it would mean *Sewing With Nancy* would be aired on six ABC affiliate stations around the state.

After a round of negotiations, we had a contract.

Earl Zieman

"Once Nancy was on TV in a bigger way, we had to move out of the chicken house. We worked there a year at least. I know we worked there through the fall and winter because we got some use out of the heater we installed in the place."

About that time, I also acquired a couple new underwriters as well—Gingher Scissors and Pellon joined Pfaff in helping to pay production costs.

Sewing With Nancy was already airing on the Satellite Program Network when ABC affiliate stations throughout Wisconsin began airing it as well. With increased exposure came skyrocketing orders for Nancy's Notions.

It wasn't long until the chicken house was too small.

Rich began looking for a location for Nancy's Notions. We wanted a facility large enough so we could be there a while and grow into it gradually. Also, on our list of "must haves" was office space so we could finally put a degree of separation between our professional and personal lives.

Rich found it in a building on DeClark Street in Beaver Dam. It had been a Gardner Bakery distribution site, but it had been empty for some time. List price for the building was one hundred-fifty thousand dollars—far too costly for us, and even more so when necessary remodeling costs were factored in.

In 1984, the United States had been going through an economic downturn. Interest rates were sky high and property wasn't moving quickly. The owner lived in Florida and we wondered if he might be motivated to unload it.

"Offer them seventy-five thousand," I suggested to Rich. He did, and they accepted.

Nancy's Notions would have its own home.

Chapter 13

❧

"Be pretty if you can, be witty if you must,
but be gracious if it kills you."
– Elsie De Wolfe

Sometimes people ask, "What's it like to be Nancy Zieman?"
I'm tempted to respond, "Good. What's it like to be you?"
I know they mean, "What is it like to live a life of celebrity?"

Truthfully, I live a pretty quiet life; part of my life just happens
to include a job on television. In order to maintain that job I must do it
well—not unlike the millions of others in the workforce. But, as a television
personality and public speaker, I recognize that people are curious and want
to know me better.

For viewers of *Sewing With Nancy,* I am a presence in their homes.
That is, however, a one-sided presence without interaction; an in-person
meeting completes the connection.

Please, let me assure you that I enjoy meeting people. From my
position behind the camera, I don't see those viewing *Sewing With Nancy.* A
face-to-face introduction and exchange helps me keep in touch. In-person
meetings are when I get to complete the connection as well.

But, many people don't know how to say hello to someone they
see on television. They think of the experience as somehow different from
meeting anyone else. While greeting me they may laugh, avoid eye contact,
act intimidated, or even get teary. Actually quite often there are tears and I
find that humbling. Sometimes I get teary, too. For example, when someone

tells me that they watched *Sewing With Nancy* with their terminally ill mother or while recovering from surgery, and that my program encouraged them—that means a lot to me.

For some, the experience of meeting a public figure seems to suspend common courtesy. People have poked me with umbrellas and slapped me with rolled magazines. "You're Nancy Zieman," one woman declared while poking me with a cane. Yep! I was aware of that before the bruise, thank you!

I have also learned that people will say the most outrageous things. One woman told me that she had watched me gain weight and lose weight over the years and that there was a time when I was really fat. So, even if that were true, how could I respond? I think I thanked her for sharing that with me.

Actually, "thank you for sharing that" is a phrase I have found quite useful. It helps deflect statements that are negative or uncomfortable. To respond to some statements is an invitation to a no-win situation and I have learned how to sidestep issues and questions that are, quite frankly, none of the asker's business.

I'm often asked questions about money and the most frequent money question is how much it costs to produce an episode of *Sewing With Nancy*. I never answer that question. First of all, the answer is confidential information. But secondly, even if I revealed the price tag for production, those unfamiliar with television would have no frame of reference for understanding the figure. So I usually say, "A lot!" and leave it at that.

Over the years I have come to understand that people want to know the breadth of producing *Sewing With Nancy*, and are less interested in the minute details.

I suspect that there is a perception that I am a wealthy woman. That perception has more to do with Hollywood than reality. I'm not an A-list actor on a prime time show. I'm a sewing teacher with a how-to program. Instead of receiving a wage for being on *Sewing With Nancy*, Nancy Zieman Productions pays for air time.

People are curious, too, about health issues. I've become something of a poster child for Bell's palsy over the years. That has been my choice, and

I'm pleased when I know that people are encouraged by my story.

Quite a number of people have told me that they had Bell's palsy, but that it went away. "Good for you!" is my usual response. Since Bell's palsy has been a huge factor in my life, I'm sure they don't mean to celebrate their blessing at my expense. Instead, they are simply expressing their experience as a means of forging a common connection between us—a shared challenge.

Aside from Bell's palsy, I tend to keep health issues to myself. This book is the first time I've talked openly about some of the physical challenges of my life.

There are always people who consider it their responsibility to correct me, to show me the error of my ways. One man wrote to inform me that I had been using the word "utilize" incorrectly. Utilize, he informed me, is when a product is used in a way it is not intended to be used. He was right. I changed how I used the word.

There are occasions when I believe people take issue with my methods or techniques simply because it makes them feel important to take on a well-known teacher. If they use a different technique than mine, that's fine with me. Their way may indeed be better. My usual response is, "Thank you for sharing that with me." Most people don't mean their comments in a negative way. They simply want to talk to me.

More often than criticism, I get praise. While I am glad that my efforts are appreciated, accolades and gushing compliments make me more uncomfortable than criticism. That probably stems back to childhood when our parents taught us it was never acceptable to brag. The teachings of our family, church and society reflected the Biblical admonition for an individual *"not to think of himself more highly than he ought to think"* (Romans 12:3). Believing too much in the praise, or too much in the criticism, creates an imbalance that bogs forward movement.

Humor helps deflect sensitive questions and laughter forges a bond between people. As a minor example of using humor, at one appearance recently—a quilting event—someone asked if I had made the blouse I was wearing. I teach sewing; if I had made the blouse the admission would have been an opening for admiration of my work. But, if I simply said no (as was the case) that might have prompted those in the audience to question whether I walk what I talk. So, I replied, "No. Even Rachel Ray goes out to dinner." Everyone laughed and the laughter connected us.

Humor helps me deal with touchy situations, both externally and internally. I try to be nimble enough in my thinking to come up with an on-the-spot humorous response to a ticklish question or off-the-wall statement. That doesn't always happen. But, I have learned to take things lightly. People are generally good at heart.

But, sometimes they don't see me as a real person.

One time I arrived in Paducah, Kentucky, for the annual American Quilter's Society quilt show after a very long and difficult day. My flight had been delayed and I had missed a connecting flight to Paducah. I needed to be there, so I rented a car and drove for five hours. It was toward evening when I arrived, tired, hungry, and with a horrible headache. I caught the trolley toward downtown, hoping to find a restaurant without a sixty-minute wait as was the estimated time for a table in the hotel restaurant.

After eating, I caught the trolley back to the hotel. Six women got on the trolley with me, and when they realized they were riding with Nancy Zieman, well, the only word I can think of that fits is "swarm"—they were all over me. I thought I was okay. I know I said hello and exchanged a couple of niceties, but evidently my response was not what was expected. When I returned home, I got a scathing letter from one of the women.

"We are your audience," she wrote, "and you were not gracious."

I stewed over that letter for a while. She had no idea what I'd been through that day, and no idea how I felt. I wanted to write back accusing her and her companions of being rude, demanding and insensitive. But, then I cooled down. How could they have known? Yes, perhaps they were insensitive, but they were excited about meeting me and I had let them down.

During the early 1980s, as Nancy's Notions grew, Rich was instrumental in developing a customer service policy that at its core acknowledges that the customer is always right and that satisfaction is guaranteed. So, instead of responding in kind to her letter, I wrote back acknowledging that I had been rude and expressing that if we met again, I hoped the meeting would be more pleasant.

When I'm in public situations, there are days when exhaustion and frustration reach critical mass. So, I sometimes step out of view and indulge in a good thirty-second cry before starting over. It is amazing what a relief valve that can be. I've also learned not to dwell on something because it becomes an irritation akin to a pebble in your shoe, and who needs that?

Over the years, I've learned diplomacy by making mistakes and by trying to put myself in the shoes of those I meet. As a general rule I try to treat everyone I meet as though they are my best friend. I have learned to bite my tongue.

My staff is helpful, too. They watch carefully, and sometimes remind me of an "appointment" in order to help me withdraw from an uncomfortable situation. If that ever happens while you're talking with me, don't take it as a rejection—I do have genuine appointments and they remind me of those as well.

For those who are curious, here are some things about me that may be of interest.

I'm an early riser, up around 5:00 a.m. most days. On the flip side, I'm also an early-to-bed person and can barely keep my eyes open past 9:30 p.m. I guard my rest and try not to slip below seven hours of sleep each night.

In the mornings I sit for a few minutes with a cup of coffee and a devotional. My days always go better when I start them in gratitude for my blessings and in a receptive mode for guidance.

Often I'll sew or quilt in the early morning. My sewing room is steps away from where I spend time in devotions, so it is simple to slip in there for a few minutes of quiet pleasure. I always have a couple of projects going, usually landscape quilts.

I'll often bake in the mornings, too. Bananas on the verge of being overripe are quickly transformed into banana bread. I may put something together for dinner that evening, too. Rich is a great cook and he loves to grill (he does so year-round), but I'm usually the one who makes casseroles or lasagna. If I know that a neighbor or friend is sick and could use a boost, I make extra for giving.

A-Z Quick Bread

2 cups of diced, chopped, or puréed fruit or veggies (Anything from A to
Z . . . applesauce, bananas, carrots . . . pumpkin, raspberries, strawberries,
zucchini)

1 cup of canola oil
4 eggs
1 tsp. vanilla
2 cups unbleached flour
1 cup whole wheat flour
1 cup sugar
1¼ tsp. baking soda
1¼ tsp. baking powder
2 tsp. cinnamon
1 cup chopped walnuts

Heat oven to 350° F. Mix fruit/veggies, oil, eggs, and vanilla. Add remaining
dry ingredients; blend. Then, stir in walnuts. Lightly grease two bread
pans. Divide mixture into both pans. Bake for 55 minutes. Test doneness
by inserting an uncooked spaghetti noodle into the thickest section of the
loaf. If the noodle comes out dry, remove from the oven. Cool in pan for 15
minutes; remove loaf from pan. Enjoy!

P.S. A cup of chocolate chips is a tasty addition to banana or
pumpkin breads.

Since I like swimming, and because of leg issues, I can't exercise as
most people do. I swim year-round. Summers I do it at home. During the
nine months of Wisconsin's poor outdoor swimming weather, I swim at a
YMCA near my office.

On days when I'm not traveling or recording, I'm usually in the office by 8:00 a.m. I leave the office for lunch because changing scenery gives me a break that helps clear my thoughts.

Office workdays end between five and six o'clock. I try not to bring work home or work on weekends.

Unless it is business related, Rich and I rarely eat out in the evenings. We prefer our own home; during meals, the television is off, and we talk. The "No TV" rule is something we initiated before we had children. We need time to be a family and talking together over a meal is one of the best ways to maintain the ties that bind.

In public, I mention my family, but keep anecdotes to a minimum. They have their own lives and can speak for themselves.

My Wisconsin upbringing came with the legacy of a northern accent that some people find harsh. Over the years I've consciously worked at minimizing those tonal inflections. For example, I try not to hit my Ts too hard, something that Wisconsinites tend to do.

I've also tried to eliminate regionalisms—phrases and words that pepper the speech of those living around me. Wisconsin may be a rarity in that people often ask, "Where's the bubbler?" instead of, "Where's the water fountain?" Back when I first started traveling, I asked for directions to the "bubbler" of someone in Atlanta, and received a blank stare.

Because I want *Sewing With Nancy* viewers to identify with me, I try to be more neutral in my choice of words, phrases and tone.

In the early years of *Sewing With Nancy* just after we started airing on PBS, I received some death threats. I will not give the person's name, but will say that a number of letters came from a convicted serial killer serving a life sentence for murder. The threats arrived in the mail at Nancy's Notions. I knew about them but never read them. Rich and Paul Shonts, our operations manager, hid them from me because they did not want me to be upset by the contents. There were a few death threats by phone as well, but they were capably handled by our staff.

Most of the threatening communications occurred during the 1990s. There were a number of prison inmates who wrote, and one who declared an intention to visit when he was released. He did show up at a seminar in Florida, and I greeted him. It was evident during our handshake that he was suffering from mental challenges; I never saw or heard from him again.

During the 1990s, when I received numerous threats, Rich took them seriously enough to install a security system in our home. I have no clue what about the 90s brought out those with ill intent. Things have been mostly quiet since then. I'm aware of safety and security issues, as any woman should be, but I'm not afraid. Sometimes people drive by our home very slowly, but our home is no mansion and I hope they're admiring the flowers. Our neighbors and the people of Beaver Dam don't perceive me as anything special.

If you picked up *Seams Unlikely* because you expected a "tell all" exposé, I'm sorry to disappoint you. Actually, I'm not all that sorry. There are some things I never discuss. For example, unless it involves quilting or sewing, what happens in our marriage is not for public knowledge.

Rich is the love of my life, my husband, father to my children, and my partner.

People often wonder how he feels about playing a secondary role to mine and some—kindly, or not so kindly—even refer to him as Mr. Nancy. In reality Rich has never played a secondary role. We are partners. Initially the idea for Nancy's Notions was mine, and it was my decision as well to produce *Sewing With Nancy* myself, but he was instrumental in growing Nancy's Notions far beyond what I could have envisioned. Someone had to be president, and someone vice-president. My name was on the business, so the title of president fell to me.

Rich is a gifted man, capable in so many ways. He is a visionary who sees growth opportunities long before others, and already has the next step in mind. But he's also practical, and knows how to take calculated risks. At times he has pushed me beyond my comfort levels, and in return, I know I have frustrated him to the edge of tolerance. But secondary? Never!

Sure, Rich and I have had our conflicts. That happens in marriages, but it happens, too, among business partners, and we were both. We had to learn how to work with each other. Part of that involved recognizing each other's strengths, and having the wisdom to stay out of each other's territory.

In the 1980s and 90s, I wore high heels much of the time. Those heels could be dug in pretty deep when I needed to hold my ground.

Look at it this way—if Rich had continued in a career with Herberger's, it is unlikely that the company would have ever carried his name. And it is not likely either that he would have become president of the organization. He is a man who serves by making possible the success of others, and in doing so he has become an incredible success in his own right.

The community of Beaver Dam recognizes those qualities in Rich. In 2012, he was honored with the community's Citizen of the Year award for his multiple contributions over the years. Organizers of the event asked me to say a few words and because I'm not good with the gushy stuff, I wrote a poem.

⋙⋘

Citizen of the Year Introduction

When I got the call to introduce the Citizen of the Year,
I had to decide what were the most important details for you to hear!

It wouldn't be that this citizen prefers a wardrobe ever so bland.
You might recognize those 14 black shirts that hang
neatly filling his closet span.

It also wouldn't be interesting to know that he hates
clutter on the counter top.
Nor that it drives me crazy when my purse is lost;
could it be stored with the mop?

Nor would it be interesting to know that he
frequently borrows my tape measures to plan
What building or office needs an expansion,
be it small or be it grand.

But it might be fascinating to learn that if a problem
seems to have no rhyme or reason.
He can easily solve it by riding his lawn mower,
providing it's the right time of the season.

It also is motivating to know that this citizen
takes his role as part-time volunteer
As serious as if he were paid thousands of dollars a year.

Some of you have realized that our citizen loves the
challenges faced by volunteer groups.
The downside is that he'll call frequent meetings until you
feel like you're jumping through hoops.

His dedication cannot be questioned whether the group is large or small
For he works very tirelessly for the betterment of all.

He didn't want extra family or friends to be part of tonight.
His reasoning, "It's my job," and I guess that's his right.

So on behalf of our sons, Ted and Tom, and friends who are not here,
I congratulate Rich Zieman, as the Citizen of the Year.

❦

I often describe myself as the Betty Crocker of Nancy's Notions and *Sewing With Nancy.* I'm the face—the public persona. Although I'm the one people see, I am definitely not the whole story. Behind that "face" is a body of people who support what I do.

I have been, and am, privileged to work with some of the world's most capable and caring people. They are not related by blood, but they are family. They have surrounded me with warmth and concern and I always want to give the same in return.

After leaving Minnesota Fabrics I worked for a short time for an employer who was critical and inconsiderate. I learned then, when an employee is made to feel insignificant, they do not produce. From that one bad employer, I learned how not to be when running a business. Perhaps I deserved some of the treatment I received, but it was not an encouraging environment. When there's negativity, employees become afraid to make decisions, afraid to move forward in their jobs.

I want to honor people, not dishonor them. People are one of God's greatest gifts to us; we're here to enrich each other, not tear each other down. That said, I have had to have frank discussions about expectations with employees and people with whom we did business over the years. I've had to fire people and it grieved me to do so. Not everyone is suited, from an attitude or skill point of view, for the positions they hold.

I never like confrontation and sometimes I avoid confrontation long past the point where it should have occurred. As an employer there have been occasions when I did not reprimand people when I should have done so. I held off because I thought they would improve. But when someone is not doing their job, it hinders other employees and creates a negative influence that especially affects people who aren't naturally assertive.

Several years ago, I was in Cincinnati presenting a seminar. Late in the morning I returned to my hotel room to catch my breath. As the elevator doors opened to my floor, I could see a housekeeping cart near my door and heard music. As I walked down the hall, the music became identifiable as the theme music for *Sewing With Nancy*. Did I leave the television on? I wondered, but I knew I hadn't.

My hotel room door was open, and at the exact time that my on-air self was saying, "Welcome to *Sewing With Nancy*," I stepped around the cart and entered the room. A slim woman wearing a hotel uniform was watching the television while she worked. At my entrance, she turned toward me and her eyes went wide. Then she screamed.

What's it like being Nancy Zieman, you ask? I hope I am the same in person as I am on-air, but like the woman who screamed, sometimes I'm startled by both.

Chapter 14

❧

When Rich joined Nancy's Notions in 1983, we were like explorers approaching a strange new land. There was a lot of excitement, but we didn't know what we would find in unfamiliar territory.

Rich's first major undertaking was to help move the mail order side of the business to the chicken house on the farm. By the fall of 1984, he needed to find a new location for the business. When he offered the owner of the former Gardner Bakery distribution center half of his asking price, the man immediately accepted. We were under contract within twenty-four hours of making the offer.

Getting financing for the building and remodeling was not quite as straightforward. When our application was presented to the loan board at the bank, we were notified that the bank would be pleased to make the loan—at fourteen percent interest!

Rich recalls that it was a Friday morning when he got the news. As he talked with the bank president with whom we had made our application, Rich asked if he had presented Nancy's Notions' sales or marketing plans to the loan board. The man admitted he had not. So about 4:00 p.m. that afternoon, we stood in his doorway, just to see if he remembered us. He did, and invited us in.

Rich asked for a few minutes of his time and said we wanted to talk to him about Nancy's Notions and the future. The man was cordial. He invited us into the conference room and we pulled out our accounting books and marketing plan, showing him that Nancy's Notions was a solid company and our potential for growth was good.

That was 1984 and even though I had been producing *Sewing With*

Nancy for less than a year, between television exposure and seminars, our business had boomed.

Rich Zieman

"The whole atmosphere changed. Since Nancy's Notions had a woman's name on it, they hadn't really been interested in working with us."

Mary Luedtke Rebman

"Nancy is so modest about things that it was quite a while before I was aware of what was going on with the business. When Nancy and Rich moved back to Beaver Dam, that was the first I was aware that they were building a business in a chicken coop. I don't even think I saw one of those programs— *Sewing With Nancy*— for a long time."

Even if they don't know the details of how it happens, most people receive catalogs they've never requested. Those catalogs come as the result of one company renting another's mailing list—either directly or through a mailing list broker. By mid-1984, Nancy's Notions was distributing thirty thousand catalogs, a very significant number considering that I had never rented mailing lists. Names and addresses were collected by handing out flyers at seminars, and offering the catalog on television.

"Wow!" the man said. "I didn't know any of this."

The loan was approved at an interest rate lower than first offered—thirteen percent, only one point lower—Rich began making arrangements for remodeling.

There was one major problem that had to be addressed before anything else could be done to the building. It had served as a distribution site for baked goods. Trucks drove in one end of the building and out the other, baked goods were loaded inside, out of the weather. Trucks were also re-fueled while there and gasoline tanks were buried on the grounds. The first expense of remodeling was seven thousand dollars just to unearth the tanks.

After that, walls to create offices and warehouse space went up inside the metal shell of the building. The DeClark Street project was Rich's first building project and he worked alongside a general contractor. That was the last time we would ever need a general contractor—

Rich handled those responsibilities from that time on, and saved us a great deal in the process.

In April of 1985, Nancy's Notions moved from the chicken house at the farm and from the office in our home basement into its new home on DeClark Street in Beaver Dam. The space in our new surroundings felt luxurious by comparison to what we had been using. This new facility also included a retail outlet for Nancy's Notions that featured all the products from the catalog plus Pfaff sewing machines. Phyllis Winter worked there, editing transcripts during slow times in the store.

I remember that it was very cold and that Ted wore snow boots to the grand opening of Nancy's Notions, held on April 10, 1985. I wore a gray suit sewn especially for the occasion, feeling the cold more keenly than usual that day because the skirt of my suit had no lining. The jacket was lined, and I had also sewn lining for the skirt, but then a little problem arose.

The little problem was Teddy. Only two and a half years old then, he had already been "helping" me sew for a long time—sitting on my lap while I sewed, helping to guide the fabric and remove pins as I stitched.

I finished the skirt, but had no time to hem it just then, so I laid it over the sewing machine. When I returned to finish, I discovered a long cut in the skirt. I stood in shock for a moment then asked Teddy, "What did you do?"

"I made a pocket," he said proudly.

There's no way I could be angry with a child who innocently believed he was helping, but still it was a major blow. I made a quick trip to the local fabric store, purchased more fabric and whipped out another skirt. But, there was no time to make another lining.

When my parents arrived for the grand opening, I told them the story. My father lifted Teddy into his arms and asked, "Teddy, did you cut Mama's skirt?"

"Yes," Teddy admitted, holding tight to his grandpa's shoulder for comfort, "and Mama cried."

Our grand opening celebration continued for three days during which I gave several seminars. It was modeled, in much smaller scale, after the few consumer shows that were springing up around the country.

For the first time our grand opening allowed customers to shop with us in person. In addition to the retail area, the warehouse area had chairs set up for seminars and tables filled with products.

On the first day of the celebration, we held a small reception at which we served coffee and sandwiches made by my mother-in-law, Elaine. Friends, family and visitors from the community filled the building and we had three large coffee pots going when the power went out. It wasn't off throughout the entire building, just the warehouse area where I was about to give a seminar. While I waited with some anxiety, Rich and several others rushed around trying to get the power restored and looking for extension cords as a temporary solution.

By the time the three-day event was over, everyone who helped was exhausted. But, we had learned something very valuable that weekend. With seminars as a draw, and tables filled with products for shopping, the weekend was very profitable.

Our grand opening was a three-day opportunity to reach out and touch the sewing community. It also gave us an injection of income that started Nancy's Notions off in its new location on solid financial footing. The next year, when we needed to meet sales goals, we held another event like it, and again the following year, and again… For almost three decades the event has been a destination for those who love sewing.

That was the beginning of Sewing Weekend.

Back in 1982, Nancy's Notions published a book I'd written: *Slacks "Pivot Guide" Fitting Book with Pattern.* A successful book in spite of its lengthy title, it was re-printed in 1983, 1984 and 1985. In 1984, we also published *The Busy Woman's Sewing Book*, which, as the subtitle claimed, was a guide to sewing a workable wardrobe with efficient, yet professional sewing techniques.

Along with the benefits of advertising Nancy's Notions on *Sewing With Nancy*, I was discovering that books were popular. I needed to write more of them. To write more of them I needed help.

Even today, many who watch *Sewing With Nancy* programs want

Phyllis Winter
(Colleague)

"The transcripts were printed on colored paper. A big decision was what color to print a transcript on. Eventually Nancy decided she wanted to make that product better looking."

a book or booklet that explains and reinforces what they saw on the program. In the early days we offered transcripts of the programs—the spoken words from the program were turned into step-by-step instructions. They were loose leaf pages, three-hole drilled and stapled in the upper left corner.

For a few months Phyllis Winter had been editing my scripts from *Sewing With Nancy*, putting them into written form. She had replaced a friend of hers in that position and just prior to our move to DeClark Street, Phyllis joined us three days a week. After the move, she worked in our new retail store where she capably assisted customers with purchases; but she also continued editing transcripts.

Phyllis had a degree in home economics and had taught junior high and high school students for several years. Her background was helpful when translating verbal instructions to print. She worked closely with Laure Noe, a graphic designer who created illustrations to accompany the text. In the days before computer design, Laure had the words typeset and then manually pasted up the pages for printing.

Phyllis Winter

"Nancy had educational material that no one else offered. It was hard to put a monetary value on the booklets. We didn't want to charge too much, and didn't want to give them away either. Every now and then we would have discussions on price and value."

At the end of every episode of *Sewing With Nancy* I offered viewers a transcript of the show. We also sold them in the Nancy's Notions catalog along with a binder to help organize the loose-leaf pages. In fact, we also offered binders already filled with *Sewing With Nancy* transcripts.

But, they weren't attractive. They were educational materials, but they were, quite frankly, boring to look at. So, we took the same information and packaged it into booklets.

Over the years we kept improving that

material—the information that came directly from *Sewing With Nancy* programs. Eventually they became books. Today a companion book is available for every *Sewing With Nancy* series or episode. Some are authored by guests on the show, while others are created as a result of the show.

For many years, Phyllis Winter coordinated books, and her job gradually expanded and evolved to include printed materials of all kinds, product selection for catalogs, and catalog production.

Trade shows and consumer shows are alike in that they are shopping opportunities. In a consumer show, the end user of a product is the one who shops, usually purchasing one or two items they need for their own use. At a trade show, though, the customer is a retail business that, in turn, sells to those who use the product. In order to allow retailers a reasonable mark-up to the consumer, sales at trade shows are generally in multiple quantities and are offered at lower prices per unit.

Both are temporary marketplaces. Businesses come to one central location to meet wholesale or retail customers, eliminating the need for them to make the rounds of various far-flung shops. Those businesses (usually referred to as vendors) set up booths—each a mini store—where they present their products or services.

Ed Moore

(Colleague)

"I met Nancy in 1995 at a trade show. Nancy completely understood the value of education. She wasn't stuck on her opinions and was continually willing to look at new ideas and concepts."

Our first trade show was in San Francisco, an event organized by the American Home Sewing Association (AHSA). By 1985, we had started selling videos of *Sewing With Nancy* programs through our catalog. We were also interested in selling the videos to other retailers and one of the best places to do that was at a trade show. We submitted the required proposal to the AHSA and learned we were qualified to only sell videos at that show and could not distribute our catalogs. So, we developed video and book sell sheets, crude in design by today's standards.

Our neighbor, Kathy Hasson (now Kathy Hasson Gittus) had worked with Rich as a clerk in the domestics department at Herberger's.

After Rich left Herberger's and Nancy's Notions started growing, Kathy came to work with us for a while, doing light bookkeeping. That was a part-time job, and she left for a full-time job elsewhere. But when we started planning for the consumer show in San Francisco, she was available, so I invited her to accompany me to the show.

Kathy Hasson Gittus

(Colleague)

"When I joined Nancy's Notions direct marketing was wide open territory. Today it is all about statistics on customers. In the beginning we simply knew that there were people out there who needed what *Sewing With Nancy* and Nancy's Notions had to offer."

Videos were very new and expensive in the mid-80s. They were a hard sell at that trade show, but we almost paid our expenses. We learned there certainly wasn't any profit in wholesaling videos and decided to concentrate on selling them in the retail market.

Kathy and I worked well together at the show and as soon as we returned home, I hired her to promote *Sewing With Nancy* videos and TV shows. For a number of years she attended trade and consumer shows. Kathy was a graduate of the University of Wisconsin-Madison where she had earned a degree in geography. Later, though, she returned to UW-Whitewater for a degree in marketing. Today she is vice president of creative services for Nancy's Notions.

The grand opening celebration for the DeClark Street building proved the value of connecting in-person with the people who purchased our products. I was on television, and traveling to teach seminars, but everyone on our small staff all agreed that we needed to participate in consumer shows.

Consumer shows attract people whose interests are focused in a specific area. They target people who are potential customers for products—new and familiar—related to that interest. For example, auto shows attract those interested in new vehicles. Home shows showcase what's new in products for building, decorating, remodeling and improving. In our case we were interested in consumer shows that appealed to those who enjoyed sewing, making fabric crafts, quilting, and embroidering.

For consumers such shows offer several advantages. While moving from booth to booth they can compare prices and the quality of items. They have an opportunity to view new products and possibly even see them demonstrated. In one location they can purchase what they need and walk away with information on what they may want in the future. And they can ask questions. Consumer shows provide an opportunity for the public to talk with representatives of various businesses.

It works the other way around as well. A consumer show is an opportunity for businesses to make contact with their customers—past customers as well as current and potential customers.

Consumer shows with sewing as a focus offered classes on various topics taught by teachers recognized for their expertise. Attendees could also view exhibits relating to sewing and shop at booths operated by vendors whose products served their interests. I taught at several consumer shows, then began exhibiting and selling Nancy's Notions products at them as well.

Earl Zieman

"Going to consumer shows—that was one of the best times of my life. I got to see the country and meet a lot of people."

Initially, the Nancy's Notions booth at consumer shows consisted of a banner at the back of the booth, a few books, a few products and a small cash box. After a while I needed help; fortunately Earl and Elaine were willing.

Earl and Elaine were good with people. Both of them had a way of drawing people in, engaging them in conversations that inevitably turned toward the tools they needed for sewing. The two worked together harmoniously. Elaine sold product and made change for sales; Earl handled the heavy lifting and passed out catalogs. Always, they collected names for mailing lists.

The first major consumer show in which Nancy's Notions exhibited was at the Sewing & Stitchery Expo in Puyallup, Washington, a thirty-minute drive from Seattle. Held at the fairgrounds in Puyallup, still today it remains the largest sewing expo in the country.

I had exhibited at smaller regional sewing events, but this was the first national event—a big deal. Earl, Elaine and I flew to Seattle and took a cab the rest of the way. It was a last-minute decision to attend; all the quality hotel rooms were taken. We stayed in a low-budget, old-fashioned motel. The bathroom in our shared room was in the process of renovation and was a disaster. Regardless, the event was successful.

All of the product had been shipped in advance of our arrival and the day before the show we set up our little ten-foot booth. At the back was an eight-foot Nancy's Notions banner. We had tables stacked with books, catalogs and a few notions.

Thousands of people attended the three-day event. I presented an hour-long seminar twice a day; afterwards, those who had been at the seminar flocked to our booth. We sold books—lots of books—and handed out catalogs with an attached coupon. By the end of the third day we were totally exhausted, but at the same time exhilarated at the response.

Most sales were cash along with a few checks. Items were priced for sale in whole dollar amounts to avoid the need to handle coins. Elaine learned that wearing a skirt with side pockets was helpful. She'd keep a wad of bills in her pocket and give the customer change right on the spot rather than going to the cash box.

Earl's job was to hand out catalogs. By 1987, *Sewing With Nancy* was airing both on cable and on the Public Broadcasting System (PBS). It was one of the few, if not only, sewing and quilting shows in most markets. Often people walking by the booth would comment, "Oh, I see her on TV."

Earl, holding a stack of catalogs would step out of the booth, practically into the aisle, and ask, "Do you order from her catalog?" If the answer was, "No," he would respond, "Well, if you don't order, she can't stay on TV. So why don't you take this catalog and order."

Earl was a farmer-turned-salesman and he was good at it!

Chapter 15

As **Rich and I settled in to working together** at Nancy's Notions, we divided our territories of responsibility into two main categories—operations and marketing.

Rich had oversight of operations. Under operations were the logistics of merchandising, order processing, order entry, obtaining and moving product, administrative responsibilities including accounts payable and receivable, human resources matters, plus facility and maintenance.

Under the umbrellas that each of us held were department managers who were responsible for those areas.

I oversaw marketing. That included production of *Sewing With Nancy*, catalog production, seminar presentations, advertising in trade or consumer publications, consumer shows, books, public relations, customer service, spokesperson responsibilities and branding.

While those distinctions seemed clear cut, there were challenges.

Rich is great at problem solving and creating solutions. He applies his business sense with an eye toward the end result. I'm more process oriented, looking at what I need to do at that moment to achieve a desired result. In that regard, we're a pretty good team—most days!

Working together was often difficult and there were plenty of anxious moments

Rich Zieman

"There was a bit of overlap between operations and marketing. Nancy and I had to learn how to work through that. One beautiful thing about our business was that you could distinguish between the two, although it took us a few years to figure out how to make it work."

191

accompanied by disagreement. Mixing marriage and business is a challenge for most couples. We were not alone, but that was small comfort at the end of the day.

Direct mail, at least from our vantage point, was still a burgeoning arena, but there were very few business models for us to follow. Television and catalog marketing combinations like *Sewing With Nancy* and Nancy's Notions were rare and we felt as if we were charting new territory. We both had ideas—lots of ideas. Rich liked to dabble in marketing and I liked to give my opinion on building expansion.

During the high growth years, when we added onto the building seven times and expanded our direct marketing, Rich and I had difficulties staying out of each other's areas of expertise. Lots of money was being spent to expand. Whether justified or not, I felt mine was the greater load of responsibility since I was the company figurehead and in charge of the creative, revenue-generating areas.

Adding to my tension was the fact that royalties on book sales were used to pay for much of the expansion. I had written those books, not on company time, but most often at night after Ted was in bed. For several years it seemed that I worked day and night and saw nothing for my efforts.

At staff meetings the tensions between us sometimes surfaced. Those staff meetings were also carried to the dinner table or into the "executive board meetings" held while getting ready for the day— toothbrush or shaver in hand. In the evening we couldn't say to each other, "So what was your day like?" We already knew. There were arguments that arose from separate expectations and others that simply stemmed from the irritability of exhaustion.

We got our wake up call one evening at the dinner table. Ted, seven or eight at the time, interrupted our heated corporate exchange by saying, "Hey guys—I'm here!" We knew then that business had to stay at work.

When it was time for a decision, each of us deferred to the partner who was overseeing the area in question. Usually compromises were made which made the new direction more palatable, but I was not necessarily gracious about losing!

When I first appeared on television, the production was barely

Rich Zieman

"I can remember telling Nancy that I'd heard that within a year or two about twenty percent of all households in the United States would have Beta or VCR players. So, I told her, why don't you find someone to put your lectures on video, then we can sell them. I was thinking that organizations like community colleges would want them, and individuals, too."

above home video standards. A move to a production studio in Milwaukee improved quality slightly, but I terminated that arrangement when I discovered I was being lied to and charged more than double the going rate.

In 1984, I moved *Sewing With Nancy* production to WKOW, an ABC affiliate television station in Madison, Wisconsin, about an hour from Beaver Dam. With an attractive set, good equipment and a professional production crew, the end result was a video production we could promote while holding our heads high.

Rich had an idea—re-package *Sewing With Nancy* programs and offer them for sale as instructional videos.

Why not? We already had the recordings. VCR equipment had been introduced in the early 1980s. Although at first they were expensive (our first VCR player, purchased in 1984, was six hundred dollars) we decided to do it. We offered VHS tapes initially, followed soon by Beta and Beta II.

By the end of 1984, Nancy's Notions was offering VHS and Beta tapes of *Sewing With Nancy* episodes for $39.95 each and they were selling well.

During the early years of taping at WKOW, Rich went along to the studio in Madison, joining me and Donna Fenske. Often while we were taping, Rich went to the Madison-based business that duplicated VHS tapes for us. On the ride home our station wagon was filled not only with the samples, sewing machines and sergers for the show, but with VHS tapes as well.

I have a series of especially fond memories from that era. On taping day afternoons Earl and Elaine relieved Joan by taking Teddy with them to the farm. When Rich and I returned from Madison, Elaine had dinner ready and three generations of Ziemans sat down together for a delicious meal. After a long and demanding day, being with family set things right again.

The move to WKOW also brought increased exposure. In addition to weekly programming on the Satellite Program Network, six ABC affiliate stations in Wisconsin began airing *Sewing With Nancy*. In 1985, a new cable station, Tempo TV, requested the program as well.

For some time I had been eyeing public television, thinking that *Sewing With Nancy* would be a perfect fit for their educational focus. I had tried to make contact with the Public Broadcasting System (PBS), but had been unable to make inroads. Soon after Tempo TV requested *Sewing With Nancy*, Nebraska Public Television also contacted me to ask how PBS stations could air the program. Their request cleared the road of obstacles to being on public television in markets across the nation.

I think I would have danced for joy had I not just undergone another knee surgery—fortunately, this time, a minor one to remove more cartilage from my "good" knee.

A pilot designed to PBS standards was produced by re-editing an episode and deleting the six minutes of commercials. In place of commercials I had a six-minute segment called Mail Bag that featured hints from viewers.

The *Sewing With Nancy* pilot was accepted and we were on PBS! Initially there were only a handful of stations—twenty-five to thirty percent of the markets—but it was a great start! For a short time we were on three markets—SPN, Tempo TV and PBS—plus the ABC affiliate stations in Wisconsin.

The advantage of cable TV was that we could include commercials, both for Nancy's Notions and for our underwriters. Yet, the costs of broadcast time on cable were escalating each year. Of course, catalog sales and sponsorships offset those costs, but when I looked toward the future, I could see that we would soon be priced off the air. By contrast, public television was, and is, a more reasonable venture. (By the way, most people think that I get paid to be on television, but it's the other way around—I pay. Often I'm asked just that, "How much do you get paid to be on TV?" Oh, funny!)

Sewing With Nancy is an independently produced series and public television doesn't own the programming. With that said, there also were no restrictions for the PBS distributor. Program managers at public television stations might have chosen not to provide a slot for my show because I was also on cable, but that's something I'll never know for sure. When word spread about the popularity of the show within public television circles, the show was off to the races, reaching market shares comparable to *This Old House*.

The Mail Bag segment of *Sewing With Nancy* was a good concept. The trouble was that episodes with the Mail Bag segments were taped in advance, long before PBS viewers knew there was such a feature, so for the first year, I made up the hints giving what I thought were legitimate tips with generic names. When viewers actually did watch the segments, tips and sewing hints started rolling in.

Viewers of the Mail Bag weren't the only ones lagging behind. The garment industry had been using sergers for a long time before the popularity of knits began pulling them into the home market as well. I wanted to introduce viewers to the advantages of serging, so in 1984 I ordered my first serger by mail. But, a mail-order serger did not include hands-on lessons in how to use it. When I introduced serging on *Sewing With Nancy*, my demonstrations were lifted from the pages of the manual. I was learning along with everyone else.

It is fortunate that there is a span of time between recording an episode and when that episode is broadcast. On more than one occasion, that span of time has given me opportunity to stay an-instructor's-leap-ahead of my on-air students.

In its infancy it seemed that television took itself so seriously. Aside from live recordings of variety shows where (to the delight of their audiences) comedians occasionally lost their lines and their composure, bloopers were hidden from the public. After all, we were the experts—to admit our failures or "mis-speaks" would be akin to knocking ourselves off our own pedestals.

Fortunately we take ourselves a lot more lightly these days. My thirtieth anniversary special contains several colossal blunders and bloopers from the early years of *Sewing With Nancy* that have survived. One involves Mail Bag.

I was trying to introduce a hint sent in from a viewer in Virginia. Seated at a small table, I began…

"This hint comes to us from Alice Magneolus…" but I had mispronounced the name. Stop. I tried again.

"This hint comes to us from Alice Magleonus…" not right either. Stop. I practiced saying her name correctly a few times. "Maleogus. Maleogus. Maleogus." Try again.

"This hint comes to us from Alice …," Stop. I had totally forgotten the name. This time I slapped the heel of my hand against my forehead in 'I-could-have-had-a-V-8' style. "Maleogus. Maleogus. Maleogus." I recited again before tapes rolled again.

"This hint comes to us from Alice Magleonus…" Stop.

Over and over I tried, but couldn't say the name correctly. Finally, on about umpteenth take, it worked.

"This Mail Bag hint comes to us from a viewer in Hampton, Virginia. Alice Maleogus writes…" and I went on to give the hint.

When it just won't work, go a different direction.

Alice, dear Alice, if by chance you are reading this book, I want to both apologize for brutalizing your name, and thank you for the laughter and joy those bloopers have generated over the years—that is, once we got past wanting to hide them.

At one point I planned a series on sewing for children. What could be better when talking about sewing for children than to have children on the program? So, we rounded up five pre-school children including Donna Fenske's and Chris Stam's children, plus our son Ted. While I was seated on a sofa, holding a toddler, I began my introduction to the program.

Our son Ted was an active child, and a climber. As tapes rolled and I began talking, Teddy stood beside me on the sofa. But as I talked, he began fidgeting. As he began fidgeting, I became nervous. As I became nervous, I began talking faster. As I began talking faster, other children joined Teddy in fidgeting. He finally climbed, or fell, off the front of the sofa and came around to jump on again from the back. It was like herding cats!

I've watched that blooper many times over the years, and although I know I somehow made it through, the antics of those children were so attention-grabbing that I'm still not sure what I said. I'm certain no one else knew either. From that point on, I was very cautious about including children as guests.

I am a sewing teacher. Sometimes coming up with twenty-six episodes of *Sewing With Nancy* each year can be a challenge. But, after a couple of experiments with expansion into other areas, I settled back into focusing on sewing. I tried a couple of programs that included cooking (I am, after all,—I reasoned—a home economist). Called one episode "Sew Entertaining," and demonstrated how to make table toppers, napkins and other items, along with giving recipes and doing about five minute's worth of cooking. I got hate mail.

I also tried an exercise episode, thinking to combat the sedentary effects of sitting and sewing. It bombed, too. I am a sewing teacher.

When I am preparing for *Sewing With Nancy*, I'm concerned that viewers get good, solid information that they can use in a practical way. I rarely think about what I would like to receive.

There are times when I look in the mirror or see "The Look" on someone's face, that I wish my face were normal. I haven't done it many times in my life, but in late summer of 1987, I remember praying, "Lord, if there's a way this could be resolved, I would certainly appreciate it."

The first week of September, I received a letter that helped answer that prayer.

I didn't need to think about it. With shaking hands I picked up the phone and dialed Dr. Balliet's number. He was not available so I left a message asking that he return my call. I remember I was in the art room at Nancy's Notions when the call came. He couldn't guarantee results, he said, and he asked questions, then said he would like to meet with me. I made an appointment.

The Neuromuscular Retraining Clinic was at the University of Wisconsin Hospital in Madison and was part of their Department of Rehabilitation Medicine. After meeting Dr. Balliet I went through an

"My wife (Tamara) and I are avid fans of your TV programs... Because my profession involves the retraining of facial paralysis, I could not help, but notice the reduced function of the right side of your face. Please don't consider this a solicitation (since we are a non-profit facility). I thought that you should know that my clinic, here in Madison, is one of only three in the world that specializes in the retraining of facial paralysis on a post-acute basis, *i.e.,* many years (up to 45 years) after injury or disease... If you are interested, please feel free to call me at the office..."

analysis in which three doctors watched, and stared at my every move, from wrinkling my eyebrow to closing my eye.

Then Dr. Balliet developed a plan for me. I worked with Jackie, a physical therapist who taught me how to strengthen latent muscles to take over the job that the dead cranial nerve can't do. When function could not be improved, I was taught techniques to disguise the disability.

For those who suffer with lingering effects from Bell's palsy, there's something that occurs called the Bell's Flip. The body has protective mechanisms. With a paralysis like mine, when the eye is closed, since the lid has reduced function and doesn't close completely, to protect itself the eyeball flips up so it is not exposed. In normal function, the eyeball remains behind the lid, but for me, the white is exposed because the eyeball rolls back. So I had to train myself to close my eye while forcing my eyeball to remain in position with the lens forward.

Those exercises are hard work! Like pumping iron with an eyeball. I may only move my eyeball a millimeter, but it feels as though I've been exerting tremendous effort. I continue to practice those exercises. The results were amazing—the exercises are called Face Saving Exercises for good reason.

Speech was another area addressed during therapy. When I learned to lead with my right side and follow with my good side, by doing so my facial movements appear more symmetrical. It has been many years since I went to that clinic, and Dr. Balliet has moved to Pennsylvania, but Jackie is still at the University

Hospital and as the Bell's palsy poster child, I refer many people to her. It isn't just those who've had Bell's palsy who are challenged by facial paralysis. It happens also to those who may have had an injury or tumor that required severing of the cranial nerve.

For about a year I went through a whole series of steps to improve my facial function and it proved to be an encouragement. Teddy was five years old that year and I had him watch me as I did my eye-closing exercises. His job was to tap me on the shoulder when my eyeball flipped up. As I practiced I gained a sense of what to do to stop it from flipping. I know the exercises helped, and Teddy helped, too, by giving me the knowledge of what I was doing. It's in my subconscious now. I continue to work on forming words in ways that improve the look and symmetry of my face.

I will be forever grateful that Dr. Balliet took the time to contact me to offer help.

I love consumer shows because they offer an opportunity to talk with customers. With television, you think you know who is watching, but there is no response. But when talking in person, you can read faces and really know what they are thinking.

But doing consumer shows is like having a big party, and then being faced with clean-up afterwards.

I started doing consumer shows in 1981, while I was the only staff member. When Earl and Elaine became involved, they attended shows six to eight times a year. As we got bigger and bigger, we enlisted a man from our team at Nancy's Notions to travel with us to help set up and take down our booth. During the show he helped with sales. The women who traveled to the shows set out our products and created product displays. It took teamwork and was also hard work.

Donna Fenske often went, as did Diane Dhein from Nancy's Notions. We wanted someone in the booth who could answer sewing questions and although they were great with people, neither Earl nor Elaine sewed. Since I wasn't able to be at every show, Donna, Diane and I took turns.

In 1987, while delivering information for printed materials to Laure Noe, the freelance artist we used, I slipped on the ice outside her home. The knee without a kneecap was badly sprained and bruised. I was outfitted with a removable cast and told to take it easy.

Good advice, but Kathy Hasson Gittus and I were scheduled to attend the American Home Sewing Association trade show in Long Beach, California. I was in pain, and even with the removable cast, could shower only with help. So at the last minute, Rich was wrangled into the job of assisting me. All hotel rooms near the convention center were filled, so poor Kathy booked a room farther away, at a much less desirable hotel.

That flight to California was the first time I was bumped up to first class. I was moved there because my left leg stuck straight out and I needed more space than coach would afford me.

Travel while wearing a leg brace is a definite challenge. At that time John Wayne Airport (now Orange County Airport) didn't have jet ways and I could not walk down the narrow stairs that were rolled to the plane's door. So, I had to wait until everyone else had deplaned.

The catering company supplying food and drinks to the plane had cabin access via a door opposite the passenger departure door. Food and drink carts were raised or lowered from cabin level on a caged platform with a scissors-like lift mechanism.

My mode of departure involved being wheeled in a wheelchair to the platform where I rode to ground level with my leg protruding forward. Seeing Rich and Kathy waiting for me, I waved as if I were the homecoming queen in a parade. That's the closest I'll come to that honor. It was the only way to make light of an ungraceful exit from the plane.

Knee pain is my constant companion. My first knee surgeries were in the pre-arthroscopic era and during the last of those surgeries my left knee cap was removed. Although I was told that I would never be able to bend my knee more than ninety degrees, I have fared better than that, but I was plagued with shooting pains in my leg. In 1991, when visiting my local orthopedic doctor, he told me, "I went to a seminar and they were talking about you. Well, not you specifically, but about the symptoms you have."

He went on to explain a procedure called denervation. In layman's terms, when nerves are cut as mine had been, they sometimes form a

Phyllis Winter

"Nancy never complains. After one surgery she had this device that circulated cold water over her knee and she had to carry it around. She just did it! Some people would have stayed home. She'll say, 'Well, it wasn't that bad. We got through it.' She always downplays everything and doesn't want people to feel sorry for her."

neuroma at the ends and those neuromas produce unexpected shooting pains. The neuromas could be surgically removed, he said.

I looked forward to a reduction in pain, so my doctor made arrangements for me to undergo surgery at Johns Hopkins Hospital in Baltimore, Maryland, which was the only place where that type of surgery was being performed.

For insurance reasons, the surgery could only be performed on an outpatient basis, but I needed to remain nearby for follow-up care. So, as she had done many times before, my mother became my caregiver and accompanied me to Baltimore.

I was among the first one hundred people to undergo that surgery, which was performed by a plastic surgeon skilled in operating in minute detail. I had only two neuromas; other patients have many more. After the surgery I was discharged—drainage tubes and all. Mother and I fended for ourselves in a hotel room. We read books and worked crossword puzzles during the day and our spirits were lifted by a couple evening visits from my mother's first cousin and his wife who lived in Baltimore.

Thankfully, that surgery was successful and even though I still live with pain, I rarely have the lightning-bolt shooting pains that I experienced before the surgery.

Deanna Springer

(Colleague)
"On my first flight I had nothing to gauge it against, so I was fine."

Deanna Springer joined our staff in 1989 and several years later started working with us at consumer shows. We were glad to have her.

Deanna had never flown before. In 1999, on Deanna's first time out, we flew in a DC10 and experienced extreme turbulence—the worst I've ever known. Donna Fenske and I were practically hanging on for dear life while a couple rows ahead Deanna was calmly reading a book. On the ground we drove into the storm that had been hitting Washington State for almost two days. Our hotel, where the advance crew for Nancy's Notions was already staying, was without power and water was flooding in under the door. We used Glo-sticks for light.

The most exciting story about consumer shows took place on February 28, 2001—set up day for the huge consumer show in Puyallup, Washington.

John Nickel and Deanna Springer had flown to Seattle on Tuesday, the day before. With a couple of hours to spare, they quickly visited Old Seattle and rode the Space Needle elevator to the observation deck for a view of the city.

Afterwards they rented a U-Haul truck, drove to the Roadway shipping terminal, and loaded the six skids of Nancy's Notions materials we had shipped there for show inventory.

Wednesday morning they were in line early for set-up at the Western Washington Fairgrounds in Puyallup where the show is held. While they waited their turn, they admired the cloudless skies and lovely view of Mt. Rainier, an inactive volcano about forty miles southeast of Puyallup.

When it was their turn, John backed the truck near the entrance while Deanna headed to the booth. The booth wasn't far—perhaps thirty feet inside the entrance—a very good thing when transporting heavy skids of product. It looked as though things would go smoothly.

Deanna and John had a system. She remained in the booth, setting it up and putting things in order, while John unloaded the skids onto a two-wheeled cart and transported our supplies to the booth. Once everything was inside and John had moved the truck, he joined Deanna to finish the set up.

We always went to consumer shows prepared to hit the ground running. That included arriving with start-up cash for making

Deanna Springer

"When snow dust started falling from the ceiling it hit me what it was. Earthquake. People around me were crawling under their folding tables, but I grabbed The Trust Fund and ran for John."

John Nickel
(Colleague)

"Deanna grabbed me and I said, 'If we're gonna go, we're gonna go together.'"

Deanna Springer

"It sounded like a giant shaking a piggy bank. There were lots of metal light poles and other metal poles—I thought they were going to fall over. Mt. Rainier was right there and thinking of Mt. St. Helen's, I thought, 'Don't make the mountain mad!'"

John Nickel

"She had a death grip on me!"

change. We kept that cash in a locked briefcase and referred to it as The Trust Fund.

Deanna was busy in the booth when she began hearing a sound that seemed to be coming from the floor above. We're northerners and northerners who love hockey are acquainted with the sounds made by a Zamboni machine that smooths ice on indoor rinks. That's how Deanna describes the roar and sweep sound, but it grew louder and louder, becoming a loud, syncopated bump, bump, bump. It was an earthquake.

When the truck began swaying side to side as he was unloading boxes of merchandise, at first John thought some fellow vendors were indulging in pre-show shenanigans. But he recognized the shaking as an earthquake by the time Deanna burst through the entrance doors, and sprinted toward him across the asphalt. They tossed The Trust Fund into the cab of the truck and even had the presence of mind to lock the doors before moving to an open area.

They stood there together, arms wrapped around each other, clinging not just for comfort, but for balance. Shorter than John, Deanna shifted her grip to his belt and hung on. The ground below their feet moved, and although the asphalt beneath them never broke, shock waves made it seem as though they were standing on the ocean. As the quake went on the roar increased.

Today, that earthquake is referred to as the Nisqually Quake. It occurred at 10:54 a.m. Pacific Standard Time and registered 6.8 on the Richter scale. Its epicenter was about twenty-four miles from Puyallup and records indicated it lasted about forty-five seconds.

Deanna Springer

"John and I are like brother and sister. First thing he did after we agreed not to talk about it, was to tell the first person we greeted upon our return to Nancy's Notions. So, I guess we can talk about it now."

For John and Deanna holding to each other, it seemed to go on for several minutes. When the shaking subsided, they stood for a while before slowly moving apart. As they composed themselves, they agreed as colleagues to not talk about holding each other.

Donna Fenske, Mary Mulari (a frequent guest on *Sewing With Nancy*) and I were on a flight to Seattle and the plane was already on approach for scheduled landing at 11:00 a.m. Suddenly, the pilot announced we were being diverted to the airport in Portland, Oregon, and made a very sharp turn to the left. Donna almost landed in my lap. Just before landing we were told there had been an earthquake.

Once on the ground, I asked Donna and Mary to handle luggage while I sprinted for the Hertz counter. I arrived just in time to get the last rental car!

Cell phone signals were down in the Puyallup area so we couldn't reach Deanna and John. Deanna found a pay phone and called Nancy's Notions, though, and told our receptionist, Loie, that they were fine. Through the course of that day, Loie became our intermediary, passing messages from one to the other. Through Loie, Deanna and John learned we had been diverted to Portland and were attempting to drive to Puyallup.

There was a lot of chaos. We got on the road, headed toward Puyallup, but when we neared Olympia, Washington, heavy traffic turned to gridlock. Just before we came to a complete stop, I saw a road to the right and exited. The rental car map was not detailed, and not of much help. When a truck that had exited ahead of us turned onto a smaller road, on impulse (or divine guidance, possibly!) I followed it. The truck wound its way up and down and around through the mountains (I later learned we were on Mt. Rainier) always heading in the general direction of Puyallup. There were mud slides and roads closed along the way, but I stuck with that truck and eventually we all arrived safely in Puyallup; it was evening by then.

Deanna Springer

"We were not allowed back in the buildings for several hours until an engineer could be brought in and deem the buildings safe. We left the fairgrounds and went to lunch, watching live reports on the TVs at a Ruby Tuesdays restaurant."

There was still some shaking going on.

Gail Brown, another frequent guest on *Sewing With Nancy* over the years, joined us for the event. She lives in nearby Hoquiam, Washington, and drove to Puyallup. An aftershock that night brought a mirrored door in her hotel room crashing to the floor.

In the restaurant, John and Deanna looked at each other in shock when they learned that Old Seattle, where they had visited the day before, had suffered extensive damage. If that weren't enough, a troop of Girl Scouts was trapped in the Seattle Space Needle for hours after the quake.

As soon as John and Deanna were able to get back in the building at the fair grounds, they finished setting up the booth. It was ready when we walked in the next morning. In spite of the earthquake, the show opened on time. There were some differences. Windows sported neon pink masking tape Xs and aftershocks had everyone on edge.

One would think that a natural disaster would keep customers away, but that show was one of our best ever. Of course, it became a company legend as well. When we left from the Seattle airport at the end of the show, we noticed that the plate glass windows in the traffic control tower were gone and that the structure was empty. Instead, a trailer like those used on construction sites was suspended in the air by crane and ground traffic controllers were working in it.

A lot of Deanna's responsibilities in the 1990s involved coordinating consumer shows. She carefully weighed costs and worked hard to make our presence at shows profitable.

Doing a consumer show is costly. The term "drayage" has its origins back in the era when dray horses pulling wagons moved goods the short distance from a shipping terminal to their destination. Although the horses are gone, drayage charges continue and they are usually based on weight— the heavier the product, the greater the drayage charges. Major consumer shows require vendors to use union labor to unload their product and move it to a booth on the floor of the consumer show. Deanna was good at thinking outside the box. She came up with creative ways to save money, including renting trucks and driving them ourselves, and bringing a hand forklift to move things rather than pay someone else to do it.

Nancy's Notions did several consumer shows every year until 2007, but nothing—ever!—came close to the drama of the 2001 show in Puyallup.

Chapter 16

✲

On the _Ed Sullivan Show,_ a variety program that aired on CBS television from 1948 through 1971, one guest performer was a man who kept plates spinning on top of poles. He ran from pole to pole, quickly giving each plate a turn to start it spinning before moving to the next pole. With all plates spinning, he started over. As the first plate began to wobble, he gave it another quick turn to keep the momentum and moved to the next and the next.

That's how I felt during the last half of the 1980s.

Kathy Hasson Gittus

"When _Sewing With Nancy_ moved to PBS and became nationwide, the Nancy's Notions mailing list kept growing. Postage was cheap then, and printing was inexpensive. I don't think there was a business plan—a five-year or ten-year plan—we were just trying to keep up."

Nancy's Notions was experiencing phenomenal growth. Our April 1985 move to 1010 DeClark Street occurred almost simultaneously with an expansion in the number of households reached by _Sewing With Nancy_. At one point in 1985, the program was broadcast on the Satellite Program Network, Tempo TV (another cable network), ABC affiliate stations in Wisconsin, and approximately fifty percent of Public Broadcasting System (PBS) markets. Huge increases in the number of _Sewing With Nancy_ viewers caused corresponding increases in the number of requests for Nancy's Notions catalogs. Increased distribution of catalogs generated increased orders for products.

Additional mail required more people; more orders meant more products and more people to process and ship orders. We hired, and hired, and hired again. At the beginning of 1985, our staff totaled around eighteen; by 1990, Nancy's Notions had more than seventy-five employees.

My father-in-law, Earl, was our warehouse manager, and my mother-in-law, Elaine, still served as office manager, but we added more people to staff the retail store, open mail, process orders, pack orders, handle events, order merchandise, work at consumer and trade shows, assist with books and catalogs and provide administrative support.

Data management became an issue very early on.

Using Mom's high school graduation typewriter, when I first started Nancy's Notions, I typed names on Avery label templates with thirty-three spaces for names. Then I photocopied the template onto actual labels for the mailings.

For my reference, I applied labels to index cards and filed the names alphabetically. When an order was received, I'd make a note on the index card if a change to the name or address was needed. It was an awkward way of handling direct mail, but pretty typical in the early 1980s.

In the beginning Nancy's Notions orders came primarily through the mail. We added to the card list for every new customer, but after orders were processed, we filed them by the customer's last name in boxes—each labeled with a letter. That way, if the customer called or wrote with a question, the order could be quickly pulled for reference. Sometimes there were several boxes for each letter of the alphabet.

Our cumbersome system needed help and Rich came up with a solution. Figi's Cheese House—a gift cheese and specialty foods company in Marshfield, Wisconsin—maintained computerized mail lists for their direct mail customers. He made an arrangement with them to do the same for us. Once a quarter Rich loaded boxes and boxes into our station wagon and drove one hundred-fifty miles north to Marshfield. At Figi's, he unloaded the boxes and carried them to the third floor where data entry clerks were busy entering everything.

Today, less than three decades later, even casual computer users know the basics of sorting data. Not only that, but the internet has changed data transfer from driving and lugging boxes to e-mail attachments and pressing, "Send." But back then, when one of the top executives at Figi's asked Rich, "How do you want names sorted—by the total of the order, or by the product ordered?"—Rich realized that before long things would need to change at Nancy's Notions.

We bought our first computer in 1986, an Apple SE with an itty-bitty screen and a twenty megabyte hard drive. Phyllis Winter, who by that time was in charge of catalogs, used it for desktop publishing. Initially we thought a small portion of our catalogs could be generated on computer, but Phyllis taught herself how to use the software, generating the whole catalog on computer—a considerable undertaking on her part. We thought we were hot stuff, and we were, in comparison to typesetting. With tower and screen in one compact unit the computer had the advantage of portability and Phyllis often took work home to finish it there.

Phyllis Winter
"Kathy Hasson Gittus needed marketing promotions materials and she would sit next to me telling me what to do on the computer. Finally Nancy said we needed another computer for Kathy."

At one point I took the plunge and purchased two computers similar to the one Phyllis was using. Kathy got one and I took the other. Computers revolutionized how we prepared materials.

Many of our early hires—Chris Stam, Donna Fenske, Scott Stanton, John Nickel, Kathy Hasson Gittus and Phyllis Winter—who grew into management roles, made it possible for Nancy's Notions to succeed. They were, and still are, as dedicated as Rich and I were. As an example, Phyllis took ownership of the catalog department. Like her co-workers, she was dedicated and went beyond what was expected. I am confident that start-up companies succeed when there's a loyal team, a team who are friends as well as co-workers.

Nancy's Notions was growing so fast. Orders were pouring in from across the nation. We were continually ordering greater quantities and

Rich Zieman

"Our second Sewing Weekend was bigger than we expected. To show employees who worked so hard that they were appreciated, I took some money out before we counted the sales and slipped some bills into Thank You notes for each staff person. The note said, 'Take your family out to dinner.' That was the one and only time I didn't report all sales."

expanding our product line—and adding staff.

At the grand opening of the DeClark building a year earlier, the teaching and retail event that accompanied our celebration was a success. We did it again in 1986, officially naming it Sewing Weekend, and promoting the event to our mailing list. It was successful beyond our expectations. Sewists came from everywhere, some long distances. Along with seminars that I taught there were presentations by guest teachers. Again, there was opportunity to shop for Nancy's Notions products. We decided to keep it up and that event is still held today early in May.

Just over a year after our move to DeClark Street, we realized the building was too small.

In January of 1987, Rich negotiated the sale of the DeClark Street building and purchased land in a Tax Incremental Financing (TIF) development in Beaver Dam. Work to construct a new fourteen thousand square-foot home for Nancy's Notions began that summer at 333 Beichl Avenue.

Our ground breaking for the new facility was held on a cold and miserable day in April, and our grand opening was scheduled for October 1. Construction of the new facility was estimated to cost two hundred fifty-two thousand dollars and I was starting to sweat the mounting expenses.

At the time we were building a house for ourselves. Most people, when they're building a new home, have the time to choose their lighting fixtures, faucets and finishes. Not me! I was so busy that Rich handled most of those decisions. I am thankful that we have compatible tastes.

We moved into the new building in August 1987, leaving behind the "luxurious" space we had outgrown in less than two years. A couple months later our family moved into a new home as well.

The new Nancy's Notions facility was huge and allowed us to

expand the retail store. A local fabric store left Beaver Dam, so we began offering fabric in the retail store, then later began offering it in the catalog as well. Diane Dhein joined us and managed the store. A former fabric store owner, she eventually began replacing me at some seminars. Today she works as an editor, preparing the books and printed materials so critical to the success of Nancy's Notions. Pat Hahn joined us in the late 80s as well, coming on staff as a part-time writer and editor who soon became full-time. She still works in the writing department and is responsible for developing books from *Sewing With Nancy* programs. Today Pat, Donna Fenske and I are the three who usually travel together to *Sewing With Nancy* recording sessions.

Selling fabric gave rise to a new service, the Personalized Shopper Service. Started in 1988, Nancy's Notions staff, Mary Neff and Sue Tamminga, helped customers match and coordinate thread, lining and interfacings with the new fabric line.

In 1987, we began offering a video club and promoted it by developing a single sheet that listed thirty-two *Sewing With Nancy* videos. The program was patterned after video rentals in stores, only ours was via mail order. Over a twelve-year period it grew to a sixty-four page catalog with over two hundred-twenty titles and eighty presenters. We were way ahead of Netflix.

Since videos were expensive, the video club was an ideal way for customers to watch our *Sewing With Nancy* television episodes—and eventually other videos—at an economical price. If they couldn't watch *Sewing With Nancy* in their home, we would bring it to them. After a few years we offered a club membership at $7.95 a year, giving the member a discounted rate on rentals. Education drove sales and that was an ideal way to educate and inform customers.

We eventually disbanded the video club over taxation issues. Since the videotapes were rented, the tapes were considered our property. Having property in other states would have resulted in Nancy's Notions being required to pay sales taxes in every state where we sent rental videos. In short, it would have opened a Pandora's Box of paperwork.

In 1988, before the era of internet information, we started a newsletter called *Nancy's Notions News*. Coordinated by Kathy Hasson Gittus and mailed to preferred customers (those who actually ordered from Nancy's Notions), it continued until 2006 and was highly successful.

Nancy's Notions News was designed as a sales and informational mailer that was mailed between catalog mailings. Initially, January and July were the months when the newsletters were mailed.

Printed by a newspaper publisher, a neighboring business to our new Beichl Avenue address, the format was much larger than our new digest-sized catalog (5½" x 8½"), and was a size common for newspaper sales pieces. The increased size allowed us to give in-depth product information and showcase products. We wrote feature articles, including some about Nancy's Notions staff members, offered new products four times a year and tested new product lines. In regards to the testing, for example, we learned that just because Rowenta irons were of interest to our customers, that doesn't translate into sales of Rowenta toasters. Live and learn!

When I watched that *Ed Sullivan Show* performance as a child, even though I was not involved in keeping the plates spinning, I felt the tension when they began to wobble. That's probably how it felt for our staff on many occasions.

That era was a lot of fun, but there were tensions as well. Mostly we experienced coordination issues. With so much to do and job responsibilities expanding every other day, we often had difficulty identifying who was responsible for what.

Computers not only revolutionized the preparation of printed materials, but they also had the capability of revolutionizing how we handled orders. In 1988, within two years of getting our first computer, we computerized operations, thereby eliminating the need for Rich to make his quarterly trek to Figi's and back. Rich and Paul Shonts, hired in 1987

Phyllis Winter

"The staff was open and there was interchange. We joked a lot. There were things we disagreed on, but Richard and Nancy tried to keep people positive and working together. It could get stressful at times, but for the most part we interacted and had our family jokes because we all kind of grew up together as a family."

Rich Zieman

"The growth we had and making all that work was the fun part of the job."

Earl Zieman

"I never learned how to use a computer. Elaine saw it coming that she would have to use a computer and she retired."

Rich Zieman

"There was a plant in the office that had died. After Kathy and I had an argument, or didn't see eye to eye, one of us would take that plant and put it on the other person's desk as an apology. I haven't worked with Kathy since 2002, but last year on her birthday, by way of a reminder, I gave her a dried floral arrangement—an ugly dried floral arrangement."

to oversee order entry, order processing and the warehouse, worked with a small software company in Indianapolis that specialized in meeting the data needs of business-to-consumer organizations.

Making the transition to computerized operations was not easy, and some were not willing to go there. Elaine decided the dawn of the computer age was the perfect time to finally retire; Earl continued to work for a while, but stepped back from his warehouse manager's position to let someone else work the computer. Their absence left a huge void that I still feel.

Computerizing operations meant that we could now analyze more detailed information and at greater speeds than ever before. That information gave us customer profiles that helped us plan promotions and identify other products we might want to sell.

Kathy Hasson Gittus and Rich periodically had disagreements over what came under the marketing category of the business, the realm in which I had oversight, and what constituted information that fed into the operations side of the business, Rich's realm. Sometimes their disagreements became heated, but any argument was short lived. Rich and Kathy are like brother and sister.

Rich knew that his father would not want to continue working forever. In 1985, before Nancy's Notions embraced technology, Rich went to the guidance counselor at Beaver Dam High School and asked if he knew of someone he could groom for the position

John Nickel

"I was a punk teenager when I started. Once I had a little money in my pocket, I started partying and showing up for work late. I got the 'sit down' conversation from Richard. He told me 'If you're not going to be here on time, you're not going to be here at all.'

Not long ago, I sat down with a teenage boy hired to work in the warehouse. He was coming in to work late. I told him, 'If you're not going to be here on time, you're not going to be here at all.'"

of warehouse manager. The counselor recommended John Nickel. John had just graduated high school, but was without plans for the future when Rich hired him.

John worked alongside Earl; he assisted in the warehouse and helped with trade and consumer shows. He became warehouse manager when Earl stepped down and today is still warehouse manager at Nancy's Notions. John considers Earl to be the grandfather he never had. An enthusiastic young man, he learned quickly, absorbing from both Rich and Earl.

Most Nancy's Notions staff members have had multiple positions. In the early to mid-80s, managerial positions were given almost exclusively to current employees. The results were mixed. Many who were good at their current position rose to the occasion and were able to handle a new managerial position, aided in the transition with training sessions and guidance from Rich and others.

But sometimes a competent employee did not fit the role of manager, and we discovered that after the fact. We all have our strengths and weaknesses. As we became more cognizant of the fact that not everyone wants or should be given a managerial role, we tried a variety of posting and hiring scenarios.

Step One—post a position internally. If we thought an individual would fit that role we would ask him or her to apply for the position, but would not guarantee his or her selection.

Step Two—advertise in the Beaver Dam newspaper.

Initially, I believed that promoting from within was the best way to go. My reasoning was that doing so would save a lot of the need to explain processes; plus, the individual would already know the Nancy's

Notions way.

I eventually changed my mind. When an opening became available for a retail store manager position, I was totally opposed to opening the position outside of Nancy's Notions. After my opinion was expressed, however, no one paid attention to what I had to say. We hired Lynn Helbing whose background was in retail management with Herberger's, the same department store chain where Rich had once been employed. Lynn had no fabric, sewing, or quilting experience and I couldn't envision how she would handle the position. Lynn joined the staff in 2001 and since then has done a stellar job.

Catalogs. Catalogs. Catalogs. The backbone of Nancy's Notions' growth and success has always been catalogs.

From my first 8½" x 11" flyer printed in black ink on colored paper in 1979, to the multiple page full-color shopping extravaganzas of recent years, catalogs have been a dominate factor in Nancy's Notions' appeal to customers.

At first the selection of which products to offer was easy—I wanted to make it possible for attendees at seminars to purchase what I used. As demand grew, we started writing manufacturers to ask them to send samples for us to consider adding to our product line. Eventually, we no longer had to ask. Nancy's Notions' reputation prompted manufacturers and distributors to send us product samples hoping we would want to include those items in our catalog.

The first flyers were illustrated with simple line drawings. Then we went to black and white photographs.

Bonnie Arndt was a freelance writer and photographer I had met several years earlier when she interviewed me for an article in the *Milwaukee Journal*. For many years, until we moved to full-color catalogs, Bonnie did our catalog photography.

In the early days Laure Noe worked for us on a freelance basis as well. She had a small child and preferred to work evenings and weekends at home, so I would drop things off at her home at the end of the day or end of the week. Laure joined the staff as an in-house graphic designer later on, but in the early years before we designed catalogs using desktop publishing

Bonnie Arndt

"We set up a studio in Nancy's warehouse. I provided lighting equipment and background screens, she provided tables and other props. My degree is in journalism and in news editorial; it is not in photography. My photography had mostly been used to illustrate news reporting. I learned a lot and grew in understanding lighting, angles, backdrops, depth of field and artistic technical things. It was wonderful."

software, she "pasted-up" the individual elements of catalogs.

We had a lot to learn about printing. At first, we used one printer for everything—catalogs, flyers, promotional pieces, and transcripts.

On one catalog, the black and white photos were too dark and both Rich and I were upset when we saw it. The printer refused to do anything about it, and it would have cost too much to reprint, so we reluctantly mailed it. We had no idea that as printing customers we had the right to go to the printer for a press check of ink and quality before the press run started.

While attending a seminar, Rich met a printer from Sun Prairie, about thirty minutes southwest of Beaver Dam. The printer courted us, and in the process educated us as well. He eventually got our catalog printing business and Phyllis Winter began doing press checks for print runs.

Over time, we transitioned from black and white catalogs to a mix of black and white and color pages, then eventually we evolved to full color. Bonnie Arndt decided to move on from product photography and Dale Hall, another freelance photographer, did our photographs.

One of our most successful catalogs along the way was one in which I wrote a narrative across the top of the pages. It was difficult to do—getting the text positioned over the proper product—but for years people at events have told me that was their favorite catalog, and one they've kept.

After orders and operations were computerized, the next step was to make it more convenient for customers to order by phone. In early 1990, we took a huge step and offered a toll-free "800" number for orders and customer service. That move positioned Nancy's Notions as a forerunner in the sewing and quilting industry. It also meant additional staff to answer phones and take orders.

Computers made our "800" number possible. With just a few keystrokes orders could be entered and customer questions answered. In its heyday, the Nancy's Notions call center had twenty-five people answering phones.

Rich Zieman
"Our goal wasn't to build a bigger building for Nancy's Notions, but as the need arose, we built."

Our mammoth fourteen thousand square foot building wasn't quite enough, and in 1989, Rich coordinated the addition of five thousand square feet for more retail store space, plus additional warehouse space. Nancy's Notions staff began realizing that when they saw Rich walking around with a yard stick, construction couldn't be far behind.

I'm not one to rally around the flag when it comes to causes. There are things I feel strongly about, but I'm not a forceful in-your-face kind of person. I would much rather accomplish things quietly, by diligently proving my point with kindness. Kindness always goes a long way.

The women's movement is an example of what I mean.

During the bra-burning era when the women's movement had the hard edges of revolution, I had my own troubles to overcome—the effects of Bell's palsy, surgeries, blood clots. I was just trying to live.

I wasn't against the women's movement and was interested in facets of it. For example, I believe in equal pay for equal work.

At Minnesota Fabrics, women in management were so underpaid. My salary was half that of an assistant manager, but I was expected to do the same work. There were very few women in managerial positions. In my role as home economist for my store, I was expected to be the "face" that drew customers into the store, but I was paid scarcely enough to live on.

From childhood, my parents instilled in me the will to work hard and do a good job. By the time Rich and I married, it was no longer expected that I would be a stay-at-home mother. I was more determined than ever to make something of myself, to show people I could achieve.

My resolve didn't center on being a woman, but on being a woman with a physical limitation. If I had been blessed with a symmetrical face I'm sure I would have been driven, but perhaps not in the same way. I wanted people to get past their first impression of me—to realize there was much more to Nancy Zieman than an asymmetrical face.

When we tried to get our first loan for Nancy's Notions in 1982, we talked to local bankers and they turned us down. It was obvious that they did not take seriously my career as a sewing teacher and entrepreneur who sold supplies to those who sew. I believe that had I been a man in the sewing business the loan application would have been regarded more seriously. So there were two strikes against me: 1) my activities were sewing related and therefore deemed to be of a lower class; and 2) I was a woman.

When the bank turned us down for that first loan, my mother-in-law went to them and showed the bank officers evidence that we were depositing large amounts of money in their bank—money they were using to their advantage. We proved we could do it.

Sales turn heads. Numbers make a difference.

There is one thing that women of our generation didn't have, and that was a sense of camaraderie. Men had that on the baseball field, basketball court and battlefield. But women were trained to care for families—their personal unit—and weren't trained to include others. We needed to learn how to encourage each other to achieve.

Perhaps elements of that encouragement aspect are behind the reasons why, by the end of

---

Entrepreneurial Woman of the Year Award Program

Each year WWE bestows its award upon a Wisconsin woman who through her ingenuity and hard work has created a successful business enterprise, and who best demonstrates the entrepreneurial spirit through her business, personal and community service accomplishments. While this evening we honor our winner, we also recognize the accomplishments of all women entrepreneurs, in Wisconsin and elsewhere, many of whom have overcome great obstacles to build their dream.

the 1980s, I received a number of awards.

In early 1988, I was at a trade show in Puyallup, Washington. It had been a busy day and when I returned to my hotel room around 8:00 that evening, I was exhausted. When I closed my door, I saw them—a dozen roses.

Momentarily confused, I found the attached card. It was from Rich.

"Congratulations on being named Wisconsin Woman Entrepreneur of the Year."

I called home and when Rich answered I said, "What?" He explained and as he talked, I vaguely remembered completing some forms requested by an executive at the Wisconsin Power and Light Company, the electricity supplier in our region. I filled out forms by request often, and once completed, I usually forgot about them. I did not recall that the forms meant I was being considered for honor.

The next morning I took the roses to our booth at the trade show so we all could enjoy them.

The award was a bigger honor than I expected. Sponsored by the Wisconsin Women Entrepreneurs, an organization of independent business owners and corporate officers, the award honored female achievement in the business realm. The ceremony was a formal event held in Milwaukee at the prestigious Pfister Hotel. I was expected to speak.

Mary Luedtke Rebman

"I didn't know about the award until later. It was quite an honor—a deserved honor. We're a quiet family. We were proud, but we're not braggers by any means. I'm sure Nancy knows how proud we are."

I worked hard on that speech. Some of our key staff members were in attendance; Rich's parents were there, my parents attended, and, of course, Rich was by my side.

Kathy Hasson Gittus attended that evening. She was a friend before becoming a co-worker and will always be a friend, first and foremost. Our offices were next to each other and I often bounced ideas off of her—I valued her opinion. Yet, if she disagreed with me, she didn't hesitate to voice an opinion or set me straight. Feisty? Yes. Given to tears? No way! But that evening, at the banquet while I delivered my speech, she cried.

It was humbling to accept the award, humbling to realize that others recognized that our achievements had bridged a divide. Nancy's Notions was an encouragement to others, an example of the camaraderie of the battlefield—only this time it was the battlefield of the business world.

A few months, later I was notified that the Alumni Association of the University of Wisconsin–Stout, was awarding me the 1988 Outstanding Young Alumni Award.

Less than a year later, I received a Wisconsin 4-H Alumni Award for, "distinguished leadership in business and community pursuits." Making that honor especially sweet was the joy of being introduced and presented the award by a lovely young woman, my sister, Gina.

Although I received a few other awards and recognitions over the next few years (among them induction into the Virtual Sewing Hall of Fame); my season of honor came to an end on June 22, 1991, when I was awarded the national 4-H Alumni Award. The organization that had encouraged and supported me as I set my feet on the path of my career honored me as an encouragement to other young people who were discovering their own paths.

A circle had been completed.

Chapter 17

❦

Football and Sewing Seminars

Several years ago, I was asked to list three things that most people don't know about me. My answers: I teach Sunday school, I sneeze every time I walk down the soap aisle at the grocery store, and I'm a die-hard Green Bay Packer football fan.

I don't have to explain the first two listings and perhaps the third isn't that difficult to figure out, either. But, there is more to my liking of football than meets the eye.

Knowing and really liking football was ingrained from childhood. Although I grew up only forty-eight miles from Lambeau Field in Green Bay, I didn't attend a Packers game until much later in my life. Still, I've rarely missed seeing one.

I remember my dad regretfully telling the story of missing an opportunity in the 1950s to purchase Green Bay season tickets. Part of Packer lore is the decades of waiting it requires to slowly climb the list to purchase season tickets at Lambeau Field. But in 1957, Lambeau Field, where the Packers still play today, was brand new. There was no lottery or waiting list for tickets. That first year, the cost of a season pass was fifty dollars, but unfortunately that was not in the family budget. Attending games also did not mesh with Dad's occupation as a dairy farmer, or our family's Sunday morning church dedication. Yet at least once a year, Dad would lament, "In 1957, I could have purchased season tickets for fifty dollars!"

The Sunday schedule at my childhood home during football season included my dad driving home after church as fast as possible (church was only four miles away) to catch the opening kickoff on our black and white TV or to listen to it on the radio. In the 1960s, Green Bay television stations "blacked out" the games within fifty miles of the stadium to encourage people to attend the games—they don't have to do that anymore!

If the game was at home in Green Bay, we had to listen to the radio broadcast. I distinctly recall listening to the "Ice Bowl," the 1967 NFL championship game between Green Bay and the Dallas Cowboys. With my head buried in my hands and holding my breath as if it would help, we listened while Bart Starr ran the infamous quarterback sneak into the end zone. My brother, John, and I jumped and screamed with delight—the game was won.

If you're wondering where I'm going with this, it's that presenting sewing and quilting seminars is a lot like playing football. Granted, I've never actually played football (not unless you count flag football in high school gym class), nor are there fifty-three people on my team—I'm generally solo when traveling to present a lecture or seminar. Yet, parallels can be drawn between playing football and preparing for and presenting lectures and seminars.

Before I go further, I must state that I truly enjoy and look forward to presenting seminars. Interacting with an audience hones my teaching skills and allows me to feel the pulse of what viewers and consumers want and need. But, I purposely keep the number of events per year at a manageable number of between eight and ten. Since the arrival of our second son over twenty-two years ago, I make a conscious effort to limit the number of yearly engagements. If I accepted all of the speaking requests I receive, I would be traveling around thirty-five weeks a year—an impossible schedule to keep while tending to other business responsibilities, not to mention the toll on one's health and most importantly, family.

The lecture and seminar part of my business life began in 1975, when I was the home economist for Minnesota Fabrics in Homewood, Illinois. Since then, I've lectured or demonstrated in church basements, town halls, basements of stores, county extension meetings rooms, libraries, high school auditoriums, stores, and convention centers or hotel meeting rooms. Set-up, lighting, and audio/visual equipment varies with each venue.

The Playing Field

Now back to football. All wannabe football players begin by playing the game, learning the basics in Peewee football or something comparable. My indoctrination into learning how to teach via lecture or demonstration began at Minnesota Fabrics. For six weeks in the fall and spring, each in-store home economist was given a lecture schedule. Using an outline provided by the store's regional home economist, our task was to prepare a sample garment or project, create step-by-step samples, and then present the topic three different times in one day. The next week the schedule repeated with a different topic. It was a grueling schedule. Most of the preparation had to be done on my own time.

Aside from giving demonstrations in 4-H or taking a teaching techniques class in college, I learned teaching skills "on the field" in front of a group. The most consistent complaint I received was that I talked too fast, a characteristic that still haunts me when nervous.

Minnesota Fabric seminars were much like a pick up game in sports. When it was time for the morning seminar, a few racks of fabric were moved to the side and thirty chairs, plus a six-foot table, were set up. I was ready to go. After an hour-long seminar, the "classroom" was disassembled and then set up again for the next class at 2:00 p.m. The process repeated for the 7:00 p.m. event.

Unfriendly Referees

In the early years of Nancy's Notions, I was often asked to speak to groups of home economics teachers. In the 1980s, sewing was still taught in most high school and middle school classrooms. To maintain their teaching certification, teachers were required to earn a certain number of credit hours each year by attending seminars or classes.

As a young, green presenter, I remember one group of seasoned teachers from Winnebago County, Wisconsin, my home area. They sat in the audience with crossed arms, looking at me as if to say, "Teach me something I don't already know." It felt like playing on a field where unfriendly referees were looking for a foul.

After the talk, I called my mom to tell her of my intimidating experience. She asked, "Did you talk fast?" Yes, I had to admit, my propensity to talk fast when nervous kicked into full gear.

Third Down and Long

Many speaking room arrangements present a "third down and long" situation. A football team has four tries to advance the ball ten yards in order to keep the ball for another opportunity to score. But, I only get one try, and sometimes it seems like third down and twenty-five yards to go when the lecture arrangements are less than stellar.

When it seems impossible that the room or lecture hall set-up will work, a creative playbook is needed. As an example of what I mean, I always travel with elastic. That may seem logical since I teach sewing, but I reserve a length of elastic and use it to tie a hand-held microphone around my neck when a lavaliere microphone is not provided. It seems that at least once a year the hosting facility sets up a podium and hand-held microphone for me to use. (Ever try to sew one-handed while holding a microphone?) Even though the setup sheet my office provides gives specific instructions, the facility doesn't take heed. In their defense (football pun intended), not too many lecturers at a hotel or convention center are teaching sewing or quilting.

Left Tackle

At large venues, I make sure I have a left tackle along for safety. As explained so clearly in the book and movie, *The Blind Side*, the left tackle's job is to protect the quarterback. I'm the quarterback (ahem!) in this example. Some (very few!) people leave their manners at the door and I've been slapped with rolled magazines, followed by a giggle and a shout, "You're Nancy Zieman." Often I've had cameras shoved in my face, and have been cornered in the bathroom for an autograph. Once, from a bathroom stall, I even heard cheering from a woman who was "so excited to sit on the same toilet seat as Nancy." Ninety-nine percent of the time people are respectful, yet if I'm at an event where I'm likely to be recognized, walking and talking with another person provides a barrier of protection.

Training Camp

Weight training should have been a requirement for my job. Hauling and lifting bulky, heavy suitcases has kept my upper arms in shape. My seminars as of late cover two different topics with two- to three-hour presentations on each topic. Support materials are needed and there's no choice, but to pack them along. I pride myself in strategically packing *to,* but not *beyond* the fifty-pound airline limit. Last week, when checking luggage at the airline ticket counter, my suitcases weighed forty-seven pounds and forty-nine pounds respectively.

No-Huddle Offense

It takes me about thirty minutes to set up for a seminar. I try to pack suitcases so the materials I plan to use in a seminar are in the order they'll be used. Sometimes, though, there isn't time during packing to be so organized. The thirty-minute, pre-seminar time also gives me an opportunity to focus on what I'll be teaching and get mentally prepared for my talk.

On one occasion the organizer of the event planned a pre-game show. Much to my surprise, a musician playing a steel drum performed and the stage was filled with musical equipment. Rather than ending a half-hour before my scheduled start time as planned, the musician decided to play until he practically had to be hauled off the stage with a vaudeville hook! While setting up my samples and beginning to teach, I likened that experience, and similar ones, to a no-huddle offense, a hurry-up offense— understandable even if you detest football.

The no-huddle offense is often adopted by seminar speakers at consumer trade shows as well. At the Sewing & Stitchery Expo in Puyallup, Washington, only fifteen minutes are allotted between the time one speaker ends and the next starts. It's a scramble! In short, I've learned to be prepared for the unexpected.

False Start

A false start is a common issue on the football field. It happens when one team jumps off sides before the ball is snapped or kicked. The penalty is only five yards, yet once I had a false start in Rochester, New York, that could have cost me the game!

It was a snowy February day, when I flew into Rochester. The local PBS station sponsored the event. My plane was three hours late, so I was driven directly to the convention center. I set up my samples and worked with the members of the camera crew who were to record the event and project close-up images of my samples onto a large screen. I quickly changed clothes, had enough time to apply fresh make-up, and then walked onto the stage before an audience of four hundred people. The lighting was such that it was difficult to see the audience, but from the introductory applause and excitement in the air I could tell it was a full house.

After a normal introduction and review of what I'd be showing them that day, I started to demonstrate by stating, "And now I'll show you how to sew this." Sitting down to the machine with the close-up camera focused on the needle, I suddenly realized that the machine wasn't threaded nor was there thread in the bobbin case. The once enthusiastic crowd silenced. My face flushed and my pulse quickened. What to do, what to do? The little voice in my head said: Tell a blonde joke.

"Why don't they let blondes work in the M & M factory?" I asked.

There was a pause and silence.

"Because they throw out all the W's!"

Laughter. I ended up telling two or three other blonde jokes while threading the machine and winding the bobbin. By then I had the audience back on my side. What started as one of the worst false starts of my career turned into a blonde joke tradition for my seminars.

Interception

I don't think that I have to explain the football term interception. What you think is yours is suddenly taken away. The memorable interception in my seminar life happened in Corpus Christi, Texas. My seminar luggage didn't arrive. My flight arrived in the early afternoon, but my luggage was in no-man's land.

After learning that the airline could not guarantee arrival of my suitcases in time for the evening event at a fabric store, I immediately asked the store owner for space and a sewing machine to make samples. An employee and I cut and stitched like mad women. A crowd of one hundred fifty attendees would probably understand, but even so it would be a difficult two hours.

Just as the attendees were arriving, so did my luggage. The store clerk pressed the samples in my suitcases and I used a combination of new and old samples during my demo. This was also the experience that taught me to travel in clothes that would be acceptable to wear when presenting. No more blue jeans for travel.

Blitz

A blitz is when the defense rushes toward the quarterback with the intent of sacking and tackling him to the ground. The kind of blitz I experience is much more friendly and kinder than a football blitz, but it happens when I'm setting up for seminars and there is a rush toward the stage.

I understand that attendees want to get their books autographed. Most people commonly approach me by saying, "I don't want to bother you, but could you sign this for me now?" I always set aside time at the end of seminars for autographs and photos, so I ask if they'd mind waiting until later.

Interference

When a football player whose job is to catch the ball is excessively pushed, pulled, or manhandled while trying to catch the ball, the referee will call, or should call, interference. (Sometimes the foul is called on the offense, not only the defense, but I digress.)

If only I'd had a referee during a seminar in Florida! The sponsoring store had an open bar in the back of the lecture hall. That was both a positive and a negative. On the negative side, the group was distracted when fellow sewists and quilters waltzed in and out carrying various libations in fancy glassware. On the positive side, I got many more laughs than usual during my presentation. I'm not opposed to anyone enjoying a drink of choice, it is just that there is a time and place for everything!

Audible

Unlike teaching via television, when giving a lecture I can see the reactions of the audience. In person I can see when the proverbial light bulb turns on as individuals grasp my simplification of a once tricky or difficult technique. But often the flip side occurs, and I see only blank stares.

My mind immediately thinks audible. A coach on the sidelines usually tells a quarterback what play to run; the quarterback hears the coach over an earpiece in his helmet. But sometimes, the quarterback on the field changes the play based on what he sees and calls something different—that's an audible.

When I haven't described the process well enough, I have to change course, detailing the technique or process in a different way. An audible on a lecture stage is a great learning experience. I've learned how to clarify and breakdown sewing and quilting instructions. I generally don't quit explaining until I see the frowns disappear from faces, a luxury not afforded on a playing field.

Burn time off the clock

In the fourth quarter of a football game, the offensive side with the highest score generally tries to burn time off the clock, calling plays that eat up as much time as possible in order to keep the other team's offense off the field. The hope is, of course, that the game will end with the score in their favor.

That comparison really came to mind when I didn't read the seminar description before packing and traveling to an event in Ohio. I had thought that I was presenting two, one-hour seminars to different audiences and had packed accordingly. When I was introduced to the group, I'm sure I took on the look of a deer in headlights when the announcer said that she'd draw names for door prizes after the two-hour seminar.

Taking a deep breath, I began teaching and teach I did, giving one of the most thorough seminars in my life while purposely burning time off the clock. People later thanked me for the in-depth description of, for example, needles—which size to use when—and other techniques that

228

I would have discussed only briefly under normal conditions. That near fumble has prompted me to always double-check my itinerary and to pack a few extra samples—just in case.

A hero on and off the field

A number of years ago, I was in a connecting airport waiting to board an airplane to Birmingham, Alabama. Hungry, I ate an apple and waited until the last call to board. When it came, I threw away the apple core and arrived at the gate just behind a tall man. With gentlemanly courtesy, he stepped back and motioned for me to go first. I stood motionless for a second, smiled, and then proceeded to walk ahead of Bart Starr, Green Bay Packer quarterback from 1956 through 1971, and my childhood football hero.

While we were walking through the jet-way, I was tempted to stop and thank him for giving our family so many afternoons of enjoyment. I wanted to thank him, too, for setting an example of living an honorable lifestyle in a career where many are after fame and glory. Since he had been waiting in a corner of the gate area before boarding, I knew he preferred not to be bothered, so I continued to walk to coach class while he took a seat in first class. On the very unlikely chance that Mr. Starr is reading this book, may I extend the thank you that I wish I had said years ago.

Touchdown!

Interacting with my audience after finishing a seminar is like the joy of a touchdown. While there is no jumping in the stands or chest bumps, there is a great feeling of satisfaction knowing people have learned new skills and techniques.

Legendary Green Bay Packer coach Vince Lombardi is quoted as saying, "When you get in the end zone, act as if you've been there before." After more than three decades of receiving appreciation touchdowns, I have been in the end zone before—and for that I say, "Thank You" to my audiences.

Chapter 18

❦

When I was in college, one of my goals was to work for
a pattern company. I could envision my life in that role—see myself
studiously at work drafting patterns, confidently discussing the merits of
garment design around a conference table, striding along the streets of New
York in a garment I designed. But, the dreams of youth don't always come
true as envisioned. I had an interview with Simplicity my senior year in
college, but was not offered a position.

Irene James had been a colleague and friend for a long time. I first
met her in the early 1980s, when she and I were both Sew/Fit instructors,
freelance home economists who presented seminars around the country. We
also worked together briefly, developing a few products, called Sew•Paks,
which I later sold through Nancy's Notions.

Irene had faith in me and was eager for my success. She had a
connection within The McCall Pattern Company, known to most sewists as
simply McCall's. Irene's contact was Gail Hamilton, McCall's Vice-President
of Marketing. In 1989, with Irene paving the way through an introduction
to Gail, I made a proposal to McCall's. My proposal was to develop a series
of patterns modeled after my self-published book, *The Busy Woman's Sewing
Book*. By the time I made my proposal to McCall's, that book, published
first in 1984, had been printed and re-printed over and over and was still
selling thousands of copies.

The day I presented my proposal I was nervous and struggling to
not let the quaking show. I'm afraid that my less-than-confident walk along
the streets of New York that day was nothing like the dreams of childhood.
When I reached McCall's offices on Park Avenue and met Gail, her

business-like demeanor helped, but I still felt slightly intimidated being in that realm. As Eleanor Roosevelt is quoted as saying, "No one can make you feel inferior without your consent." I had consented.

The people I met around the conference table were corporate dressers, confident, articulate—they looked great. Somehow I made it through the presentation without embarrassing myself then I left the materials—designs for individual patterns for the Busy Woman's jacket, blouse, pants and skirt—with them and went on my way.

After I left, my proposal was taken for review to Bob Herman, the president of McCall's. He phoned me to say that they were interested in carrying my patterns, but that first he wanted to inform Pati Palmer who was also an independent pattern designer, a sewing teacher and partner in Palmer/Pletsch Company. Pati was big as a pattern designer with McCall's and they didn't want to risk their relationship with her. I waited, and then got the news—my patterns would be published by McCall's. Finally, I was working not *for*, but *with*, a pattern company.

In my initial proposal, I presented a design concept for the covers of the pattern envelopes. I turned to Laure Noe for help. Remember, that was in 1989 and Nancy's Notions had been designing catalogs on computer for only a year or so. Laure is a great graphic designer, but she had not yet made the leap to computer design. Everything she did was by paste-up method.

Laure went to work, using graph paper with a quarter-inch blue grid as the base for her paste-up. When McCall's sent a proof of the pattern for me to review before publication, that blue grid was still in the background. They thought it was a great design feature and were enthusiastic about its cutting-edge appearance. In reality, it was the opposite. We used it because we were unacquainted with technology.

Stitchers are often curious about how pattern concepts are presented. Here's a very quick explanation: In my work with McCall's, I presented design concepts. Those concepts were illustrated and included notations of design elements. Often a sample garment accompanied the proposal. Then, the McCall's team evaluated the design concepts based on past sales or current trends. If the design was accepted and the process moved forward, their team drafted the patterns, selected fabrics, and sewed garments for photography. On occasion my sewing studio was asked to stitch the garments. If that happened McCall's sent notes to say what lengths sleeves or hemlines should be to accommodate the long, lean models used by the fashion industry. After that, the patterns were sent to me for review. My staff and I made samples, taking photos of each step. Those photos later became the basis of computer-generated illustrations. Having those photos at hand also made my task of writing the instructions so much easier. My signature "Notes from Nancy"—found in all my sewing and quilting books—were added, along with "Timesaving Notions."

Sometimes when I attended meetings at McCall's, I left Beaver Dam around 3:00 a.m. and drove to Madison where I caught a 5:00 a.m. flight to New York. Our meetings were usually in the early afternoon and I caught a flight home that evening. I did that to save time and money. To be prepared for delays, I usually carried a few toiletries and personal items with me in the same travel case as my business materials.

I always wondered what I should wear to New York meetings with the McCall's staff. For those who sewed, they were, after all, the cream at the top of the fashion industry crop. I wanted to fit in. Shortly after I began working with McCall's, I selected a jacket that I thought appropriate for that day's meeting. That was the era when the actress Linda Evans was a fashion influence and my jacket, with its gold metallic threads, reflected that style. In the conference room at McCall's, though, the lead designer raised one eyebrow and asked, "Going to the theater?"

Oops! Instantly, I knew I was overdressed. He didn't seem to hold my naiveté against me, though, because much later he introduced me to his son at a trade show and said, "This is Nancy, one of the nicest people I know and I really enjoy working with her." And I felt the same in return.

The mechanics of a pattern company are fascinating. We often met in a merchandising room (I also heard it referred to as the "brain room") where the walls were lined with vertical—about six-foot-high— bulletin boards that swung on hinges like the super-sized pages of a book. McCall's pattern covers were tacked to the surfaces of those boards, sorted in categories by sales.

Nearby was a fabric library where current fabrics and trimmings were cataloged for reference. Of course there were also other rooms designated for drafting and grading, sewing areas, photography—in short, a fascinating place.

My meetings were generally attended by four vice-presidents: Gail Hamilton, Nancy DiCocco, Kathy Linn, and Sid Tepper, plus numerous other talented people. After my initial meeting with McCall's staff, all subsequent meetings began by reviewing sales of my line of patterns plus trends in the industry—a fascinating and educational experience. I gleaned ideas from Nancy DiCocco's marketing and analysis presentations and learned to critique Nancy's Notions' sales in a similar fashion.

There was one time, though, when I narrowly avoided embarrassment. We were in a conference room high above Park Avenue in New York, where expansive windows faced the skyline and the decision-makers of the fashion pattern industry were seated around the table.

Prior to every meeting with McCall's, my staff and I carefully prepared proposals for the designs I was submitting for consideration. There were six copies of each proposal; each included illustrations and suggestions, along with descriptions of what construction techniques I would show as part of the pattern instructions. I wanted everything to look highly professional and refined. But when I lifted the packet of proposals from the travel case that I'd carried from home that morning, a pair of panty hose came along for the ride. Quickly, I grabbed them, stood a little as I passed the proposals in my hand to the next person, and stuffed the panty hose beneath me as I sat down again. I hoped no one had noticed, and it seemed no one had. If they had, they graciously ignored my faux pas.

At first, I was intimidated by the McCall's staff, but soon began to feel their equal, which I was. They welcomed me into their fold and I will always be grateful.

Much has changed since McCall's first began carrying my patterns. All of the original people I worked with are gone now, but working with McCall's has been a nice ride. Sewing itself has changed.

Just recently a McCall's staff member told me that craft patterns have become their best sellers. For some time interest in home garment sewing has been dwindling. For that reason, I have taken some time off designing for McCall's, something I did another time as well.

My association with McCall's has been one of the most validating of my career. I couldn't figure out what Gail Hamilton first saw in me, but over the years she was my best cheerleader in that company. She took me under her wing in the beginning, paved the way for McCall's to sponsor *Sewing With Nancy*, appeared on television with me (most often for episodes on serging), opened doors for me within the sewing industry, and most importantly, became a valued friend.

To be sure, the dreams of youth don't always come true as envisioned. Instead my dream of an association with a pattern company became reality in much different packaging than I could have imagined. Different packaging, but dream-come-true—that's been the story of my whole life.

Over the years, I've lost count of how many books, booklets, and pamphlets bear my name. There are a lot.

The first was *The Sew/Fit Manual*, a four hundred sixty-eight-page tome of tips and time-saving techniques prepared under Sew/Fit founder, Ruth Oblander's, direction. Ruth, Doris Ekern (another Sew/Fit colleague) and I were listed as co-authors. We sold the books while giving Sew/Fit seminars across the country. The life of an author isn't as profitable as many believe—I had to purchase the books from Sew/Fit at the same price as non-authors bought them.

In 1982, I self-published *Slacks: "Pivot-Slide" Fitting Book with Pattern*, or rather Nancy's Notions published it—I was the only staff member back then. Over the next several years we reprinted that book numerous times. It was followed by *The Busy Woman's Sewing Book*, a volume that was co-published by Nancy's Notions and Open Chain Publishing. And so it began…

Transcripts of *Sewing With Nancy* could be considered books as well. Early on, Phyllis Winter worked with those, re-writing my television

Phyllis Winter

"Every few years Nancy wanted to revamp books to make them more valuable. The information in them was always very good. Whatever Nancy did was always very easy to understand. When we wrote directions we tried to make sure we had very good directions."

scripts into a narrative that presented that episode's instruction. Today Pat Hahn is the one who prepares books from *Sewing With Nancy* episodes.

Over the years those materials became more attractive. They went from being cheaply printed to being nice little books that can stand alone or as reference companions for *Sewing With Nancy* episodes sold through Nancy's Notions.

There is a book available for every *Sewing With Nancy* series. If there's a guest and that guest already has a book on the topic, we don't do one, but if they do not have a book, we generate one. In that case, the guest and I are listed as joint authors.

Pat Hahn attends *Sewing With Nancy* recording sessions with Donna Fenske and me. She sits in the control room, taking notes on a laptop computer while tapes roll. Later, Pat compares my script, the video from the episode, and her notes to prepare text for a twenty- to

Pat Hahn

(Colleague)

"My husband saw an ad in the Beaver Dam paper for a part-time writer and editor for Nancy's Notions. I applied and got the job, then went to full-time not long afterwards. That was twenty-four years ago."

twenty-four-page book on the topic. Topics that span two episodes are often combined into one. Since episodes are recorded long before they are aired, companion books are usually available by the time viewers see the program. If a book is generated, the royalties go to me and copies are sold by Nancy's Notions.

Pat is our grammar guru and over the years she and I have worked on many books together. She worked as a high school home economics teacher for several years and for more than forty years has led a sewing group in her local 4-H community.

I remember first teaching Pat how to write a book. That was in 1991 and we were working on *Let's Sew! A Beginner's Sewing Guide* that Nancy's Notions published. I had decided it was going to be ninety-six pages long (a number divisible by sixteen, the number of pages printed at one time on an offset printing press). Pat stood beside me while we worked on a conference table. I'm a visual person, so I divided the ninety-six pages into sections with each section representing a different aspect of the book's focus. Then I began allocating information to each section.

My method of preparing materials for books isn't something I was taught, but something that I adopted because it worked for me— block it out and lay it out. At my elbow, Pat watched as I cut and pasted, shuffled and re-positioned until the conference room table was filled with pages, at which point Pat exclaimed, "I get it now!" And she did. From that point on she was doing books like a pro.

Pat works with our artist, Laure Noe, who is a phenomenal sewing illustrator. Laure sews, and because of that has a greater understanding of how to design illustrations so the reader will understand. Laure began working with me on a freelance basis in 1983, long before computers entered the picture. When computers came along, at first Laure resisted going to computer-assisted design, but once she got the hang of it, she was unstoppable. She also finally agreed to come on staff with Nancy's Notions, leaving her freelance days behind.

Let's Sew! A Beginner's Sewing Guide was the last major book self-published by Nancy's Notions. In October of 1992, Oxmoor House published *10-20-30 Minutes to Sew*, a hardcover book with skyrocketing sales. All in all, I worked with Oxmoor House on the publication of twelve books, three of them co-authored with others.

Book royalties through Oxmoor House were significant money over the years. They were like having a bank account that we didn't have before. The first royalty check we used personally, the remaining payments were used to fund the expansion of Nancy's Notions building projects.

Krause Publications became my publishers in 2002 and our relationship continues to this day. Aside from books created as companions to *Sewing With Nancy* programs, I have authored and co-authored thirty-three books and re-prints of earlier books.

Rich Zieman

"When you're in business, most of learning is what you learn on the job, not in college."

Several years ago Rich and I were invited to address students in the business administration program at Virtebo University in LaCrosse, Wisconsin. Goal of the presentation was to give students who would face business decisions in their careers the opportunity to learn from us. We prepared a PowerPoint presentation to accompany our comments, and in the process of putting that together we finally defined some of our experiences—personal as well as business. We learned from ourselves.

In the dramatic growth years of Nancy's Notions we were so busy that there was little time for reflection. Time away from the business needed to be devoted solely to family and to rejuvenation—not business reflection.

With the clarity of hindsight, and keeping in mind the frenetic growth Nancy's Notions experienced during the 1990s and into the 2000s, here are some of the things we learned.

Know your customer

It wasn't always easy to determine what products Nancy's Notions should offer. In the beginning those decisions were mainly mine, but as the company grew I reached out to staff members for input. We came up with profiles of five imaginary women, each representing a distinct market. We named them after me, the Nancy in Nancy's Notions.

N – Nadine: a sewist who creates gifts for others

A – Amy: an embroiderer who likes to embellish garments, gifts and décor

N – Natalie: a garment sewist, the market I originally targeted as a freelance home economist

C – Connie: a quilter

Y – Yvonne: a die-hard sewist who enjoys all types of sewing, quilting and embroidering

Those names helped us determine which customers might use various products, and how we could further meet their needs. Were we heavily weighted toward Nadine's, for example? Were we meeting Connie's needs by providing enough products and inspiration for quilters?

The NANCY distinctions were applicable beyond products offered through the catalog, and later through on-line ordering. They impacted *Sewing With Nancy* programming, what we offered at trade and consumer shows, the content of seminars, considerations for books, and more.

Market to co-workers as well as you market to your customers

Chris Stam

"Nancy's Notions was a family-run business and we felt like part of the family. In return you try to make your family successful."

Most of the time people tend to think that customers are external to a business, those people who need to be courted into purchasing, mostly through advertising. But there is another category of customer that must be considered—employees.

Over the years we added many new staff members. Although some had college degrees, many did not. We were more interested in honesty, integrity and a willingness to learn than we were in impressive degrees. Many of those people remained with us for decades and are still with Nancy's Notions today. We learned from them, included them in decisions. By working side by side we got to know each other very well.

Without the support of a cooperative, enthusiastic staff Nancy's Notions would never have grown as it did. Rich and I learned early on to give our staff members the information they needed to perform their jobs. They knew if the company was making money—if their efforts were profitable—and they knew if something didn't work.

When an employee makes a mistake, they know. They don't need to be reminded, or punished. They need to be encouraged to continue growing in their job.

In the wake of being named Wisconsin Woman Entrepreneur of

the Year, Nancy's Notions ranked in the top fifty "Largest Women-Owned Businesses in Wisconsin," a list maintained by the Wisconsin Department of Development.

I was just the choir director—other people sang the music that got us recognition. Good employees are a company's greatest asset.

Value and react upon customer feedback

When we offered an "800" number for ordering and opened a call center, phone operators began fielding customer service issues. But for as long as there's been a Nancy's Notions, there has been customer service.

As the years have gone by we've received countless letters, calls, and e-mails from customers and viewers of *Sewing With Nancy*. I can honestly say that most communications are favorable, but for those who have a problem, we learned to get on it quickly. Situations not addressed are situations that fester.

Rich Zieman
"Many companies have paid time off separated into categories and require employees to take them according to set parameters. We decided to put all the days together and call them personal days."

To draw attention to new products in the catalog, we added a yellow "swish"—a colored highlight over the name of the product. (New! Magnetic Pincushion) One of our customers called us upset because, for Christmas, her husband had ordered every item that was highlighted in the Nancy's Notions catalog. He thought she had done the highlighting, and she in turn, didn't like her gift. We stood by our policy of one hundred percent satisfaction guaranteed, and the products were returned.

Care about your employees

Rich deserves a great deal of credit for designing employee benefits that were both flexible and fair. We didn't have a human resources director until the late 1990s, so those functions were under Rich's direction. He took a good look at vacation time, paid holidays and sick days. His philosophy was that adults know how to handle their time so he pooled paid time off into one category and let people take it when they needed it.

Although outwardly Rich's approach seems matter-of-fact, most staff members who came through the big growth years of Nancy's Notions see him as someone with a soft, family-oriented core.

Kathy Hasson Gittus

"Rich and Nancy made it possible for me to work half days at full pay for months. They even fed my dog."

In 1993, Kathy Hasson's husband was ill and for six months was hospitalized at the University of Wisconsin Hospital in Madison, fifty miles away. With a small child at home, Kathy soon became exhausted by traveling back and forth, trying to work full time and care for her child. Rich arranged a rotation of employees and friends to drive Kathy back and forth to Madison until her husband's death later that year. Several years later she re-married, becoming Kathy Hasson Gittus and we rejoiced with her at her wedding.

Value and implement employee ideas

As we grew and grew, and people moved from one position to another, some communications issues arose. They were mostly based in enthusiasm. Staff members wanted success so badly that they were eager to give input and hopeful that their suggestions would be taken seriously.

Have defined areas of responsibility and decision-making if you have a business partner

Dean Luedtke

"I believe a lot of the work ethic Nancy has came from our father. He was a man who believed in faith, family and a firm handshake."

Some of our staff members have told us that it was difficult to know which of us to go to for direction—me or Rich. I know that's true. When we worked together, it was not always pretty and we were always trying to determine where the lines of authority were. Determining who makes what decision is difficult, but I think Rich and I have both mellowed over the years.

If you're married to your business partner, leave your work at work

I often say that we had board meetings while brushing our teeth. Although Rich and I tried to make an agreement that we wouldn't bring work home, sometimes that was easier said than done.

But, there's a bigger reason than husband and wife not to do it. Children don't need to overhear heated board meetings.

Be prepared to and for change

When Nancy's Notions moved into the fourteen thousand square foot Beichl Avenue building in 1987, there were eighteen employees. By 1990, there were sixty, and the by end of the decade that number had topped one hundred twenty.

Along with growth came a corresponding need for more space. We added on to the Beichl Avenue building numerous times.

Scott Stanton
(Colleague)
"It was hard to keep up with growth— new people, new equipment, new computer systems and software. It was go, go, go! For a while, there were fifty percent increases in business every year."

1990: 20,000 square feet of warehouse and office space

1992: Addition of a new 2,500 square foot retail store

1993: Added 24,000 square feet to the warehouse and shipping area

1994: Interior remodeling and expansion of office areas and the retail store

1998: Addition of 15,000 square feet to the warehouse

2000: 17,000 square foot addition to the warehouse

2001: Additional 600 square feet to shipping area and seven thousand one hundred square feet to the retail store

By the end of our fourteenth year on Beichl Avenue, Nancy's Notions was filling over one hundred thousand square feet of space.

Two other bits of information that we passed on to young

entrepreneurs in training are self-explanatory: Be honest and truthful in all aspects of your business, and Trust in God—you'll sleep better at night.

Chapter 19

❧

Joan Woods

"One year Beaver Dam Lake was drained, probably to fix the dam. Ted and I were pirates, treasure hunters. We walked out on the dry lake bed and found spoons, cups and bottles. We did that a couple times before they filled up the lake again."

Ted Zieman

"The employees all just watched, hoping I wouldn't fall. They watched out for me and there was a lot of unproductive employee time because of me. John didn't like it. He kept telling me, 'No, no, no.'"

As Teddy grew and entered school, we dropped the name Teddy and began calling our firstborn by a more mature Ted.

The joy of our life, he was an active child. Joan Woods, who started caring for Ted part-time as an infant, was full-time by the time Nancy's Notions moved into the DeClark Street building. Joan often helped dispel Ted's abundant energy by taking him on walks, sometimes expanding his imagination along the way.

Joan was great with Ted and his childhood was enriched by her presence. It was also enriched by Earl and Elaine who spent a great deal of time with their grandson. He accompanied Earl and Rich on errands and he loved the Nancy's Notions warehouse. Early on, Ted discovered that climbing on the "stacks" (the tall industrial racks on which boxes of products were stored) was great fun. It was also dangerous, so the staff watched with some anxiety while he climbed.

We moved in 1987, from the Oneida Street house where bins for Nancy's Notions products had once lined the basement walls.

John Nickel

"As soon as Ted came into the warehouse he was a monkey at the top of racks and on top of boxes. He made me nervous."

Ted Zieman

"I remember our house being built—it seemed so big. Our first meal there, I remember, was chicken. The ceiling and walls were in, but the electrical work wasn't finished. My parents brought in white lanterns and I remember looking up at the ceiling and thinking it was so tall."

At the same time that a new building for the business was being constructed in a business park in Beaver Dam, our own home was being built just outside town. Rich was acting as general contractor on both projects.

The house on Oneida Street had only two bedrooms and we strained for space, especially when it also housed the business. Our new home was much more spacious— two-stories, three bedrooms, two and one-half baths with plenty of yard for an active boy like Ted to enjoy.

Joan came to take care of Ted when he was about six weeks old, and remained with us through our second child as well. At first, she didn't drive, and walked from her nearby home, but when we built a new house and moved, Joan learned how to drive.

Soon after moving to our new home, Doris Walter also joined the circle of our family.

With the schedule that Rich and I maintained in those years, we found it impossible to meet the demands of keeping a home clean and orderly. When we returned home at the end of a busy day, we wanted to spend time with each other and with Ted. For a while, we tried to keep up (people ought to be able to clean their own homes, right?), but finally we decided to get someone to clean.

Doris came to us on the recommendation of a friend. She worked on Tuesdays, giving our home the deep cleaning we had no time to perform. It was absolutely wonderful to walk in the door late Tuesday and see that things were in order and spotless. Between Joan and Doris, they gave me the ability to do what I do. Doris still comes on Tuesdays, and it

Rich Zieman

"For a while my parents owned some land along a lake near Shawano, Wisconsin, where they camped on occasion.

Soon after Nancy and I married, a huge summer storm blasted through that area and where there had been three thousand trees, only about two hundred remained standing. Since the storm had cleared the land, my parents had a small house erected on the property and spent a lot of years working on the landscaping. Nancy and I would go there, but when Ted was born, we didn't go as much as before. That was also when Nancy's Notions took off and it was hard to get away."

is still wonderful to come home that evening to a spotless home.

As a family we liked spending time together. We loved the outdoors, especially loved swimming and picnics, and enjoyed trips with just us, and with friends.

There was room for a pool at our new home, but we knew it would have to wait for the funds to build it. In 1991, I signed a contract with Oxmoor House for the publication of my book, *10-20-30 Minutes to Sew*. When a check arrived for an advance on book sales, Rich said, "There's the pool!" and we put it in. The pool and the porch of the pool house are our vacation cottage. Instead of driving to a getaway retreat, we walk a few steps out the back door.

Our back yard became a center of enjoyment for us, and a place where our children and their friends could hang out— under the watchful eyes of adults.

Ted's birth had been by emergency Caesarean section and my recovery was lengthy.

Our family did not feel complete; we wanted another child. Rich and I weren't the only ones—Ted was eager to be a big brother.

In the late 1980s, I had a miscarriage. Although it was an early pregnancy miscarriage, it was difficult, both physically and emotionally. That miscarriage was followed by another. After consulting with physicians, Rich and I considered adoption.

Through a friend we heard of Bethany Christian Services, a

reputable adoption organization that assisted American couples in adopting children from foreign countries. Especially vulnerable, we learned, were children born into some of the Far Eastern cultures. Our decision was not a snap decision, but the product of discussions and prayer that went on for years. In the end, we knew that sharing our lives with a child from a foreign country was the best direction for us.

We began the adoption process in 1989 and expected that most likely we would adopt a child born in South Korea. Adopting a child requires filling out forms, undergoing psychological tests, site visits by social workers trained to evaluate whether the home environment will be suitable, and more papers. Since Joan would be a caregiver for our adopted child, she was also interviewed. By the time we were through the process, I believe Bethany Christian Services may have known us better than we knew ourselves.

Then, at the end of December 1990, we were notified that the adoption program in South Korea was closing and it was highly unlikely a baby would be assigned to us. What disappointment! It seemed that all the evaluations, paperwork, anticipation and arrangements had been for nothing. In sadness I gave away all the baby equipment—bed, changing table, jumper chair and the baby clothes.

It was generally our custom to let the phone ring during dinner time, but one evening toward the end of April 1991, when it rang, I answered.

"Hello, Nancy, this is Julie, your social worker. Remember me?" she began. "A little boy was born in South Korea on February twenty-sixth. He's yours if you want him!"

Immediately I called to Rich to pick up our other phone. When Rich was on the line, Julie said that the little boy might have "Sun Downers Syndrome" as his head was large, a possible indication of disability. Julie said we'd be able to meet with her the next day—see a picture, review medical records, consult with our family doctor—and then make a decision.

Imagine our excitement. One minute we were eating grilled chicken, and the next we were learning a baby was waiting for us in South

Korea! What followed was an evening of calling our parents, talking to Ted about the baby, and thinking about the possibility that the baby was disabled. But, we decided, biological parents don't have a choice as to whether or not they will accept their child if it is born with a disability and we didn't want that choice either. Sight unseen, this little boy was ours and that was that.

The next night the three of us traveled to the offices of Bethany Christian Services in Waukesha, near Milwaukee. We were presented a folder for our review. Included was information on the baby's length, weight, head circumference, and there was one precious photo that showed the baby's hands and uncovered feet. In that photo, a card with a number—his identification number—was laid at his feet. It was the only photo of the first six months of his life. He had been given the name Jung Huh by an adoption worker at the offices of Holt International in Korea.

The next day we met with our family doctor. Dr. Bush studied the medical records and the photo which had been taken for the purpose of medical analysis. He paid special attention to Jung Huh's hands and feet. The baby's fingers and toes were long, but not webbed—something that might indicate health issues. Finally, Dr. Bush announced, "He just has a big head, that's all!" He smiled and said he couldn't wait to give him his first check up.

We were thrilled. Eight-year-old Ted was wildly excited and wanted his brother to be named Tom.

Rich and I solidified a plan that we had already discussed. Under the requirements of the adoption agency, one parent needed to be full-time for a period of three months after the child's arrival. Since Nancy's Notions was built around my presence on television and at seminars and public venues, Rich would be the

Ted Zieman

"I knew for a long time that I was going to have a brother and I remember going to the doctor for shots in case a baby came. I think the shots were because Tom was coming from Korea. I was at the airport when he arrived and was so happy to have a little brother. I loved him a lot and didn't resent him. I was instantly in love with my brother."

stay-at-home parent for the first several months after our son's arrival.

The months went by during which a conflict over production of *Sewing With Nancy* demanded my attention. Summer arrived, along with notification that our son would be arriving at Chicago's O'Hare Airport on August 17, 1991.

That was a Saturday, a beautiful summer day. In Beaver Dam, we packed the car with a car seat, baby bottles, outfits and other things we thought we'd need for a baby. Near Chicago, we met Gene and Viv Sekel, good friends who had been in our wedding. We went to lunch, but I was hardly able to eat.

In 1991, before the era of airport restrictions, we were able to meet the plane at the arrival gate, so the five of us made our way to Gate E9. We didn't know beforehand, but also, at the gate were two other families awaiting babies. The plane was delayed several hours; I paced up and down the concourse, and we waited and waited and finally the plane landed.

Impatiently we watched as it taxied to the gate and the jet way was positioned. It seemed to take much longer than usual for the completion of arrival arrangements, but finally people began deplaning.

I don't know why I expected our baby to be first off the plane, but that didn't happen. We looked with anticipation at every person who exited the jet way, but no one emerged carrying a baby. Finally a businessman on the flight walked to our group and asked if we were getting babies. When he learned we were, he said, "This is wonderful," and stayed with us to watch.

Someone, I don't recall who, cried, "Here come the babies!" and there they were—three babies carried by three escorts.

Expecting that the moment when we received our son would be as full of red tape as the adoption process had been, Rich and I were prepared with our adoption folders in hand. There was a social worker who validated who we were, but when the actual moment came, the woman carrying Tom simply announced, "This is the Zieman baby," and handed him to me. I could feel tears welling up, starting from my toes; it was the most glorious feeling ever.

The businessman was taking in the scene along with others who were also enjoying watching the transfer of babies. All three families receiving babies wanted to live in the moment, so with our children in our arms we remained together in the gate area for some time.

Tom arrived wrapped in a navy blue blanket. He wore a little Korean outfit and rubber shoes. We were handed a brown bag containing one baby bottle and a pamphlet about South Korea. A few minutes after his arrival, while we were snuggling him in our arms, a Northwest Airlines flight attendant approached and asked for the return of the navy blue blankets that belonged to the airline.

Tom was about six-months-old, when he arrived. We call that day Gotcha Day! and we celebrate it with as much enthusiasm as Tom's and Ted's birthdays. We thought we were prepared to videotape the event, but when Gene Sekel began taping, the battery was dead, left on accidentally while recording a little preamble video. So we have only about fifteen seconds that show the baby coming in the arms of the caregiver. The rest is wonderful memory.

We named him Thomas Jung Huh Zieman, using his Korean names as his middle name. Everyone calls him Tom.

Tom had been in transit for thirty hours and was quite groggy. Viv's parents lived near O'Hare Airport so we drove to their home where I gave Tom a bath in their bathroom sink and changed him. Their grandchildren were visiting that day and after Tom's bath we put him into a jumper seat and the children sat around him. Tom was amused!

Viv's mother made dinner for all of us, but I could hardly eat. Although I'd had a baby before, there's something vastly different about being handed a six-month-old child. I was overwhelmed with great excitement and also was concerned about taking care of a baby who wasn't a newborn, and who already had loved, and was loved, by another mom—a foster mother.

Beaver Dam was a three-hour trip from Chicago. Rich drove while Ted and I sat in the back seat with Tom between us. At one point I looked across Tom to Ted and there were big tears in his eyes. "This is the most wonderful day of my life," he said. That moment is so precious

"In the beginning with
Tom we used a lot
of sign language and
Tommy learned by
associating things. I
would point to myself
and say 'Joan.' He
couldn't say Joan and it
came out as 'Jo-Un.' It
is amazing how much
kids understand. Tom
was shy at first until
he was about a year
old, then he talked and
talked and talked."

Lois Kurtz

(Colleague)
"When they got
Tommy, Nancy was
so overworked and so
busy, but when Tommy
came through the door
she was a mom and
had the biggest smile
on her face. He could
jump onto her lap
and do whatever he
wanted on her desk.
That's the happiest
I ever saw her."

to me. Even though there are eight years of life
between Ted and Tom, they have been the best
buddies.

Tom slept much of the way back to
Beaver Dam from Chicago, waking to cry
only once, about ten miles from home. At
first he had his days and nights mixed up,
understandable for someone who had been
living on the other side of the world. That first
week all three of us stayed at home. Yet with
Tom's mixed up sleeping schedule, by the end
of the week I was so exhausted that I could
scarcely say my name. I took another week off.

There were adjustments. Ted had been
an only child for eight years, and suddenly
things were different in his home. A baby was
diverting our attention. Near the end of that
first week, he came into the house with some
friends and sat on the couch.

"Look Steve," I heard him say. "I've
had this sliver in my finger for three days and
my mother doesn't even care!" I did care and
promptly removed the sliver, but apparently
Ted was feeling just a little put upon.

One of the challenges in adopting
a foreign child is communication. Tom had
heard Korean all his life, so we used sign
language to bridge that divide. Even at six
months old children understand. He didn't
understand our words, plus his foster mom had
dark hair and eyes. I'm sure in his little mind
he was trying to figure out what in the world
had happened to him. In his early pictures, he
often looked bewildered, not sad, just as if he

were wondering, "Who are these people?"

After Tom's arrival, I made a decision not to travel as extensively as before. I cancelled appearances at a lot of events. To remind myself, I had a sign made that read, "Just Say No."

Lois Kurtz joined our staff in 1988 and was my secretary at that time. Often while I talked on the phone with someone who wanted me to make an appearance, Lois would be in the doorway mouthing, No.

Nancy's Notions was built around me. The business depended on sales and it was a huge risk to pull back from appearances. When I spoke at an event such as a trade show, people came back to our booth and purchased items. Even so, I began attending trade shows every other year instead of annually. Extended travels were dramatically shortened to no more than two or three days.

During the months that Rich was a stay-at-home parent he did a great job. We bonded as a family. Joan stopped by on occasion so Tom could become accustomed to her before Rich went back to work, but Rich was the lead parent during that period. It was then that Rich learned he really loves to cook and even after returning to work he frequently made meals.

All in all, I think our sons led very normal lives, with the exception of their mother being on television and traveling. I was home much more than I was gone; Rich was consistently there. We ate meals together and talked. For many years Earl and Elaine ate evening meals with us as well and ours was an extended family.

Sometimes I wondered: Is this the way I should be a mother—having someone come

Tom Zieman
(Son)

"I've known since very young that people recognized my mother because of the TV show. But when people recognized my mom when I was with her, it never seemed important to her, and therefore it was not important to me. She didn't expect to be treated differently even in Beaver Dam. I am impressed by her grace and humility. When people in Beaver Dam refer to her they usually connect her with something she's done as an act of service, like visiting them when they were in the hospital."

into my home, taking care of my children? Should I be flying off to work? But, I didn't plan on the life I had, and didn't strive for it. An opportunity simply presented itself and I took it.

I remember calling home once from a public appearance trip and having Ted tell me, "Mommy, come home. I miss you," then sobbing into the phone. Then he handed the phone to Rich and went off to play.

Rich assured me, "Ted is fine; he's playing with the neighbor." Meanwhile, I was crying on the other end of the phone line. Ted knew how to play me, which generally assured him that I would bring him a treat upon my return.

Ted and Tom grew up to be great guys. I am proud of them—very proud. Do I regret not spending more time with them? You bet!

Rich and I were from different Christian backgrounds—I had grown up in a conservative Lutheran church, he had been raised Presbyterian. Before our marriage, unless we were visiting our respective families, we didn't attend church together. When we moved to Beaver Dam, we settled on Peace Lutheran Church. Rich began singing in the choir, and when Ted was three years old, I started teaching third grade Sunday school. I enjoyed working with the children and almost three decades later, still do.

Attending church on Sunday was not an option. Even while on family trips we tried to find a church to attend. Church, and the spiritual needs it filled, became the footings of our family's foundation.

Holidays have always been fun and important for us as a family. The Fourth of July is an opportunity for a pool party, as are

Tom Zieman
"When I was little and company came, my parents would make me stand and say hello to our guests."

Doris Walter
(Cleaning Lady)
"There is a Bible in the house that is visible. I work mostly for Christian people, but a Bible is sometimes hard to find, and I'm the cleaning lady. I dust places most people don't see. Not only is their Bible visible, but it looks as though it is used."

Memorial Day and Labor Day. New Year's isn't as predictable as other holidays, but we always enjoy spending time together.

Barbara Luedtke Eckstein

"Oyster stew at Christmas was a German tradition. Nancy likes it pretty well. It came from both sides of the family—maybe it was Norwegian."

John Luedtke

"Oyster stew is mandatory. It's a Northern Norwegian heritage and we had to have oyster stew during Christmas. Mother would get cans of oysters and then she would be cooking that oyster stew on the stove mixed with milk, butter, and oysters. One Christmas, she forgot to put in the liquid from the can and it didn't taste very good. I make oyster stew now."

Thanksgiving is also spent with family, along with a feast centered on a turkey.

Easter is church-centered and usually we're up early for a sunrise service.

Christmas, though—Christmas is all about family tradition. When I was a child on Christmas Eve, we'd attend church for a children's service. Since we were in a farming community, that service was held at 8:00 p.m. to avoid interfering with milking. Sometimes we didn't eat until close to 10:00 p.m.

The traditional Christmas Eve meal in my family was centered on oyster stew. My mother made it early Christmas Eve day and warmed it when we returned from church that evening.

Christmas Eve, still today, belongs to immediate family. On Christmas Day we get together with a wider circle of family to exchange gifts and share a meal.

I use my mother's recipe for oyster stew, handed down through several generations.

❧

Oyster Stew

Three cans of oysters or a quart of fresh oysters
½ stick of butter
½ gallon of milk
Salt and pepper

Christmas Eve morning, in a Dutch oven or

Gina Luedtke Crispell

"I hated that oyster stew! It was fishy and buttery. The next day we had ham—that was better."

Ted Zieman

"We always have oyster stew on Christmas Eve. I didn't like it at first, but I grew to like it a lot. I think it was from Dad's side and Mom just carried it on. Mom's rule is that you must take at least one 'polite bite' whether you like it or not. When Ali [my wife] first spent a Christmas with my family, I told her she had to take a 'polite bite.' 'You've just got to try a little,' I told her."

soup kettle, melt the butter, add oysters plus the juice. Heat through on stovetop until mixture comes to a gentle boil. Add 1 tsp. salt and ½ tsp. pepper.

Lower temperature on the stovetop, gradually add the milk. Heat mixture just prior to boiling. Taste test to see if additional seasoning is needed.

Remove kettle from the stovetop, cover, and let the mixture rest at room temperature until cool. Refrigerate. (Generally my refrigerator is filled to the brim on Christmas, so living in the upper Midwest, I use Mother Nature's cooler and set the kettle outside (providing the temperature is below 38° F.) Serve hot (don't boil) and top with oyster crackers as part of the Christmas Eve meal.

⁓

We have wonderful friends. Rich knew Gene Sekel as a child. They went to college together, and Gene rented a room from Rich in the house he owned while working for Minnesota Fabrics. Jeff Trader was a college buddy who also rented from Rich. When Gene began dating Viv, I embraced her as a friend. She and Gene were in our wedding. Jeff was also in our wedding and when he married Patty, she joined the circle.

When we lived in our first home in Beaver Dam, a couple moved in next door—Sarah and Roger Hasbrouck—and they became close friends as well. Over the years Rich and I have spent many, many

Tom Zieman

"We always had oyster stew on Christmas Eve; it comes from my Mom's side of the family—no idea why. I guess I've gotten used to it over the years. Maybe ten years ago, Grandpa [Zieman] was eating his oyster stew and he looked up and said, 'Y'know, I'm really beginning to like this.' I couldn't believe he had eaten this forever and really didn't like it!"

enjoyable days in their company. When our children were young, we took family trips together. On getaways without the children, Rich and I have also traveled with the Traders and Sekels, thoroughly enjoying new places and new experiences.

Every summer we tried to take a family trip, often in the company of friends and their children. Once we took a two-week trip to Yellowstone, and there were car trips to Nashville and Louisville as well. We also did weekends in Wisconsin's beautiful Door County every year, staying at an old-fashioned, not-too-fancy lodge with another family. The kids, theirs and ours, played ping pong and shuffle board between just running around.

For the most part our family was normal. I loved reading to my children—it was one of the joys of my life, and still is now that I have granddaughters. Once Ted was in school—and later Tom as well—evenings revolved around homework.

The boys were involved in soccer, baseball, Boy Scouts, and church activities. Rich and I attended football games and baseball games when Ted played, and softball games for both boys. They played catch and

Joan Woods

"I paid attention to what Rich and Nancy expected. They liked manners—saying 'Please' and 'Thank you' and 'You're welcome.' I did, too."

ball in the yard and Rich took them skiing and sledding—guy things. When they were little, we baked a lot together—cookies mostly.

When Rich and I were gone at the same time, Joan usually came to stay with the boys.

As Ted and Tom grew, they each found their own direction.

In high school, Ted attended Wayland Academy in Beaver Dam, an old, private

Tom Zieman

"My dad's parenting style was very example based. He was a good role model. I certainly knew when I was in the wrong, but so did he. We had discussions—it wasn't just black or white with Dad, there was some latitude. I never wanted to let my parents down. I knew they were good, upstanding people with good expectations. But they were very loving, and if we had a disagreement, the next day was a new day."

Sarah Hasbrouck

(Friend)

"Nancy is a wonderful mother. She connects cooking and baking with motherhood and I've seen her pack up strawberry and banana bread for Tom to take to college."

academy where small classes and one-on-one instructor attention fit his learning style. Tom, more outgoing in his ways, chose to attend Beaver Dam High School where he thrived.

Ted played baseball, golf and soccer. He was on the ski team as well. For a while he had a summer and after-school job in the warehouse at Nancy's Notions, then later got a summer job as a lifeguard.

The boys and their friends hung around our pool a lot. We tried to keep pizzas and snacks on hand and were always happy for their friends to be where we knew they were supervised.

As in business together, Rich and I had somewhat different parenting styles. We did, however, agree that we wanted our sons to be well-behaved, responsible and courteous.

In connection with discipline, I stumbled onto something with Ted. I had been wondering how I could discipline him and make an impact. So when he did something wrong, I asked, "What do you think should be your punishment?" Ted's suggestion was always more severe than I would have given. "Take my computer keyboard away for two weeks," he suggested one time. Handling things in that manner was the smartest thing I ever did as a disciplinarian with both children.

Tom was sick a lot as a child. Perhaps his little body had no immunity to America's "bugs."

As a child if I was sick my mother would sleep at the end of my bed. I did that for the boys, probably more than I should have. "Just sleep there till I go to sleep," Tom would say, and I would lie crosswise on the bed and pat his knee. Then, of course, I would fall asleep.

When one of the boys was sick on a work day, Joan would usually care for them. I am so thankful to Joan for pouring her love and concern into our children.

In 1995, the State of Wisconsin widened the highway fronting Earl and Elaine's farm, taking it from two lanes to four. The new road cut the farm in half and meant that their home would need to be torn down or moved. Earl sold the farm building site to the state and began building a new home near ours, in the same subdivision.

As a point of interest, the large farmhouse where Rich grew up was purchased from the state and the new owner moved it farther back from the road. The chicken house that had served a short time as warehouse for Nancy's Notions was cut in half and the side nearest the road was demolished. The other half remains.

By the time of the farm sale Elaine was showing the early signs of Alzheimer's disease.

Earl and Elaine ate with us six nights a week for almost three years. It was a way for Earl to cope with Elaine's illness. There were many crazy meals with the issues of a teenager, those of a grammar school-aged child, a person with Alzheimer's, and three other adults. Some meal times were absolutely chaotic, but we made it a point to always sit down, eat together, and share the happenings of the day.

Rich's sister, Mary Jo Zieman Check, who lived in Denver, had been diagnosed with leukemia in 1990. Before that time Mary Jo, an extremely intelligent woman who was bored with college as a teen, had worked for an oil company. When her health robbed her

Earl Zieman

"Mary Jo had leukemia and died when she was 49 years old.

Mary Jo's death accelerated my wife's Alzheimer's disease, making it worse than before. Elaine was lost when we moved to the new house. She couldn't find the bathroom."

Alison (Ali) Zieman

(Daughter-in-law)
"I didn't know of the Zieman family before I met Ted. It was funny because when I told my mom I was dating Ted and that his mother had a sewing show, she said, 'Nancy Zieman! I've been watching her for years and I have some of her books.' She pulled out some of her sewing books and she found pictures of Ted as a boy. My mom's a big sewer."

Earl Zieman

"My grandkids are two great kids. Tom just had his twenty-first birthday and Ted's daughters are so pretty."

of strength, she went back to college to finish her degree and then went on to graduate from law school. Leukemia claimed her life in July of 1996.

Sometimes I think that Elaine almost willed herself ill because she didn't want her daughter to die before her. Although Elaine's mind left her, her body survived her daughter's.

That was a difficult time, especially for Rich and Earl. For a time before Elaine needed more care than could be provided at home, she and Earl came to our home for evening meals. Tom especially enjoyed Elaine, sitting on her lap for long stretches. Elaine died in 1999.

My father died two years before Elaine following a long battle with cancer. I was born on Father's Day and he died on June 21, 1997, my forty-fourth birthday. I drew from his strength as a child and found my way in his example of hard work and integrity. I'd like to think that I am like him.

Earl was a continuing presence in our lives and at family events for many more years. As of this writing, Earl has been gone five months. He lived long enough to be interviewed for this book, but he slipped away peacefully on February 5, 2013—his ninety-fourth birthday.

They are all missed.

Several years after my father died, my mother married Warren Eckstein, a widower who had known my father and had, in fact, graduated with him from tiny Winneconne High School. Mom and Warren continue to live in the home where I grew up.

Joan Woods

"I don't think the boys suffered because Rich and Nancy were gone frequently. When they were together their time was quality. Sometimes it bothered Nancy that she couldn't be there as much as she wanted, but the boys were nurtured."

Ted Zieman

"There were some conflicts between my parents over business— arguments they should have in the board room that happened at home, but there was nothing that scarred me. It benefited me because I got to hear how it is sometimes. Ali and I want to try not to talk too much business at home around the table. It's just business; leave work at work if you can."

The Luedtke Farm has now been in our family some one hundred fifty-seven years, making it one of the longest family-owned farming operations in Wisconsin. Today my brother, Dean, and my cousin, Rick Luedtke, are partners in farming.

The farm stopped being a dairy operation in 1994, a few years before my father died. Today, Dean and Rick custom raise calves for dairy herds. Instead of milking twice daily, they work with two large dairies, taking their newborn calves and raising them until they are installed in a milking herd—a process that takes about two years. They have about six hundred cattle on the farm and have added new buildings to shelter them.

Ted and Tom have moved on with their lives. Ted attended St. Norbert College in DePere, Wisconsin, graduating with a degree in business.

On April 8, 2006, Ted married Alison a lovely young woman he met in college. Tom was best man at their wedding. Ted honored our request that both Rich and I would walk him down the aisle. I still get a lump in my throat remembering the moment.

Ali and Ted have given us two beautiful granddaughters—Avery, born in September 2009 and Luella, born in October of 2011. My granddaughters add a new dimension to my life and I savor the time I spend with them. There is a reason they're called grandchildren. It's a grand feeling, when they squeal with delight when they see me or

Tom Zieman

"I always knew that I wanted to join the military. There were a lot of factors, but one is that being adopted, I have had a lot of opportunities I would not have had in South Korea and I want to defend those. Also my grandfather was a veteran; he and I have a special connection."

Gina Luedtke Crispell

"Nancy was able to be a good mom and a successful business woman. Everybody has regrets, but I don't see her having too many of them."

hug me around my neck and say, "Grandma, I love you so much!"

After Ted and Ali had Avery, Ted—only half kidding—asked Joan Woods if she would move to Green Bay and take care of their children. She didn't go, but there is a strong bond between Joan and Ted and I am glad.

Ted and Rich work together in business. Ted's family lives near Green Bay; recently Ali and Ted began working together, at about the same ages that Rich and I were when we began doing the same.

Tom attended the University of Minnesota in Minneapolis where he earned a degree in Sociology of Law, Criminology and Deviance. He's also a US Marine Corps Reservist who, while on reserve duty, serves as a military police officer.

Tom was recently engaged to be married to Katelyn, a woman he met at college. They're planning a wedding in 2014. Her family is from Appleton, Wisconsin, and that's where Tom is working in his new job as police officer for the city. We couldn't be more proud of him and are thrilled to soon have a new "daughter."

Several years ago now, Rich, Tom, and I took a trip to South Korea with a group of adoptive families whose children had been born in that country. We were able to meet the foster mother who cared for Tom as an infant, an emotional experience for me.

Tom is a true-blue American and feels an association, but no strong ties, to his birth country. Still, for me there was something poignant about visiting there. His mother's decision to place him for adoption forever changed our lives, and changed Tom's as well.

We are all products of decisions and we are heirs to the actions of those before us. In moments of reflection I consider myself blessed.

Chapter 20

From its title, *Sewing With Nancy* may seem to be all about—well—sewing! In reality, though, traditional sewing is only a portion of the fabric-focused topics we cover. Although in the beginning garment sewing was the mainstay of the program, today it represents only about thirty percent of our programming. Now, serging and embroidery account for approximately twenty percent of annual episodes while quilting and quilting projects account for between forty and fifty percent. Occasionally, episodes on embellishments are thrown in for spice.

A line-up of twenty-six episodes makes a season; most episodes are broadcast twice, thus completing a full fifty-two week year. It seems that every year, as preparations begin for the next season, I wonder if I can fill another twenty-six episodes, but we always do. Sewing, quilting, embroidery and serging interests are ever shifting and new techniques and innovations keep interest alive.

Laurie Gorman
(Director)
"Nancy has a loyal fan base. Now and then she'll ask me 'Is this still working?' *Sewing With Nancy* is in the top ten programs streaming online. *Sewing With Nancy* will last as long as Nancy wants it to last."

I'm often asked how I select topics for the program. There's no rocket science to that answer—if something interests me, I believe viewers will find it interesting as well. To that end, I try to keep in touch with what's happening out there. That means keeping in touch both with viewers who are the people who sew, quilt, and embroider as well as the innovators who lead the way to change in those realms. Keeping in touch means meeting and talking with them through guest appearances, events, social media—however possible.

It continually amazes me that viewers regard *Sewing With Nancy* as more than an educational program. They see me as a friend and I am honored at the affection I receive. People take from *Sewing With Nancy* what they need. If they need companionship, that's what they take. If they desire a connection to the past, that's what they get. If they need encouragement, we're all about encouraging.

When *Sewing With Nancy* was first broadcast over the Satellite Program Network, it was available to about three million households, a very small number when considering the population of the country. Today all Public Broadcasting System stations have access to *Sewing With Nancy*; however, not all stations choose to air the show. Yet, ninety percent of the total PBS markets in the nation air the program either full- or part-time.

Today, *Sewing With Nancy* shows are also available online. Fifty-two of the most current shows can be watched via computer 24/7 at www.nancyzieman.com. This new viewing option is experiencing exponential growth.

I'm probably more surprised than anyone else about those figures. When considering career choices as a young woman, it was never on my radar screen to have a television program. I was the girl with the crooked face. I am not normal television material.

But, I'm getting ahead of my story…

People are curious about what happens behind the scenes at *Sewing With Nancy*. Underlying that question is a curiosity to know what it is like in the recording studio and in preparations for recording. But, something occurred far behind the scenes in 1990 that threatened the very existence of *Sewing With Nancy*.

As the 1980s came to an end, *Sewing With Nancy* had been airing on PBS stations for about two years and we were in fifty percent of the PBS markets in the nation. The Satellite Program Network had gone out of business and Tempo TV, another cable network that aired *Sewing With Nancy*, was purchased by the Discovery Channel. Overnight, the weekly costs of being on Tempo jumped from five hundred dollars to eleven thousand dollars and we withdrew. We were still on ABC affiliate stations throughout Wisconsin, but increasingly I was seeing PBS as the exclusive home of *Sewing With Nancy*.

To position *Sewing With Nancy* for increasing viewership on PBS, I knew that association with a public television production studio would give the program a virtual "Seal of Approval." There are many guidelines that public television programs must follow. If I had a director with a pulse on those rules, I believed that other stations would give our show a second look if they hadn't already added *Sewing With Nancy* to their lineup.

For those who may not know, PBS is a non-profit organization with over three hundred fifty member television stations nationwide. Its programming seeks to educate viewers and provide quality, commercial-free entertainment. Funding for public television stations is viewer supported through donations, through grantors who support programs, and an ever-dwindling amount of tax based support.

Because we were already on PBS it made sense to have the backing of a PBS station, so in 1990, I approached Wisconsin Public Television and made arrangements to move production of *Sewing With Nancy* to their studios located at the University of Wisconsin–Madison.

I had been with WKOW for seven years and crew members there were friends. The director and staff helped *Sewing With Nancy* grow, but we all knew that our growth was limited at that studio. A new general manager was hired halfway through my tenure at WKOW. He was an elusive man and even though I was paying the studio a substantial production fee, we never met.

We had a solid core of underwriters. Pfaff had been a faithful underwriter for many years. McCall's had come on as a sponsor of *Sewing With Nancy* in 1986 as part of a licensing agreement for my line of Busy Woman's Sewing Patterns. Gingher Scissors and Pellon Interfacings were also sponsors.

The move to Wisconsin Public Television gave us a bigger set, plus a production facility and crew with plenty of experience in producing quality programming. A new set was designed and everything was in order. Recording went well. I was excited with the results and felt we had a new home. After recording our first several *Sewing With Nancy* episodes at Wisconsin Public Television, the general manager of our previous

267

production studio, WKOW, filed a complaint claiming that Wisconsin Public Television was unfairly competing with the private sector in producing the program.

WKOW's complaint was directed to the University of Wisconsin's Board of Regents that maintains legal authority over Wisconsin Public Television. Initially, a committee of the Board of Regents investigated the complaint and determined that no such unfair competition existed. But, when the matter came to a vote, the regents reversed their own committee's recommendation and my contract with Wisconsin Public Television was cancelled.

What followed was more than two years of legal wrangling, expense, uncertainty, inconvenience and political maneuverings. Instead of moving production to a better production studio nearer and more convenient at Wisconsin Public Television, I had to move it farther away, to Milwaukee to a studio where I was not happy with the production quality.

Appointments to the University of Wisconsin's Board of Regents are political appointments. My desire to move production to Wisconsin Public Television was rejected by that group, not on the basis of legalities, but because of political concerns. There was no way to fight it. At first I tried to push back, but got nowhere. The more I tried to press through, the more anxiety and frustration I felt and the more legal fees mounted. So finally, I let go and a semblance of peace returned. It was still inconvenient to make a longer trip to receive lower-quality production, but I could sleep at night.

In December of 1993, new members of the Board of Regents replaced departing members whose terms were ending. The matter was presented to the regents again, and they voted to honor a contract for the production of *Sewing With Nancy* at Wisconsin Public Television. Under the new contract Wisconsin

Note

Since Wisconsin Public Television is now a co-producer of *Sewing With Nancy*, at the beginning and end of each episode an announcer says: "*Sewing With Nancy* is a co-production of Nancy Zieman Productions and Wisconsin Public Television."

Public Television is a co-producer of *Sewing With Nancy* and I could not be happier!

While the conflict was underway and correspondence flew back and forth between lawyers, *Sewing With Nancy* celebrated ten years on television by producing a sixteen-month calendar. Each month featured a video topic with coupons for Nancy's Notions products. Viewers of *Sewing With Nancy* were oblivious to what was going on in the background.

But after the Board of Regents' decision that allowed our return, when we walked back in the studios of Wisconsin Public Television, I felt like crying with joy.

Plans for each episode begin months, and sometimes even a year, before recording. I'm constantly on the lookout for good program ideas and the concept for a program is fleshed out over a period of time. But when it comes down to an actual episode, I write a script and we work from it.

Every episode has both a number and a title. The number is primarily for use by PBS and is a reflection of where that episode is in the sequence of all episodes of *Sewing With Nancy*. The title, however, is a brief description of what the topic will cover. At least it should be brief, along with being interesting and descriptive. After I titled one two-part series *Fitting the Bodice with Pivot and Slide Techniques,* my colleagues Donna Fenske and Pat Hahn yawned, then they rebelled. We now collaborate on titles, referring to our good-natured competitiveness as "Name That Tune."

That script is a map of the episode, divided into segments of minutes and seconds. Actual content for each episode of *Sewing With Nancy* aired on PBS stations or through online streaming is twenty-six minutes, forty-six seconds long. The remaining three minutes and fourteen seconds is allocated to local grantors and for transitions between programming to announce things like upcoming programs. Tucked into the twenty-six minutes, forty-six seconds of content is one minute and thirty seconds that is allocated for grantor or sponsor recognition. By contrast, half hour programs on commercial television contain about twelve minutes of commercial time. So, think of it this way: If *Sewing With Nancy* were on commercial television, our actual program time would be shorter and we would have less content. Ya gotta love public television!

My greeting and introduction of that episode's topic are allotted forty-five seconds during which I also introduce any guest who may be with me. I think you get the idea—each episode of *Sewing With Nancy* is carefully timed. Unless something is being broadcast live, in television there is no such thing as running long or ending short. Precise timing is critical. Sure, I can go over on time or under on time on a segment, but the very last segment must end as the floor manager gives me a "ten count" hand signal—10-9-8-7- . . . 2-1. I must end with his motion of a closed fist, the signal signifying my time is up.

Sewing With Nancy, I always say, should actually be called *Sewing With Donna, Kate, Pat, Laure, Diane, Erica, Diane, Lois and Deanna.* I may be the one hosting the program, but I have a support staff of highly experienced people who make it possible.

Donna Fenske has been part of *Sewing With Nancy* since she joined the Nancy's Notions staff in 1984. An excellent sewist with a creative and logical mind, Donna creates many of the step-by-step samples used on the program. She is present at the planning and recording sessions and makes certain that all materials are ready to go and are arranged in the sequence in which they will be used. Between "takes" (the actual recording) Donna prepares the set for the next segment. Common to many like-mind individuals, Donna and I frequently don't need to verbalize what we're thinking. A smile or glance at each other will signify what's needed—perhaps an extra sample, more details, or to scrub (eliminate) a technique or project. Donna is my much-needed and valued extra right hand.

Each mini-series is planned up to three months in advance. Yet there are times, when it is a three-week push to get prepared. Some series come together easily, others can be a challenge. The day before recording, we meet in my offices to go over the specifics of what will happen the next day. A copy of the script is passed around the conference table. If a guest is appearing on that episode, they are part of that meeting. Step-by-step samples are reviewed and tweaked if necessary. We discuss camera angles and go through everything that will happen while tapes roll. We compare samples and identify potential problems. You might say it is a step-by-step process that leads to step-by-step instruction.

Before a guest appears on *Sewing With Nancy*, I ask them to select garments in solid colors to wear on camera and to avoid prints which may not be as pleasing to the camera as are solids. I tell them that blue, green, purple, pink and yellow are TV-friendly colors, but I leave it to a guest to decide what, specifically, to wear. Years ago black and white were out; now things have changed, but I stick to medium tones for jackets, blouses and scarves because they are pleasant on camera. I have enough solids in my wardrobe that I can usually mix and match with whatever the guest selects. As a base, I often wear black slacks and possibly a black shell beneath a jacket, sweater or blouse. If possible, I wear something constructed as part of that episode's topic.

While we're on the subject of clothes, let me add that I do most of my wardrobe shopping online. While traveling, occasionally I'll do some shopping, and I have a friend that I enjoy shopping with, but I'm easily overwhelmed by options and have to be in the right mood. I'm tall, but not dainty, and outlandish styles don't fit with my personality or body type, so I stick with garments that are classic in design.

Also, I do my own nails. There was a time when I had my nails professionally done, but making and taking time for manicure appointments during a recording week are not generally high priority. Viewers also used to ask me what color nail polish I was wearing, and I decided to take the focus off my fingernails and back onto the subject matter by using clear nail polish.

On recording days Donna Fenske, Pat Hahn and I—joined by a

guest if one is scheduled for that program—make the trip to the studios of Wisconsin Public Television. Pat is a writer and editor. She is the one who monitors a teleprompter to help me stay on track while filming. She is also responsible for creating a small book from that episode if one is needed.

I'm somewhat tense on recording days (I prefer to call it focused). At home, while going through my morning routines, I'm thinking about what is to come. On recording days there is one routine that I skip: I don't apply makeup before leaving home—that will happen at the studio. So, not only am I focused elsewhere, but I don't look very good either.

I meet Pat and Donna at Nancy's Notions around 7:00 a.m. and together we load everything needed for that day's recording into our vehicle. Donna usually drives, giving me additional quiet time to review the scripts.

Our loading scene became the source of one of our favorite anecdotes about *Sewing With Nancy* production. The topic of a two-part series was bridal wear and we were transporting several wedding gowns plus the supplies, samples and notions needed for one of the episodes.

At Nancy's Notions we loaded everything into the back of our van and headed out. But just a couple minutes later, at a sharp curve in the road, the hatchback on the van swung open and everything spilled across the road.

There was a collective shriek from all of us and Donna quickly braked and pulled to the side of the road. Pat and I were out and running before we stopped. We went for the gowns first, stooping and grabbing. Fortunately they were protected in garment bags, and the roads were dry and clear. We laid them carefully in the van and went back for the notions and supplies.

Aside from the adrenalin rush caused by our panic, things could have been so much worse. We were blessed that day with good weather and dry conditions. The biggest challenge facing Donna and Pat was to put the samples and materials needed for that day's recording back into the order in which they would be needed—something that took considerable time.

A few days later, when once again driving past that spot on the road, something caught my eye and I stopped to pick up a spool of thread we had missed. Then I found a button farther on. A few sequins glittered in the grass where they twinkled as motorists passed.

Ever since that day we have double checked that doors are latched and locked before we leave Nancy's Notions—and ever since that day we have referred to our adventure as The Runaway Bride.

If that story carries the overtones of romantic comedy, there is another that does as well.

One day a package arrived in the mail containing a romance novel. On the cover of *Keeper* by Patricia Gardner Evans (Silhouette 1994) was the image of a shirtless, well-muscled, and handsome young man—a hunk!

A sticky note inserted into the pages simply said: "You might want to check out page 171."

I turned to the page and read:

"What else did you do today besides doodle?"
He'd caught just a glimpse of the "doodle," L. J. in a skimpy hospital gown.

She wrinkled her nose. "Mostly slept and watched TV. The highlight of my day was learning how to do pin tucking on "*Sewing With Nancy*!" She shook her head gravely, "It was pretty much downhill after that…"

What can I add to that; *Sewing With Nancy* had finally become the stuff of romantic legend.

Over the years on recording days we've traveled through tornado warnings, rain storms, hail, ice storms, blizzards and only once has our recording day been postponed due to weather conditions. Wisconsin has a capricious climate, and Wisconsinites are a tough breed—we make it through.

As a case in point, Philip Pepper arrived from Texas for a guest appearance on *Sewing With Nancy*, emerging from the airplane into Wisconsin's sub-zero winter wearing light clothes. He had no coat, no winter boots and no cash.

He was dropped off at a local hotel where our guests usually stay. A blizzard was brewing when he arrived, and before we could have our pre-production meeting, it hit with such force that everything shut down— schools and businesses closed, roads became impassable, and restaurants that made deliveries simply weren't. The hotel had no restaurant and poor Philip was stranded, unable to go anywhere, and without even a few coins for the hotel's vending machine.

Clearly he had never experienced anything like what faced him in Wisconsin. Beaver Dam got seventeen inches of snow in that storm.

Laurie Gorman

"Wisconsin Public Television has been producing *Sewing With Nancy* for twenty-two years. In that time Nancy's seen a lot of faces come and go, but she goes out of her way to know everyone."

When we finally collected Philip, fed him, and were on our way to Madison for our recording session, he started asking, "Are we there yet?" when we were barely five miles down the slippery, snow-covered highway leading into the city, fifty miles away.

On recording days, awaiting us at the studios of Wisconsin Public Television is a production crew that includes my director, Laurie Gorman, an incredibly capable woman with a wacky sense of humor. Joining Laurie in the control room is a crew that includes a lighting designer who monitors to make certain light levels are at their best, a technical director who switches cameras as tapes roll, an assistant director who keeps track of timing using script notes; an audio engineer who monitors sound; a tape engineer who makes certain everything is recording and a video engineer entrusted with the final product.

In the studio are three camera operators and a floor manager who serves as the communications link between me and Laurie in the control room.

While Donna and Pat lay out materials for the program, press stray wrinkles, and assemble everything in sequence, I head for the green room. Green room is a term that no longer has anything to do with color; instead it is a room where performers not yet required on stage wait before and after a performance. In the case of Wisconsin Public Television, it is also the room where makeup is applied. Two swivel chairs face large mirrors flanked by lights and I sit while Vicki Fischer, the makeup artist for *Sewing With Nancy*, applies makeup for me and any guest appearing on the program.

Not often, but occasionally, we forget something. Our current production scheduling usually has us recording both episodes of a two-part series on the same day, but that hasn't always been the case.

Several years ago we recorded a three-part series on working with fleece in which we showed how to construct jackets. This was during the era of having the Mail Bag segments at the end of the show. That particular time I recorded the sewing segments for all three shows in one day—it was a full day. The next time back at the studio, three Mail Bag segments and other promotional clips were scheduled. When we returned to Wisconsin Public Television two weeks later to finish up the three-part series, I brought back the three wardrobe selections I'd worn on the respective shows—well, almost. I forgot one of the turtlenecks I had worn beneath one of the jackets.

Donna came looking for me in the green room and conveyed the bad news.

The trouble was that episodes are recorded far in advance of their broadcast date and it was summer. Stores weren't carrying turtlenecks. Cream was also not a popular summer color. Donna left the studio and scoured stores, but could not find a single turtleneck. She did, however, find a cream colored T-shirt. With a lot of ingenuity and a short amount of time, Donna cut off the bottom of the T-shirt and transformed it into a turtle neck tube that she attached to the neck. The cream-colored neck looked warm and cozy, but under my jacket, the chopped off T-shirt was very drafty.

The look of *Sewing With Nancy* has evolved through many sets. There have been seven over the years, but the one currently in use was developed by set designer Shirwil Lukes about twenty years ago and has been repainted and updated a few times since.

I like simple lines. The arrangement and mission style elements in our current set are very comfortable. A few years ago, when we switched *Sewing With Nancy's* Mail Bag segment to Nancy's Corner, Shirwil designed a small, intimate set where I can talk face-to-face with a guest or interact with a guest appearing via Skype. It too, has mission-style elements and is compatible with the décor of the main set.

While the *Sewing With Nancy* group is preparing, the production crew is getting ready as well. When camera operators are in position with headsets on, director Laurie Gorman goes through that day's "Stupid Quiz," a take off on a daily feature in a local newspaper, the *Wisconsin State Journal*. There's a lot of laughter then, and the crew relaxes. Laurie asks a question and the crew shouts back answers that are picked up by their headset microphones. The only problem is, as I'm setting up props and samples, I only hear the shouted answers. It is somewhat disconcerting, as well as comic, to hear a crew member blurt out "Benjamin Franklin" while another loudly says "Albert Einstein!" I have no clue as to the question. (Maybe you have to be there!)

Once I'm on set and we're ready to roll tape, the atmosphere is attentive, upbeat and focused.

I do my worst sewing on television. The cabinet housing my sewing machine has a custom cut insert so the machine is at a thirty-degree right angle. Instead of sitting with my nose aligned with the needle as any normal person would do, I sit slightly sideways—in fact, thirty degrees left of normal, the opposite direction from the sewing machine. That makes for a sixty-degree off normal angle. Sometimes in order to see what I'm doing, I have to look at a monitor.

Depending upon what I'm demonstrating, there is a camera over my left or right shoulder that captures what's happening while I sew. After I sew and cut threads, I look up and forward into a camera a little to my left and begin to speak.

The next time you are sewing, position your machine away from you at a thirty-degree angle, begin sewing, and while you're still sewing look up and away from the needle area and describe what you're doing. Then you'll know why I say, "I do my worst sewing on TV!"

All that awkwardness is so viewers get a more realistic impression of what is happening. In many sewing programs, camera shots come from the side of the machine or front of the machine. Those camera angles are akin to making a video demonstrating how to drive a car by videoing through the windshield or side window. Instead, our productions have the "driver's" view of someone actually seated at the machine.

As we work very hard to achieve realism, that close-up video of the needle, showing it the way a sewist or quilter would view their machine has become our signature production trademark.

The angles are not quite as awkward at a table where we show and manipulate samples and close-up views of processes. While to the viewer it appears that the camera is pointing directly down at a flat table surface, instead the surface is lower in the front and raised in the back side forcing me and guests to work on a downhill slope of, again, about thirty degrees.

Even though the angles aren't as challenging at the table, I do have to demonstrate with all pieces upside down. When I work on a project at home or in my work-sewing studio, I position the pieces facing me—just like you do. On television, though, the pieces are rotated one hundred eighty-degrees to face the camera lens. At times when I am sewing at home in the late evening, I'll inadvertently position the pieces as if I'm demonstrating on television—a sure sign that it's past my bedtime.

Sewing With Nancy programs are shown not only on public television stations, but they are also available as DVDs, and before 1997, on VHS and Beta. As of August 2011, 52 of the most recent shows can be viewed online at nancyzieman.com. This is the fastest growing viewing outlet of *Sewing With Nancy*.

Public television allows no commercials, in fact, brand names cannot be used. For example, I cannot say Velcro; instead I refer to that product as hook and loop tape. If I use a specific product on the program I must speak of it generically, by its function rather

Laurie Gorman
"*Sewing With Nancy* was the first how-to program to be produced in high definition. It was also the first to release home videos and DVDs. For a while we had to make both DVD and VHS formats. Whenever change was needed, Nancy would do it."

than its brand name. For viewers who want to know more about the products and notions used on the program, those are explained in bonus material included as part of *Sewing With Nancy* DVDs.

When we finish recording the PBS segments, we turn our attention to the bonus material for DVD versions.

Over the years I've developed an innate sense of timing. That's a natural result, I'm sure, and anyone required to conform to the rigidities of allotted television time probably does the same. I can often feel the amount of time remaining in a segment, even before the floor manager gives me visual cues. My guests don't usually have my experience, though, so there has to be a way to let them know. So, while cameras are running I give physical cues. A touch on the elbow with the back of my hand, for example, means that about thirty seconds remain. It also means wrap up your thought.

Gail Brown
(Friend)

"Nancy knows her audiences' interests because they are her interests, and she stays true to presenting what they want to learn. Many people "present," but Nancy is a natural teacher and can break down techniques into simple steps for entertaining, viewing and learning. Viewers watch and believe, 'I could do that.'"

Sometimes when guests are concentrating on what comes next, they forget. Numerous times we've had to go back and record over that moment when a guest says, "Oh!" in recognition of what the nudge meant.

The Mail Bag continued for several years, until we felt the need for some fresh air. Laurie Gorman had an idea: eliminate the Mail Bag and replace it with a segment that focuses on inspiration, information and worthy causes. I agreed and we called it Nancy's Corner. The response to Nancy's Corner has been nothing short of phenomenal.

There are two ways that we conduct Nancy's Corner interviews: In person, and via Skype. We now have two Skype cases that we send around the country to people we'd like to interview. A Pelican (hard-sided) case is equipped with a computer, lighting, microphone, and instructions. Recently I interviewed someone from Phoenix and—half an hour later—interviewed the next Nancy's Corner guest who was located in Pittsburgh.

In 1998, *Sewing With Nancy* produced a mini-series on things to be sewn, quilted, or embroidered for various causes. The concept was introduced at one of our Sewing Weekends, when a woman from Rhinelander, Wisconsin, handed me a written request that she prepared in advance in the event she would not be able to talk with me personally.

That request was for a bolt of maroon cotton fabric. A group in Rhinelander was making jumpers for girls in Haiti. Perhaps the most poverty-stricken country in the western hemisphere, girls in Haiti would receive two meals a day if they were attending school. But in order to attend school, each had to have a uniform—a maroon jumper.

That request haunted me. I could donate a fourteen-yard bolt of fabric—that would be no problem—but realistically, how many girls would that actually help? Few, was the answer.

Each chapter of the American Sewing Guild has a designated charity or sewing project and I knew about that. But I started researching other possibilities, and in the end decided to do a television episode on volunteer sewing—what we can do for others. Then one episode expanded to several.

In a small pun on my own smile, I called the series "Sew a Smile."

When the first episode aired, we began getting letters and over time received more than twenty-five thousand letters. For one of the writers at Nancy's Notions, dealing with responses almost became her full-time job. We learned of other projects. Pins and Needles, a store in Ohio owned by Jan Brostek sewed layette sets to give to financially strapped mothers taking their tiny babies home from a neonatal intensive care unit. There were comfort caps and quilts, lap quilts, sleeping bags, pillows for mastectomy patients. The list went on and on of projects that caring people were doing to help others.

There were stories, too, that were often heart-wrenching and while preparing content for the series sometimes we worked with a tissue box on the table between us.

We even asked that viewers nominate "Sew a Smile Stars"—

people who were serving others with their projects. I featured some of those "Stars" on the program.

After a while we knew we needed to connect volunteers with causes, so we pre-empted the Mail Bag segment and started featuring "Sew a Smile"—causes that people could help. As people told us what they were doing and identifying needs, we started compiling a list, offering it to viewers if they sent a postage stamp and envelope for mailing. That list included organizations and how to contact them.

The whole thing just grew and grew to the point where Gail Brown and I put together a book.

Gail has been a guest on *Sewing With Nancy* many times. She and I met nearly thirty-five years ago at a trade show and have enjoyed working together over the years. Our lives have run parallel courses. Our children and grandchildren are comparable ages. We've shared joys and sorrows and Gail is a confidant. Gail's expertise in home décor was what first brought her to *Sewing With Nancy,* and we co-authored a book, *Quick Gifts and Décor*, published by Oxmoor House in 1998.

Gail and I did several programs together on serging. In the early years before sergers had the feature of automatically threading themselves, we brought nine sergers with us to the studio in order to have one for each aspect of the step-by-step instructions that day. The threads got jiggled during our trip from Beaver Dam and Gail spent time in a corner providing first aid to thread loopers.

Creative Kindness was published in January 2000 by Reiman House, and later

Gail Brown

"*Creative Kindness* was neither Nancy's nor my most commercially popular book, but we both believe that establishing this sharing forum was a significant milestone in our professional and personal lives—one that continues to live on."

Lois Kurtz

"Nancy was always bombarded with requests for materials, fabric, donations or offers from people who had fabric, sewing machines and other materials they'd like to give away. *Creative Kindness* was a way to connect people."

by Krause Publications. It was never meant to be a profit-making book. Instead it featured simple knitting, crocheting and sewing projects along with stories and photos of what others had done. As such projects are known to do, Gail Brown and I became solid friends, connected heart-to-heart by our attempts to help others.

"Sew a Smile" was our first major attempt to use sewing and quilting to help others and the response was astounding. "Sew a Smile" morphed into a link on the Nancy's Notions website where recent information on donation projects is listed. Called *Creative Kindness* as well, that link is still there, connecting people who want to volunteer with causes that need help.

Nancy's Corner carries forward many of the volunteer aspects that "Sew a Smile" brought to light, and that segment incorporates interviews with people whose lives are encouragements to others.

My administrative assistant, Lois Kurtz, coordinates Nancy's Corner. After we got our new set for the segment, Lois scheduled a couple of Nancy's Corner guests then came across an effort founded by Rachel O'Neill called Little Dresses for Africa.

Mary Mulari
(Friend)

"Although once in a while Nancy gets lighthearted on *Sewing With Nancy*, she has a sense of humor that doesn't usually come across on television. It does in live seminars, though. She can laugh at herself. Sometimes when we're together we're just two dames doing blonde jokes."

As in Haiti, girls in Africa are often considered second class citizens, unworthy of education and investment. Rachel wanted to change that. She wanted little girls to feel that they had something of their very own, so she figured a way to make a little sundress out of one pillowcase using bias tape for neck edging.

Lois invited Rachel to come to Wisconsin and appear with me on an episode of *Sewing With Nancy*; she agreed. When that episode aired, the response was overwhelming and Rachel was quickly inundated by dresses. Nancy's Notions became a collection point and volunteers from the Beaver Dam Senior Citizen Center sort dresses by sizes before they're shipped out.

Mary Luedtke Rebman

"Nancy being funny is something that's come out in the last few years and I think Mary Mulari brought that out of her. Nancy had a great sense of humor, but we never saw it because of all her health issues and the responsibilities she had."

Eileen Roche

(Friend)

"Nancy and I design embroidery products together and that is good for both of us. When Nancy lends her name to anything huge value is added. She has her finger on the pulse of her viewers and she sets the bar. *Sewing With Nancy* is America's sewing room."

To date, more than seventy-five thousand dresses have gone through Nancy's Notions and Rachel's organization has provided more than one million five hundred thousand dresses. Her project has been featured twice on NBC's Nightly News—once as an introduction to the project, and an unprecedented second time as a follow up. I couldn't be more pleased. Those who give of themselves are the greatest people on earth, and viewers of *Sewing With Nancy* are givers.

Mary Mulari has been a guest on *Sewing With Nancy* more often than any other—forty-eight appearances so far! She and I met when Mary attended a sewing seminar I presented in northern Minnesota while Rich and I lived there. She was an English teacher then, someone who simply loved to sew.

Mary is probably best known for the sweatshirt makeovers that she started doing about thirty years ago and she's written numerous books about her techniques. We've covered a full spectrum of topics in Mary's appearances, topics that Mary claims range from A to Z—from appliqué to zippers.

We have become close friends, and more than any other person in my life, Mary brings out my comedic side. We try to get together for a getaway weekend at least once a year, and those times are full of laughter and joking. Whenever she's in town for another taping of *Sewing With Nancy,* along with work, we have a lot of fun as well.

In 2009, when Wisconsin Public Television asked me to do a

fund-raising special, I invited Mary to be my sidekick in a lighthearted adventure called, "Kick it Up a Stitch." In that production, there was no effort to teach anything about sewing. Instead I donned the white coat of chef's garb while Mary wore one of her signature aprons and we spoofed our way through an hour of "cooking." I haven't had that much fun at a recording session—ever! Recently we debuted "Kick It Up a Stitch—Second Helping" at a consumer show and who knows where that will end up. Lucy and Ethel move over—here come Nancy and Mary!

Over the years I've been privileged to have guests who represent sewing, serging, and quilting, but Eileen Roche has stood alone in the realm of embroidery. The editor of *Designs in Machine Embroidery* magazine, Eileen taught me how to embroider. That's one of the benefits of having a television program—I get to learn, too.

At the beginning of my career in sewing, mechanical machines were the only thing around, but as technology increased, so did the options for machine embroidery. At first, machine embroidery required hooping fabric and using a stabilizer. I was not impressed. But as technology improved, and more intricate computerized designs entered the picture, Eileen took me from the industrial age to the electronic age.

Today, people who have no desire to sew are using sewing machines with computerized embroidery designs. In connection with embroidery I've taken a leap from my reticent days when I thought machine embroidery was limiting, into the realm where I now have a licensed line of embroidery designs. And it all started with a guest appearance by Eileen Roche who became a good friend, and a mentor to me in navigating the embroidery world.

In 1996, I was invited by Wisconsin Public Television to host a fund-raising special on Wisconsin quilters. Eight quilters were invited to be part of that special, each representing a different style. To prepare them to teach on television, I was asked to tutor them.

Although I had often worked with quilters on *Sewing With Nancy,* when Natalie Sewell unrolled her landscape quilts, I literally gasped. I could hardly concentrate on teaching her to teach because

Natalie Sewell

(Friend)

"Together Nancy and I have authored four books on landscape quilting. I've been on *Sewing With Nancy* many times. She asked me to teach her how to do landscape quilting, but it was Nancy who taught me how to teach with step-by-step progressive samples."

Lois Kurtz

"Nancy blossomed after meeting Natalie Sewell. She started making landscape quilts right away and hasn't stopped. She always has something in progress. Nancy was worn out and landscape quilts were something that was inspiring again."

I wanted to know how to do that. The photographic quality of Natalie's quilts touched something deep within me.

As a child I loved roaming outdoors, taking photographs of woodland scenes and searching out flowers in the woods. I met Natalie after having been deeply immersed in a career for twenty years. Quite frankly, I was burned out. The thrill had gone and I either needed to get out or get better. In Natalie's style of quilting I recognized the road to getting better.

I asked Natalie to teach me, and she agreed. Landscape quilting has changed my life, and so has my friendship with Natalie Sewell. She has put me in touch with a creativity that, in turn, has nurtured me. It re-stoked my fires of passion for fabric and all the possibilities it holds. About once every three months I travel to Natalie's home studio in Madison and we have a quilting play day. We share what's happened in our lives since we last met and solve the world's problems, all while designing landscape quilts.

Gail Brown, Mary Mulari, Eileen Roche, and Natalie Sewell have become close friends as the result of *Sewing With Nancy*. All four joined me for the thirtieth anniversary special of *Sewing With Nancy*. After a long day of rehearsal prior to the next day's recording we went out to dinner together and lingered in the warmth of friendship.

I can't entirely explain the success of *Sewing With Nancy*. I know it has something to do with the fact that we need to share with each other, and in the sharing receive back more than we've given. Creating together forges bonds between people. I know that's how it has been for me.

Chapter 21

❧

Rich Zieman

"It was interesting to have people to bounce things off and if we wanted to do something we would ask them if they were happy with it. They were good thinkers and knew what we were about. It was great to bounce ideas off them."

Ed Moore

"There hasn't been another model like Nancy's Notions in the US sewing industry. Nancy is a wonderful marketer, a good copywriter and she knows how to tell the story. Information is delivered in such a way that people want the product she is offering."

A five-word question changed my life and altered its course.

When Rich and I incorporated Nancy's Notions, I was named president and secretary of the corporation; Rich was vice-president and treasurer. Those were our corporate roles in 1983, when we operated out of the basement of our home and when board meetings were convened at the kitchen table. Over the years, though, Nancy's Notions grew beyond our wildest expectations. We grew, and grew, and grew again.

By 1996, Nancy's Notions had one hundred twenty employees and a large facility. Rich and I saw a need to bring more people into the picture, people who knew our business and could serve as advisors and company protectors should something happen to either Rich or me. So, we invited our accountant, our attorney, our banker, and a retail business manager to work with us as members of a board of directors.

It was a great decision to have

them. At monthly meetings we reviewed financial reports and discussed business decisions. Their wisdom and experience taught me so much. Starting a business from scratch, growing it into a substantial entity and working with high-quality business leaders gave me the business education I didn't have.

At a board meeting in 2001, our attorney looked at me and asked the question: "What is your succession plan?"

The question shocked me and I could not answer. I wondered: Who would take over if Rich, or me or both of us, were suddenly out of the picture? And on the heels of that wonder came another: Who will take over when you decide to leave?

Rich and I began discussing options. Ted was only nineteen that year and Tom was ten. They were hardly ready for corporate leadership. Besides that, neither of us wanted to strap our sons with a direct mail quilting and sewing business.

We also discussed the option of an EOSOP (Employee Owned Stock Option Plan). We had a great team of people, but no one who stood out as a great leader who could carry on the Nancy's Notions vision.

We had a business evaluation performed. The evaluation looked at: 1) the dollar value of the company; 2) the goodwill worth of the company; and 3) the company's projection of growth and possibility. We also looked at whether we should expand by acquiring another business and not sell.

Do we grow or do we sell? We were at a crossroads.

So, we tested the waters. We looked around for corporations that might be

---

Patty Trader
(Friend)

"Nancy and Rich personify the American success story. I marvel at their ability to take an idea and move forward with it. Their success was a matter of timing, luck, some blessing—all factored with dedication and perseverance. Ethics were in their bottom line—treat others the way you want to be treated."

Donna Fenske

"I kinda knew Nancy and Rich were in a frame of mind to sell the business. It made me a little nervous."

Ted Zieman

"Beaver Dam is different because of my parents. They started a company that brought in millions of dollars a year in sales. It provided incomes for one hundred twenty to one hundred thirty people—that's a lot of jobs. Then during Sewing Weekend it brought three to four thousand people to restaurants and shopping. It made a difference to the local economy."

candidates to purchase Nancy's Notions. I visited two of those companies to inquire if there might be interest in purchasing Nancy's Notions. To my immense shock both companies jumped at the possibility. Yes!—a resounding Yes!!!—was the response. When each learned another company was interested, we were courted.

Nancy's Notions was part of our lives before we had children and I had to think about it. So entwined was Nancy's Notions in our family that it was almost as if she were a child—our daughter. I was more than attached.

I knew one thing, though. Several years before at a trade show I noticed the founder of a company working in the organization's booth. She was still there, looking exhausted and wearing tennis shoes; she must have been at least seventy-five years old. I didn't want that to be me.

My father once gave me some advice. "Don't play poker," he said. "Put all your cards on the table."

Every morning I prayed. Proverbs 3:5-6 says: *"Trust in the Lord with all your heart, and lean not to your own understanding. In all your ways acknowledge him and he will direct your paths."*

'Paths'—not a singular path—but multiple 'paths.' I remember underlining those verses in my Bible. While going through the process of evaluation, conversation and consideration, I kept thinking, 'Trust, trust, trust—you will be guided.'

By that time Rich had been working less at Nancy's Notions to give more separation between work and our family life. For so many years we had worked together and I felt the need to be able to go home evenings and ask, "What did you do today?"

It all took about six months. By mid-2002, we had made our decision.

Our decision was to sell Nancy's Notions to the Tacony Corporation.

Like Nancy's Notions, Tacony is a family-owned business with kindness as a core value. Ken Tacony, second generation leader of the business started by his father, is a unique combination of smart business and compassion. Today a third generation of Tacony children are already working for the company.

Based in Fenton, Missouri, the Tacony Corporation manufactures sewing machines, commercial and residential vacuums, ceiling fans and more.

Until mid-2002, we kept negotiations under wraps, telling only a few of our key administrative people. Outside of Nancy's Notions, only Earl Zieman and my mother knew.

We planned to publicly announce the sale in early August in coordinated statements from Nancy's Notions and Tacony Corporation. But, Earl was at coffee with friends on July 21, when his good friend, Bernice, turned to him and asked, "Did you hear Nancy's Notions is going to sell?"

Immediately Earl called us to report what he'd heard. After the initial shock, I called Bernice to ask how she'd heard about the sale and she said she thought it was common knowledge.

We called Tacony to tell them, then put together a press release for the Beaver Dam newspaper and radio station, then hand-carried the press releases to both. The same happened on Tacony's end in Fenton, Missouri. We had to announce at the same

Ken Tacony

(Colleague)

"Our personalities are similar in nature and our companies were similar in nature as well. For over ten years now we've been very compatible and we're continuing the Nancy's Notions legacy. We love the relationship. Nancy wanted to make sure that her people were going to remain in place and we are committed to being in Beaver Dam."

time. In big, bold letters, the front page headline of the July 23, 2002, edition of the Beaver Dam Daily Citizen read: Nancy's Notions Sold.

We called a company-wide meeting and announced the sale to all employees. Of course there were concerns and we tried to be as understanding as possible.

Under the terms of the sale, I was to remain as President of Nancy's Notions for a period of five years. I would also be a spokesperson for Baby Lock sewing machines and continue to produce and host *Sewing With Nancy*—very workable terms.

Once announcements had been made things got into motion. Administrative staff from Tacony came to look at our computer system in preparation to integrate our ordering system with theirs. We also took our key staff to Fenton to assess the synergy between management staffs.

For the Nancy's Notions staff things were different, but not necessarily bad. As for me, though, it was difficult.

One difficult phone call I had to make following the sale was to the people at Pfaff USA to inform them that they would no longer be an underwriter of *Sewing With Nancy*. The Tacony Corporation had purchased that right and Baby Lock, their sewing machine line, would become the major underwriter.

Rich Zieman

"Nancy felt the time was right to sell, and that Tacony was the right company to sell to. But after the sale, she was still there and concerned about the people who dedicated their careers to Nancy's Notions."

I often compare selling Nancy's Notions—a decision I made of my own free will—to that of a possible parent/child relationship. Imagine raising a child to adulthood, protecting them, celebrating milestones as they grew up, and watching with tears and joy as they married. Then imagine giving your child and their new spouse your home to live in with the condition that you are allowed to remain for a while. During the time you remain, you will be responsible for the maintenance of that home. When they move in, it is no longer

Kathy Hasson Gittus

"We were not prepared for the differences between the 'old' system and the 'new' system. Luckily, our customers were flexible and understanding while we worked to get their orders to them."

Rich Zieman

"It was hard for Nancy to remain president of the company after the sale of Nancy's Notions. She really wanted to use her creative talents more."

Ken Tacony

"Nancy is a hard working, dedicated individual with a lot of humility. Her style of leadership is 'come in the side door' and blend in. That kind of leader motivates people in a very subtle, soft way. That's Nancy!"

your home and your precious child's focus is on another relationship.

One of my concerns with the sale was that people would lose their jobs and a few did. Tacony was poised to handle much of the accounting and administrative functions from their headquarters in Missouri, so those with similar responsibilities for Nancy's Notions were no longer needed. Consolidation of efforts is commonplace and prudent in an acquisition.

On New Year's Eve, the last day of 2002, Tacony's information technology staff came in and at the end of the day our computer system was shut down and over the holiday our system was integrated into theirs. On January 2, 2003, Nancy's Notions opened with a new computer system and trouble!

Whenever a business is acquired, transition issues are to be expected. What we experienced was all part of the process. While the new computer system was ideal for business-to-business transactions in which one or two or a hundred vacuum cleaners or sewing machines could be ordered, it was not designed for consumer orders. For example, an order for half a yard of fabric was perceived as part of a product and a partial product wasn't initially accepted by the system.

Retrofitting the computer system was not going as smoothly as planned. Orders were piling up and there were boxes of envelopes with checks and order forms everywhere. Information technology staff members from the corporate office joined us in Beaver Dam to assist in the transition, yet for three months we struggled. I was so frustrated that I got shingles on the right side of my face and in my ear and I was in great pain. "Just let it go," someone advised, but I couldn't.

Communication to, and coordination with, a corporate office was foreign to me. I wasn't good at it since it was new territory. Finally I asked for someone to help me. They sent one of their key staff members to oversee the transition for two weeks to give me a break. In the end, Ken Tacony also hired Rich for a month to help through the transition.

Ken Tacony

"Nancy's Notions pushed us to get something more robust in place for an information technology platform because their internet sales were down. I invested in a more current internet retailer and things have improved a great deal. Online ordering needs to be consumer friendly, it has to be easy, you want an easy checkout—you have to have all those functionalities. Our platform was wholesale oriented rather than retail oriented."

When the sale occurred, Rich was not working full-time. As planned and as part of the agreement, Rich stepped down entirely. Some of the profits from the sale of Nancy's Notions enabled him to start Zieman Properties, a commercial real estate venture. He put his experience building for Nancy's Notions to work and today is a general contractor who oversees construction and maintenance of office buildings and other commercial space. He's in business with Ted, our son. But he set that aside for a month to put things back in order, and I think everyone at Nancy's Notions was grateful.

In the frustration of that time things still got done. We didn't miss deadlines, but I also couldn't devote the attention that was needed to *Sewing With Nancy* and other marketing efforts.

I think Ken Tacony was worried about me during that time.

Oddly, it was a weight loss program that helped see me through that time. Called "First Place for Health," I began attending the program not so much because I needed to lose weight, but because I needed contact with others. I felt as though I was trying to pull a heavy sleigh up a steep hill. There were people from all walks of life in the program and everything said in that group was treated confidentially. That program, and the women who attended, became my comfort and my counselors.

Gradually, as time passed things—including myself and the computer system—eased into place. The sale proved to be a wise business decision and I couldn't be more pleased with the outcome. I continue to work with the Tacony Corporation; they treat me like family.

Mike Schuster came to Nancy's Notions in 2004, as general manager. With a background in direct mail, he began positioning the business for new growth.

Mike Schuster
(Colleague)
"Nancy took a passion and made it into a multi-million dollar business. She took risks to see what would happen and it was all done so humbly and with caring. The culture she established is one that we're working to keep alive."

In 2005, Wisconsin Public Television and *Sewing With Nancy* partnered together to offer Quilt Expo, a three-day quilt show, educational event and consumer show held in Madison. The event was, and still is, a fund-raiser for public television. Wisconsin Public Television arranged for the venue, Madison's Alliant Energy Center, and promoted the event. *Sewing With Nancy* brought the sewing connection—a pool of teachers and the name to help promote it.

We sent out brochures, rented two halls at the Alliant Center and filled the place with vendors. Classes for the Thursday-Friday-Saturday event were about ninety-eight percent filled and there was a waiting list for vendors, but only about sixteen hundred people had pre-registered to attend. I was seriously worried.

When opening day came, an interview kept me away from the front when the doors opened. During the interview I was trying to be cheerful and gracious in spite of the fact that I knew practically nobody was coming. Vendors had placed their trust in me when agreeing to be part of an untested event, and they would hold me accountable if things didn't work out. When the interview ended, I walked toward a side entrance at the convention center with a throbbing headache.

When I opened the door, I could see the front entrance. People were pouring into the building. I stood there, feeling tears rising and I wanted to cry. 'Stop,' I told myself. 'You can't cry now—you can't.' I did some serious swallowing and went on.

Obviously people weren't accustomed to pre-registering for attendance and instead registered on the spot.

That first year nine thousand six hundred people attended and it has grown every year since. In 2012, attendance topped seventeen thousand and there's no end in sight. Quilt Expo now fills the entire Alliant Center facility instead of just two halls.

Roger Hasbrouck
(Friend)

"Nancy carries around luggage too much and she had an extremely painful shoulder surgery several years ago. The rehab was terrible. Nancy's spent a lifetime training to block out pain. She's always had body troubles—her knees, her shoulders, her face. But Nancy has an even keel, no matter what—even after surgeries."

In 2006, with one year remaining in my term as President of Nancy's Notions, I underwent another surgery, this time to repair a rotator cuff and torn ligaments in my right shoulder. That was painful.

I had a special chair that moved my arm up and down to maintain flexibility. A year later, a much less painful surgery shaved bone to prevent rotator cuff damage in the opposite shoulder.

As my five-year tenure as President of Nancy's Notions drew to a close, I prepared to move on. Leaving Nancy's Notions was not the end—not even close! Tacony Corporation had purchased Nancy's Notions, but I was still the producer and host of *Sewing With Nancy*. Baby Lock, a Tacony-owned company was an underwriter for the program—as were Madeira Threads, Koala Cabinets, Amazing

Designs, Clover and Klassé Needles—but I still controlled the content and direction.

Deanna Springer

"I knew that Nancy wasn't going to hang up her needle and retire. Before the end of Nancy's tenure with Nancy's Notions, she and I were riding from a Quilt Expo meeting in Madison back to Beaver Dam and there was a quiet time. I thought, 'This is a great time to tell Nancy that she's going to do some great things and I would like to be part of that.' At the very moment that I opened my mouth to say the words, she brought it up. I can tell you what mile marker we were at—we were on the same wavelength."

There was also Quilt Expo. The end of my time as President of Nancy's Notions under Tacony Corporation was the dawn of a new partnership for that event. My new business, Nancy Zieman Productions, would sponsor that event with Wisconsin Public Television.

I began to consider who I wanted to continue working with and two names kept coming to mind—Deanna Springer and Lois Kurtz.

Deanna had been events coordinator at Nancy's Notions and worked with me on Quilt Expo as well as *Sewing With Nancy.* With Quilt Expo leaving Nancy's Notions, Deanna's position was tenuous. So more than a year ahead of my departure, I asked if she would be interested in going along.

Rich had been preparing office space for me in a new building owned by Zieman Properties. My desk was set up and a computer was in place. My official last day at Nancy's Notions was to be January, 31, 2007, but because of accumulated vacation time I left on November 20. I had planned to leave at the end of that day, but I couldn't face the wrenching goodbyes from people I loved and respected. So, at 10:00 a.m., I slipped on my coat and pressed, "Send" on an e-mail to my friends and colleagues at Nancy's Notions. It read simply, "Bye," and I was gone.

That afternoon I went to my new office and tried to work on a new book, *Pattern Fitting with Confidence*, and while I worked, I cried.

The Friday after Thanksgiving Rich and I flew with our friends, Jeff and Patty Trader, to Miami where we spent four days. I concentrated on breathing in and breathing out. We ate at a wooden table outside and I could feel myself letting go.

I worked alone in my new office until January 2, 2008, when Deanna joined me. Seven months later Lois arrived.

Hanging behind Lois' desk in the reception area of Nancy Zieman Productions is a landscape quilt that I created during my last year of working at Nancy's Notions. There is only one tree in the scene, but many of the tree's branches extend into the borders. I named it "Branching Out" and somehow the process of designing and quilting the piece kept me focused on things to come, not on what I was leaving. Nancy Zieman Productions truly does represent a branching out beyond what I had known before.

Things seemed quiet to me at first after stepping away from the constant action at Nancy's Notions. Although Nancy Zieman Productions and Nancy's Notions are separate organizations, we still collaborate on multiple projects—*Sewing With Nancy* being the major one. The *Sewing With Nancy* team at Nancy's Notions is a cohesive unit of artists, writers, and creative people. As I've said, I am the band director, they play the music.

I often tell people I'm the Betty Crocker of Nancy's Notions. I still am. My face continues to be the one that customers associate with Nancy's Notions products and I serve as company spokesperson. When Ken Tacony's company purchased Nancy's

Notions, I became the spokesperson for several other Tacony companies as well. That includes Baby Lock sewing and embroidery machines, Koala Cabinets, Madeira Threads, Klassé Needles, and Amazing Designs.

There's a lot of work to coordinating Quilt Expo, something we do in partnership with Wisconsin Public Television. Half of the arrangements are handled through our office. Deanna Springer takes the lead on most of the education coordination, sit 'n sews, quilt contest, special exhibits, and programs while Lois Kurtz maintains records for quilt entries and teaching applications. Other aspects of show coordinations are handled by Wisconsin Public Television.

Physical issues weren't quite finished with me. In 2012, on a lovely summer day, I hung bed sheets outside. While walking from the clothesline across our driveway, I fell and broke my right femur. Instead of slipping between fresh, wind-dried sheets that evening as I had planned, I underwent surgery in which the bone in my upper right leg was pinned. My recovery took months and required extensive physical therapy. At the 2012 Quilt Expo, although I could stand and walk a short distance, I made my way around the Alliant Center in a motorized scooter.

Licensing is something that consumes more of our time these days. Being creative is what keeps life fun! Developing products and working to refine concepts and ideas charges my batteries. From being the girl few people noticed as a child, it still surprises me sometimes to realize that I'm well-known. I'm pleased to have my name associated with quality products that benefit sewists, quilters, and embroiderers.

Lois keeps everything in order and she coordinates arrangements for Nancy's Corner interviews as well. She's invaluable in more ways than I can count.

Three times a week, I write a blog. Social media helps keep me in touch with those who enjoy sewing and quilting and serging and embroidering.

Our offices have a small studio where we produce online instructional and product videos.

Books, products, DVDs, quilt shows, personal speaking engagements, blogging—it all comes back to teaching—and the possibilities are endless.

When a life is stitched together by the hand of destiny, what seams unlikely, becomes possible.

Epilogue

The *Sewing With Nancy* set is empty. Cameras are wheeled out of the way and the bright lights that illuminated the scene are cooling above me.

Guests who attended the recording of a two-part special celebrating *Sewing With Nancy's* thirty years on television are enjoying refreshments in another room. For the moment all is silent.

This is my classroom—this is where I invite viewers to follow, step-by-step, through the process of creating items that enrich their lives, in mostly humble ways.

I am so thankful for my blessings. Two fine sons, one with my lovely daughter-in-law at his side, stand next to my husband. They, and my grandchildren, are my joy and my heart.

There are others, too. My mother, friends, family, and business associates—all are important, but here in the darkened studio, I think of those who watch *Sewing With Nancy*.

It is unlikely that I will meet most of them, but they are the reason I'm here. It is for them—viewers invisible to me on this side of the camera—that *Sewing With Nancy* is created.

On an evening long ago, when I stood before my 4-H club and demonstrated how to attach a waistband, I felt a sense of purpose that has never left me.

There is destiny in the empty set of a television program, as if all one needs to do is turn on the lights and a life that surprises with its possibilities will be there, poised to begin.

Life is full of the unexpected and I am the most unlikely of television personalities.

Whatever paths I've followed, I am, at heart, a teacher.

Bye for now...